D0259736

# FAMILIES AND FAMILY POLICIES IN EUROPE

*Also by Linda Hantrais*

Le vocabulaire de Georges Brassens, vol. 1 Une étude statistique et stylistique, vol. 2 Concordance et index des rimes

Contemporary French Society

The Undergraduate's Guide to Studying Languages

Managing Professional and Family Life: a Comparative Study of British and French Women

Social Policy in the European Union

(Edited with Steen Mangen) Cross-National Research Methods in the Social Sciences

# Families and Family Policies in Europe

Linda Hantrais and Marie-Thérèse Letablier

UNIVERSITY OF
LUTON
PARK SQ LIBRARY

3402604375
306.85094
HAN

7 Day Loan

WITHDRAWN

**LONGMAN**
London and New York

**Addison Wesley Longman Limited**
Edinburgh Gate, Harlow
Essex CM20 2JE, England
*and Associated Companies throughout the world.*

*Published in the United States of America
by Longman Publishing, New York*

© Linda Hantrais and Marie-Thérèse Letablier, 1996

All rights reserved; no part of this publication may be
reproduced, stored in a retrieval system, or transmitted
in any form or by any means, electronic, mechanical,
photocopying, recording, or otherwise, without either
the prior written permission of the Publisher or a licence
permitting restricted copying in the United Kingdom
issued by the Copyright Licensing Agency Ltd.,
90 Tottenham Court Road, London WIP 9HE.

First published 1996

ISBN 0-582-24767-5

**British Library Cataloguing-in-Publication Data**

A catalogue record for this book is
available from the British Library

**Library of Congress Cataloguing-in-Publication Data**

Hantrais, Linda.
    Families and family policies in Europe / Linda
Hantrais and Marie-Thérèse Letablier.
        p.   cm.
Includes bibliographical references and index.
ISBN 0-582-24767-5
    1. Family—Europe.   2. Family policy—Europe.
I. Letablier, Marie-Thérèse.   II. Title.
HQ612.H36   1996
306.85'094—dc20                           95-45061
                                              CIP

Produced through Longman Malaysia, PP

# CONTENTS

# LIST OF FIGURES

# KEY FOR FIGURES

| | |
|---|---|
| A | Austria |
| B | Belgium |
| DK | Denmark |
| SF | Finland |
| F | France |
| D | Germany |
| GR | Greece |
| IRL | Ireland |
| I | Italy |
| L | Luxembourg |
| NL | Netherlands |
| P | Portugal |
| E | Spain |
| S | Sweden |
| UK | United Kingdom |
| | |
| EUR | Europe |

# PREFACE

Demographic trends affecting family formation and structure in the member states of the European Union (EU) would appear to be moving in the same direction, and governments are generally thought to be facing similar social problems requiring similar policy responses. Within the Union, each member state organises social welfare according to its own socio-economic and political circumstances and cultural traditions, and the place of families within national social policy reflects the different ways that governments and public opinion conceptualise family affairs. These differences may help to explain why convergence of family structures does not seem to have occurred automatically across the Union and why family policy has not been given prominence in the European political agenda for social affairs. The reluctance of the Council of Ministers to demonstrate a firm commitment in this area can be interpreted as an indication of the lack of agreement among members states over not only the objectives and content of family policies but also family policy as a concept.

Although the body of literature on families expanded rapidly across the Union from the 1980s and was given a new boost, particularly within the European context, when the United Nations proclaimed 1994 as the International Year of the Family, few attempts have been made to compare and contrast family structures and family policies across the Union.

Since the late 1980s, regular annual reports have been produced by the European Observatory on National Family Policies and the European Commission Network on Childcare and other Measures to Reconcile Employment and Family Responsibilities, and studies have been commissioned on benefits and child support in Europe. Yet, no systematic comparative analysis has been undertaken hitherto of the concepts underlying family policies at either European or national level. The present volume seeks to fill this gap by exploring how family structures, the relationship between the family and employment, and family policy are conceptualised in individual member states and at European level, by re-examining theories about the convergence of family and family policy models and by analysing national and EU policy responses to common social problems.

The book is the outcome of a collaborative project carried out between 1993 and 1995, supported by awards from the Economic and Social Research Council (R000221159), the European Commission, Directorate General V, Employment, Industrial Relations and Social Affairs, and the Caisse Nationale des Allocations Familiales in Paris, within the framework of an initiative on comparisons of family policies in Europe. The aim of the project was to contribute to a greater understanding of national conceptualisations of the family and the operation of the family policy-making process at European level and within different national contexts. Since the book deals with a large body of information that is undergoing rapid and constant change, we have not sought to be comprehensive; rather the focus is on trends and patterns of behaviour that are of interest from a cross-cultural perspective.

Our thanks are due to the three organisations that made the project possible and to our many collaborators, particularly those in Finland, France, Germany, Italy, Spain, Sweden and the United Kingdom, and at Eurostat, who generously contributed their time, knowledge and expertise. Any errors of interpretation of their reports, of other national materials and European documentation remain our own.

Linda Hantrais and Marie-Thérèse Letablier
October 1995

# PART ONE

# Constructing and Deconstructing the Family

The period from the 1960s to the 1990s saw intense social change in advanced industrial societies that called into question the core social institutions, not least the family. The extent and pace of change, the timing of key events acting as catalysts for change, as well as national perceptions of social trends, differed, however, from one socio-cultural context to another, prompting fundamental questions to be asked about the structure and role of families in society: What is the family? Is it universal? Is the State the creator or destroyer of family solidarity? Is the family in a state of crisis? Does the family exist? These questions (by Gittins, 1993, with reference to Britain; and Roussel, 1989, in the French context), echoed others that had been raised more than two decades earlier about whether the family was likely to survive (Cooper, 1972).

Although convergence has been a major theme in the European debate, authors (for example Dumon, 1994) attempting to make international comparisons soon realise how dangerous it is to assume that apparently similar demographic trends are necessarily producing similar outcomes: in this instance the decline of the family and the emergence of a 'European family model'. Historians have long demonstrated that family structures are subject to important variations over time and space (Ariès, 1948; Laslett and Wall, 1972; Flandrin, 1976), and sociologists have tended to conclude that it is more appropriate to refer to families and family models in the plural and to emphasise family diversity (Rapoport *et al.*, 1982; de Singly, 1991; Nunes de Almeida *et al.*, 1992).

The cautious approach adopted by the European Commission in the area of family affairs (see Part Three) reflects awareness at European level of the importance of family diversity and of differences in the responsibilities attributed to family members and to the state from one country to another. The concepts underlying family policies in different national contexts and the ways in which they are operationalised clearly point to the continuing importance of conventions that are firmly rooted in historical, political, economic and cultural traditions. Ideology and popular mythology play an important part in the conceptualisation of families. National definitions of the family can thus be seen as an indication of conflicting demands and expectations and as the outcome of a process of negotiation between social actors.

To gain a better understanding of the premises and realities on which family policies are based, the chapters in the first part of the book explore social constructions of the family in the member states of the European Union. They examine definitions of the family as used by statisticians, administrators, policy makers and sociologists. These different disciplinary and national definitions of the family are analysed and compared in each chapter with reference to the contexts within which they are produced.

CHAPTER 1

# Statistical definitions of the family

Statistics was one of the first scientific fields where an attempt was made to achieve standardisation of observational methods at international level. The first international statistical congress was held in London in 1853 and the International Statistical Institute was set up in 1884 (Desrosières, 1996). The Statistical Office of the European Communities (known as Eurostat) was established in 1958 to serve Community institutions and monitor policies by collecting statistics from member states. Eurostat was also given the brief of taking forward the integration of national statistical systems, supported by Council Directive 73/403/EEC of 22 November 1973 (*Official Journal of the European Communities* L 347/50, 17.12.73), which was aimed at synchronising general population censuses. Despite this long history of international collaboration and the growing need for reliable information about demographic trends in Europe, by the mid-1990s, data on households and families in the Union were still far from comparable (Eggerickx and Bégeot, 1993).

Even before statistics became a scientific discipline, European states had collected information about families and households. Initially, they required data for administrative purposes, and sources such as parish registers were used for details about christenings, marriages and deaths. Later, 'political arithmetic', as it has been described in the English context (Desrosières, 1993, pp. 34–7), was justified on social grounds: for example f analyse causes of death or track the spread of diseases in the seventeenth century. The first population census to use a family questionnaire form dates from 1841 in England and Wales (the first British census was held in 1801) and from 1846 in Belgium. Households were considered as statistical units in the first population census taken for the German Reich in 1871 (Council of Europe, 1990, p. 11).

By the mid-twentieth century, statistics on the composition of families and households, as collected in population censuses and surveys, were being used routinely throughout Europe to predict and monitor the need for public provision of services and other forms of social protection. The 1973 Directive on the synchronisation of population censuses confirmed the importance of statistics on families and households. The Commission required data from member states on the population in general, the working population, employment, households and families to be able to fulfil the tasks assigned to it by the articles on social policy in the 1957 Treaty establishing the European Economic Community.

In the 1980s, national statistical indicators were pointing to population ageing and changes in family structure due to lower fertility rates, increased life expectancy, the decline in marriage, the growth in the number of divorces and the restructuring of the labour market, as more women entered paid employment. In 1989 concern about demographic trends prompted the European Council and Council of Ministers to propose Community action with regard to family policy (*OJEC C* 277/2, 31.10.89). Article 7 of the Agreement on Social Policy appended to the Treaty on European Union, concluded in Maastricht in 1992 and signed by all member states except the United Kingdom, required the European Commission to draw up annual reports on the demographic situation in the Union. The purpose of the reports is to provide the Union with the information needed to assist it in achieving a number of objectives as set out in Article 1 of the Agreement, including the improvement of living and working conditions, the development of social protection and human resources.

The first two sections in this chapter are devoted to an analysis of the issues affecting the availability and comparability of the national data collated and monitored by Eurostat, as required by the Union. The statistical conventions adopted in different countries are examined, as are the definitions of the family used in compilations by individual member states and at European level. Although the primary aim in the chapter is to identify and compare statistical definitions of the family unit, the concept of the household is frequently used by statisticians and policy makers and is therefore included in the analysis. The remaining sections of the chapter are devoted to a comparison of data on demographic trends relating to both families and households across the Union.

## Statistical sources and conventions

In line with the principle of subsidiarity (SEC(92) 1990 final, 27 October 1992), the 1989 Community Charter of the Fundamental Social Rights of Workers and the Maastricht Treaty constantly laid stress on the need to have due regard for the different forms of national practices. By virtue of the principle of subsidiarity, the Union should act only if the objectives of a proposal cannot be satisfactorily achieved by member states themselves. In the case of the collection of data on families and households, action at Union level may be justified on the grounds that 'adverse demographic trends' and 'changes in family structures' can be identified as similar problems facing all member states (Commission of the European Communities/Directorate-General Employment, Industrial Relations and Social Affairs, 1994, p. 3). As demonstrated throughout this book, national practices in the area of family affairs, like the collection of statistical data, are, however, strongly imbued by socio-cultural, political and economic traditions, which make standardisation difficult to achieve, thereby limiting the scope for action at European level.

Attempts to standardise data collection methods across countries have had to deal with issues such as national political priorities and ideologies, the centralisation and autonomy, or otherwise, of the organisations responsible for data collection and the reluctance of some governments to accept decisions taken at supranational level (Desrosières, 1996). As a result, standardisation has probably been taken further in areas concerned with the economy (as demonstrated by the European Accounting System) than in social affairs, where consensus over the need for harmonisation has been more difficult to achieve (Hantrais, 1995, pp. 19–37).

In this section, consideration is given, first, to the reasons why standardisation of statistical sources across the Union is problematic, before examining some of the obstacles to comparability associated with differences in the national practices adopted for defining families.

### Synchronisation of statistical sources

The aim of the 1973 Council Directive on the synchronisation of general population censuses was to specify the period during which national censuses should take place: 1 March to 31 May 1981 was chosen. A schedule of statistical tables that all member states should supply in a standard format based on their national censuses was drawn up, covering demographic, professional and social characteristics of individual households and families.

Full compliance with the directive was prevented for a number of reasons. The 1980/81 census was to be the first occasion on which harmonised datasets would be collected. For political reasons – presidential elections in France and local elections in Italy – the census date was not observed in all member states (Baldwin, 1991, p. 112). In Germany, the census was postponed until 1987 due to problems concerning privacy and data protection. The proposal to conduct a general population census had to be dropped in the Netherlands under pressure from public opinion. Opposition to national censuses has also developed in Belgium, Spain and the United Kingdom, but without preventing them from conforming to the census requirement (Eggerickx and Bégeot, 1993, p. 1711). In addition, the expense involved in carrying out censuses, which by definition cover the whole population, meant that the directive could be very costly to implement in countries where the practice was not already established.

In response to the problems of standardising dates and information collected in the 1980/81 censuses, the new Directive 87/287/EEC (*OJEC* L 143/33, 3.6.87) on the synchronisation of censuses, issued on 26 May 1987, was much more flexible regarding the reference period. The Council proposed that data derived from sources other than censuses should be accepted, thereby admitting that the statistics supplied could not be wholly standardised. Since major changes can, for example, occur in birth-rates within a relatively short period of time, even if national censuses were carried out, as required by the Council, their relative infrequency (generally every ten years) and the time taken to analyse and produce the results would continue to impose limitations on their usefulness and usability.

Most countries collect information by other means and, in several cases, alternative sources could be used to replace the census, although the quantity and quality of data were not necessarily equivalent (Baldwin, 1991, pp. 112–13; Eurostat, 1994a, pp. 17–28). Germany used the micro-census which covers 1 per cent of households. The Netherlands, and also Denmark, already drew their data from administrative registers, thereby avoiding the need for direct contact with households, but with the result that they were unable to supply information on topics such as religion and education, as well as some of the details about housing and mobility that can be covered in census questionnaires. Belgium, Germany, Italy, Luxembourg and Spain also compiled registers covering some of the information routinely collected in population censuses. Finland and Sweden have used a combination of administrative registers and shorter census questionnaires (Eggerickx and Bégeot, 1993, pp. 1712–15).

For registers to be effective, they may need to use personal identification numbers, as in Finland, to assign individuals to households and families, involving procedures which can also be objected to on the grounds that they infringe privacy. Another disadvantage of registers is that they are not always so accurate as nationwide censuses, particularly when records are collected and held locally. It seems unlikely that register-based censuses could be adopted across the Union both for these reasons and because countries including France, Greece, Ireland, Portugal and the United Kingdom have not in the past kept registers of their population and could not easily reconstitute longitudinal data (Eggerickx and Bégeot, 1993, p. 1715).

In addition to census and register-based data, in most countries statistics are collected on families and households at regular intervals by other means. Sampling and sample surveys are used in Austria, Denmark, Germany and the United Kingdom to gather information about population and economic activity; labour force sample surveys are carried out across the Union. A few countries conduct family budget surveys (Denmark, Greece, Ireland, the Netherlands and Portugal) or surveys of household income (France and Luxembourg) (Council of Europe, 1990, p. 18). Materials from most of these sources are available for comparative analysis, but they too need to be handled with caution since the criteria on which they are based may vary from one national context to another.

## The impact of national culture on data collection

Whether or not data are collected at European level, national governments require regular and up-to-date socio-demographic information on the behaviour of families (birth-rates, fertility rates, divorce rates) and about family forms (size, structure and organisation) as an essential component in the policy-making process. Time series data are analysed to establish and monitor trends with a view to assessing the need for housing, schools, training, social security benefits, and other social services.

Attempts at European level to harmonise data collected in member states on demographic trends and measurements of family composition and structure are further hampered by the fact that statistics are not indifferent to the environment in which they are produced. The work of statisticians has long been subject to constraints that may determine both the type of information collected and the way it is analysed. Statistics tend to reflect the social order at a given point in time, the politically and ideologically motivated choices made by governments, as well as national or local sensitivities on particular issues. Data collected by national statistical organisations on social affairs can generally be interpreted as a response to a particular demand. Contextual information is therefore essential if international comparisons of statistics are to be worthwhile and meaningful.

The cultural embedding of statistical concepts can be illustrated by a few examples. The term 'depopulation' was introduced in France in 1870. Although Germany experienced the same phenomenon, the Germans have resolutely refused to use the term to describe it (Dienel, 1992). Some countries have decided not to ask questions on topics concerning contentious issues such as nationality or what are considered as private matters. Ireland and the United Kingdom ask about ethnicity or race rather than nationality, and in Luxembourg the response 'separated or divorced' has been removed from questions about marital status (Eggerickx and Bégeot, 1993, pp. 1719, 1721). Another politically loaded term is 'head of household'. From the 1970s, the concept of head of household was increasingly opposed on political and social grounds in several EU member states. The United Nations recommended replacing it by 'occupant of the dwelling' (a term not generally used) or 'reference person', to be identified by one of the household members, and the latter concept was subsequently adopted in most EU member states (Council of Europe, 1990, pp. 15–16). Despite general agreement over the term, national differences persist in the way the reference person is identified and recorded, as illustrated below.

### Concepts and definitions

The examples given in the previous section suggest that seemingly familiar statistical concepts cannot be properly understood unless they are located within the contexts from which they are derived and for which they are intended. Similarly, statistical definitions are no more than conventions that need to be interpreted in relation to national socio-political contexts. In some countries, families and households were defined for census purposes in the nineteenth century. Definitions have subsequently been refined, adapted and extended to other national contexts as attempts have been made to achieve standardisation across the Union. In this section, the main concepts associated with families and households are examined with reference to the definitions adopted at European level and their application in individual member states.

### *Families*

For statistical purposes, Eurostat has implemented the United Nations' definition of the family unit based on 'the conjugal family concept', as established in 1978 and then revised in 1987 for the 1991 round of population and housing censuses. According to the 1987 recommendations:

131. For census purposes, the family should be defined in the narrow sense of a family nucleus, that is, the persons within a private or institutional household who are related as husband and wife or as parent and never-married child by blood or adoption. Thus, a family nucleus comprises a married couple without children or a married couple with one or more never-married children of any age or one parent with one or more never-married children of any age.

132. The term 'married couple' in the above definition should include whenever possible couples who report that they are living in

consensual unions, and where feasible, a separate count of consensual unions and of legally married couples should be given. A woman who is living in a household with her own never-married child(ren) should be regarded as being in the same family nucleus as the child(ren) even is she is never-married and even if she is living in the same household as her parents; the same applies in the case of a man who is living in a household with his own never-married child(ren). 'Children' include step-children as well as adopted children, but not foster children.

(United Nations Statistical Commission/Economic Commission for Europe Conference of European Statisticians, 1987, p. 35)

From the statistician's point of view, the family nucleus may be interpreted as a subcategory of a household, composed of couples or singles and the children to whom they are biologically related (but also including adopted children), generally for so long as these children remain unmarried. In some cases, a family nucleus may be equivalent to a household.

Not all the requirements of the United Nations' definition have been observed by EU member states. For the 1991 censuses, Belgium included married children living with parents in cases where they were not living with a spouse or their own children. Single persons were regarded as families in Denmark, Finland and Sweden. Grandchildren living with their grandparents were considered as family nuclei in Germany, Luxembourg, Portugal and the United Kingdom (Eurostat, 1995b, table 1; Simões Casimiro and Calado Lopes, 1995, pp. 18–38).

The revised version of the United Nations' definition quoted above took account of the growing interest in unmarried cohabitation. The 1978 definition had not requested that a distinction should be made between couples living in consensual unions and those who are legally married. In 1981, unmarried cohabiting couples were recorded as family nuclei in Denmark, France, Ireland, Luxembourg, Portugal and Spain. Ten years later, Italy and the United Kingdom adapted their definitions, with Belgium, Germany, Greece and the Netherlands still not recognising consensual unions for statistical purposes.

An important source of discrepancy between countries in definitions of the family can arise from differences in dealing with the age of children. In most EU member states, no age limit was applied in 1991, whereas in Denmark, Finland and Sweden, children were considered as part of the family up to the age of 18, and in Luxembourg to 25. A change from 26 to 18 in Denmark between the two census dates produced a fall of 13.6 per cent in the proportion of married couples without children (Simões Casimiro and Calado Lopes, 1995, p. 70). France applied a limit of 25 until 1982, but it was abolished for the 1991 census

(Eurostat, 1995b, table 1). The effect was to increase the proportion of lone-parent family nuclei by 34.8 per cent (Simões Casimiro and Calado Lopes, 1995, p. 71).

## Households

Data collected in national censuses generally take private households rather than families as the unit of measurement. Eurostat has also used the United Nations' definition for the private household, as distinct from the 'institutional household', basing it on the concept of the 'housekeeping unit':

121. A private household is either:

(a) a one-person household, i.e. a person who lives alone in a separate housing unit or who occupies, as a lodger, a separate room (or rooms) of a housing unit and does not join with any of the other occupants of the housing unit to form part of a multi-person household as defined below; or

(b) a multi-person household, i.e. a group of two or more persons who combine to occupy the whole or part of a housing unit and to provide themselves with food and possibly other essentials for living. The group may pool their income to a greater or lesser extent. The group may be composed of related persons only or of unrelated persons or of a combination of both, including boarders and excluding lodgers.

(United Nations Statistical Commission/Economic Commission for Europe Conference of European Statisticians, 1987, p. 33)

Boarders are defined as taking meals with the household and are generally allowed to use all the available household facilities, whereas lodgers are sub-tenants who are renting part of the housing unit for their exclusive use.

Despite the standard definitions at international level, differences in focus become apparent when countries are compared. Most EU member states have adopted the United Nation's concept of the 'housekeeping unit', but Denmark, Finland, France and Sweden refer to the concept of 'household dwelling'. Accordingly, the main place of residence is taken as the criterion enabling a household to be defined as the aggregate number of persons occupying a housing unit and does not therefore yield information on the number of housekeeping units within a household. Because they are largely equated with housing units, the number of households is consequently underestimated in comparison with other countries. In Germany, individuals occupying more than one dwelling for professional reasons are counted twice. As a result, the number of single-person households may be inflated. Italy and

Portugal consider a unit as a household only if the people living in it are related by blood or marriage; they therefore effectively equate households with families.

While most countries base their census data on the *de jure* concept, which covers all persons usually resident in an area, irrespective of where they are at the time of the survey, Ireland and Greece adopt the pragmatic solution of counting as a household everyone present in a dwelling on the census date, representing the *de facto* situation (Eurostat, 1995b, p. 3).

The structure of households as recorded in statistics may be affected by differences in the way the head of household or reference person is designated. The household in Austria, Italy, the Netherlands, Portugal and Spain identify the reference person themselves. In Germany and the United Kingdom, the respondent entered on the first line of the survey form is designated as the reference person, but without information being collected on the relationship between him/her and other household members in the 1987 census in Germany. In Denmark, the wife is considered as the reference person when the family nucleus consists of a married couple with children. In other types of families, the status is accorded to the oldest person and, in Finland, to the person contributing most to household income. In France, the reference person is determined by using the criteria of age, sex and occupational status of the members of the household (Council of Europe, 1990, p. 16; Simões Casimiro and Calado Lopes, 1995, table 8c). From a comparative perspective, an anomaly may therefore arise when, for example, an economically inactive woman aged 50 and her 25 year-old unmarried son, who is earning a reasonable income, are living together in the woman's house: in England, she could be identified as the reference person, while this status would be assigned to the son in Finland.

## Unmarried cohabitation

Accurate statistics on the number of consensual unions are difficult both to collect and interpret even within a single national context, since the status of unmarried cohabiting couples may be a temporary and relatively unstable arrangement which is not normally recorded in registers. In addition, where liability for taxation and eligibility for social security benefits can be affected by non-marital cohabitation, individuals may attempt to conceal a *de facto* situation, and couples may have many personal reasons for not wanting to admit that they are living together without being married.

Consensual unions are generally defined according to two criteria: a shared dwelling and the fact of living together as man and wife. Different definitions are, however, observed from one country to another. The use of national population censuses, as compared with survey data, is also likely to influence findings since census data tend to focus on the sharing of the place of residence, whereas surveys pay more attention to the relationship between cohabitees. Comparative analysis over time or between countries of non-marital cohabitation is therefore problematic.

In the United Kingdom, since 1979 the General Household Survey (GHS) has identified a cohabiting couple as a 'co-resident man and woman living together within a sexual union, without that union having been formalised with either a civil or religious ceremony' (Haskey and Kiernan, 1989, p. 23). The criteria of co-residence, a sexual or emotional and relatively stable relationship (euphemistically described as living together as a couple), and the absence of formal marriage are widely accepted as the defining characteristics of consensual unions, although the information needed to identify unmarried cohabiting couples is not routinely collected across the Union.

The 1987 micro-census in Germany identified co-resident men and women who were neither related nor married to one another and unmarried children under the age of eighteen, but without being able to determine whether couples who claimed to be two one-person households were actually living in a consensual union (Council of Europe, 1990, p. 16). In Finland, the age difference within couples had to be less than sixteen years for them to count as consensual unions. Until 1991, Denmark did not count couples without a joint child as cohabitees. In the United Kingdom, couples were recorded as living in consensual unions only if they themselves stated they were living as man and wife, while in France the relationship had to be deduced from the information collected from separate census questions about couples living together without claiming to be married. Only in Portugal and the United Kingdom, however, was it possible to estimate cohabitation with a reasonable degree of certainty. Estimates for Denmark, France and Italy were less reliable, and in Luxembourg and the Netherlands, it was considered impossible to produce any data (Simões Casimiro and Calado Lopes, 1995, table 12).

### Lone-parent families

Statistical comparisons at European level of the number of single-parent families, or lone-parent families as they have come to be called, are unreliable, because the phenomenon is often conceptualised and measured differently from one society to another and because they form a particularly unstable and heterogeneous category. The United Nations recommends that a parent living alone with a child or children should be recorded separately but does not specify an age limit. Disparities between countries in statistics showing the relative importance of lone parenthood may therefore be explained less by empirical evidence than by variations in recording techniques. The absence of the age criterion means that a single-parent family could be composed of an elderly widow living with a daughter in her sixties or of a young unmarried mother with a child of two. Data from the Belgian census in 1981 showed, for example, that a quarter of lone parents were aged over 65 (Roll, 1992, p. 7).

In an attempt to formulate a standardised definition that could be used in the European context for a report on lone-parent families in the twelve member states, Jo Roll (1992, pp. 7–10) identified three main issues that needed to be taken into consideration: the marital status of the parent, the family's household situation and the definition of a dependent child. The resulting definition of lone parenthood was:

A parent who
— is NOT living in a couple (meaning either a married or a cohabiting couple)
— may or may not be living with others (e.g. friends or own parents)
— is living with at least one child under 18 years old.

(Roll, 1992, p. 10)

For the 1991 census date, Portugal, Spain and the United Kingdom were considered to be in a position to provide full estimates of lone-parent family nuclei. Other member states could provide data for most situations (Simões Casimiro and Calado Lopes, 1995, table 12). Even when seemingly comparable overall figures are available, lone-parent families can be comprised of divorcees, separated or widowed spouses or unmarried parents, whose living conditions may be very different. For statistical purposes, as mentioned above, not all countries make a distinction between separation and divorce, and Greece does not produce official figures for the number of lone-parent families, although it does record the number of divorces involving children and the number of extramarital births.

### Reconstituted families

A related phenomenon which has not yet been given the same attention in official statistics is what has been termed the multiparental family, step-family, reconstituted, blended or re-ordered family (Burgoyne and Clark, 1982; Théry, 1993; Utting, 1995). Statistical definitions of the family unit have proved to be inadequate as a tool for representing the more complex family structures that arise when households are composed of one biological parent (although both biological parents may still be alive) and a step-parent living with children from more than one marriage or a non-marital relationship. The situation is further complicated when children share their time between more than one family and household in cases where parents have joint custody. The United Nations' definition of family nuclei, as quoted above, does take account of step-children, but the lack of information in national census data about the biological relationships between respondents means that it may not be possible to tell whether children are related to the adults with whom they may be living. With the exception of Portugal, the EU member states were not in a position to identify reconstituted families in their 1991 censuses (Simões Casimiro and Calado Lopes, 1995, table 12).

The changing composition of households and families has made it necessary for statisticians to rethink their categories and to look for new ways of identifying and measuring them. Changes may occur over a relatively short period of time and can only be effectively observed and recorded using detailed questionnaire surveys or by collecting accounts of individual life histories. According to criteria that are being progressively adopted, for statistical purposes a reconstituted family can be said to consist of a couple of adults, married or single, and at least one child from a previous union of one member of the couple (Bridgwood and Savage, 1993, p. 13; Desplanques, 1993, p. 81; Villeneuve-Gokalp, 1993, p. 324). Children living with both parents and their step-brothers and sisters therefore also belong to a re-ordered family, even though their own biological family has not been broken up and reconstituted.

## One-person households

Not all couples in conjugal or consensual unions live together, and not all individuals living in the same dwelling form families or households. Two or more individuals may be 'living apart together' (LAT). Persons living alone are therefore often difficult to classify, and the term 'one-person households', used in census data, may misrepresent national situations.

In countries where cohabitation is not recognised, the number of individuals living alone may be overestimated. In Italy, an analysis of *de facto* situations has shown that consensual unions are often not admitted and that many older people registered as living alone are actually living with their children (Kaufmann, 1994, p. 938). In Germany, as already mentioned, the number of people living alone tends, by contrast, to be overestimated. When children are living away from home, as in the case of students, but continue to be registered at their parents' address, as in the United Kingdom, the proportion of one-person households or households without children is likely to be lower than in countries where students are registered at their place of residence, as in the Netherlands. The examples of consensual unions, lone-parent and reconstituted families, and one-person households illustrate the difficulties which arise when trying to collect and analyse comparable statistical data on families and households across countries, confirming the need to exercise extreme caution in interpreting information derived from different national sources.

**Trends in family and household composition and structure**

Since its foundation in 1958, Eurostat has collected statistical data from member states on a range of demographic indicators, many of which focus on family and household size and structure, based on information supplied by national statistical services and converted using a software system called SYSCODEM. Eurostat's annual publication, *Demographic Statistics*, provides a series of tables that include data on total fertility rates (the number of births to women during the reproductive period of their lives), marriage and divorce rates, and the number of extramarital births (Eurostat, 1994a).

In addition, studies have been commissioned at European level on lone parenthood (Roll, 1992), solo women (Millar, 1991) and one-person households (Kaufmann, 1994), and attempts have been made to compile data on cohabitation and reconstituted families, for at least some member states (Roussel, 1992; Kiernan and Estaugh, 1993; Meulders-Klein and Théry, 1993). In this section, information from these different sources is drawn together to illustrate various aspects of the composition and structure of families and households in EU member states, with the object of trying to identify and track the trends that have been referred to as being at the root of common problems across the Union. The period covered spans the 1960s to the 1990s, during which the European Economic Community was developing, expanding and undergoing rapid demographic change. Figures for Germany represent the territorial status as from 3 October 1990. Although Austria, Finland and Sweden did not become members of the Union until 1995, Eurostat has also calculated data for these countries using a common method.

Eurostat indicators do not differentiate between subcategories of the population in member states, a restriction which can be justified on the grounds that the inhabitants of any one nation state are subject to the same legal, social and material constraints and may therefore be expected to display broadly similar patterns of family building and family structure, as argued by Louis Roussel (1992, p. 134). Regional differences within countries in economic development and in policy implementation are, however, far from being negligible, and the legal framework may not apply uniformly across a member state, as in the case of the United Kingdom or in federal states, such as Germany.

*Family building*

The United Nations' (1987) definition of the family unit stipulated that couples should be either married or living together as man and wife, or that one or both parents should be living with their unmarried children. A family unit is thus formed either by marriage (or a consensual union) or by the arrival of children. Data compiled by Eurostat for the period 1960 to 1994 (Figure 1.1) show that, by the mid-1970s, the number of marriages per 1000 population was falling in most countries, particularly where it had been high in the 1960s. Greece, Ireland and, especially, Portugal, which peaked in 1975, were bucking the trend. By 1994, marriage rates had fallen in all countries, reaching particularly low levels in Sweden, France and Ireland, whereas much higher rates had been maintained in Denmark and Portugal. Age at first marriage had been rising everywhere since the 1960s, reaching a mean of 28.5 for women in Denmark in 1993 (Eurostat, 1995a, table F-15).

In the early 1990s, most children were born within wedlock. Data on total fertility rates, as shown in Figure 1.2, provide an indication about family formation patterns both within marriage and extramaritally. From the mid-1960s, at the same time as effective means of contraception were becoming more widely available, and legislation was being enacted in most member states to enable the whole population, at least in theory, to have access to birth control, fertility rates were declining in all countries with the exception of Greece. Between 1975 and 1994, rates increased in Finland, Luxembourg and Sweden, after having fallen to some of the lowest levels in the Union in the 1970s. By 1994, the rank order had changed substantially, with some of the countries that had shown the highest fertility rates in 1960 registering the most marked fall. Although Ireland, where abortion was still illegal in 1994, continued to record one of the highest levels, Sweden had moved from a position low down the scale in 1960 to the top, after peaking at an even higher level in 1990 with 2.30. Italy and Spain showed the lowest rates in 1994. Disparities between member states had not disappeared, although the gap between the most and the least prolific nations had narrowed from 1.56 to 0.70.

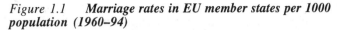

*Figure 1.1* **Marriage rates in EU member states per 1000 population (1960–94)**

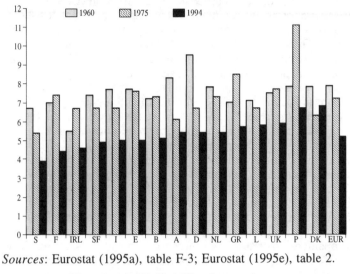

*Sources*: Eurostat (1995a), table F-3; Eurostat (1995e), table 2.

*Note*: 1993 figure for the United Kingdom.

*Figure 1.2* **Total fertility rates in EU member states (1960–94)**

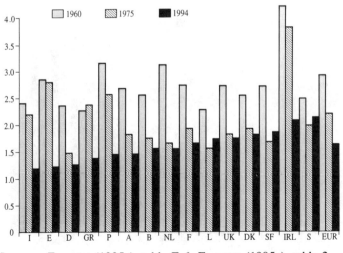

*Sources*: Eurostat (1995a), table E-6; Eurostat (1995e), table 2.

*Note*: 1994 figures are estimates for Belgium and the Netherlands.

The number of consensual unions is much more difficult to estimate, as explained in the previous section, and a full dataset is not available for all EU member states. Information covering trends in the 1970s for different age groups in some member states shows that most cohabiting women were in their late teens or early twenties. Different patterns of cohabitation could be identified across the Union. In two of the Nordic countries – Denmark and Sweden – cohabitation was well established. In Austria, Finland, France, Germany, the Netherlands and the United Kingdom, cohabitation began to emerge during the 1970s as a transitional phase before marriage. Although no statistics were available for this period, cohabitation was thought to be unusual in the south European countries (Kiernan and Estaugh, 1993, pp. 61–2).

In Denmark and Sweden, the growing numbers of consensual unions have been accompanied by particularly high extramarital birth-rates, as illustrated by Figure 1.3. In Austria, Finland, France and the United Kingdom, cohabitation would also seem to be associated with extramarital births, whereas in Germany and the Netherlands rising levels of non-marital cohabitation have not been accompanied by such a large increase in births outside marriage. Extramarital birth-rates remained relatively low in Greece, Italy and Spain and, during the period in question, the disparity between the highest and lowest rates increased from 11.8 to 46.9.

*Figure 1.3    Live births outside marriage per 100 live births in EU member states (1960–92)*

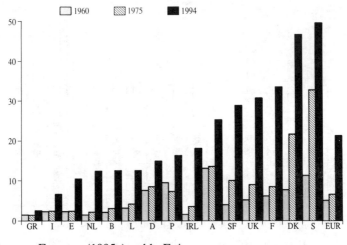

*Source*: Eurostat (1995a), table E-4.

*Note*: 1991 figure for Belgium.

*Figure 1.4* **Gross divorce rates per 1000 population in EU member states (1960–94)**

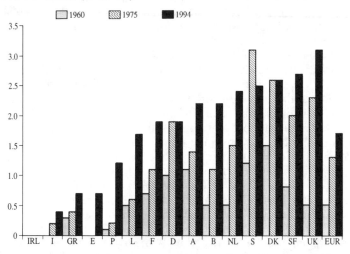

*Sources*: Eurostat (1995a), table F-19; Eurostat (1995e), table 2.

*Note*: 1993 figures for France, Germany, Italy, Portugal, Spain and the United Kingdom.

*Figure 1.5* **Lone-parent families with children aged under 15 in EU member states in percentages (1981–91)**

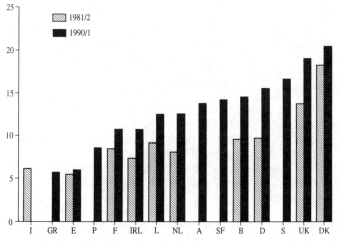

*Source*: Data supplied by Eurostat.

Extramarital births may also be associated with divorce in cases where divorcees do not seek to remarry. Eurostat data on divorce, as presented in Figure 1.4, show that between 1960 and 1994, despite a doubling in the rates in most member states, the north continued to be distinguished from the south where divorce had been harder to obtain. Here, the Nordic countries and the United Kingdom were already displaying relatively high rates by the mid-1970s. While the level had fallen in Germany and Sweden by 1994 and had stabilised in Denmark, elsewhere it continued to rise. No data were available for Ireland, where divorce was still illegal.

The fall in the number of marriages, the increase in the number of divorces and the growth in the number of extramarital births are associated with rising levels of lone parenthood, as shown in Figure 1.5. The datasets are incomplete due to problems in collecting standardised information at national level. For the 1981/82 and 1990/91 censuses, or equivalent, Eurostat data for lone-parent families with at least one child under fifteen as a proportion of the total number of families in this category place Denmark and the United Kingdom at the top of the scale for both dates, followed by Sweden for 1990/91. The south European countries recorded the lowest rates across the two census dates.

Nor do the data available at European level allow a distinction to be made between different concepts of the family: lone-parent households cannot be distinguished according to whether they are the result of births to women living alone, separated or widowed. National statistics for the United Kingdom suggest that, since the 1980s in the countries displaying some of the highest levels, lone parenthood has increasingly become the result of divorce or separation, including the breakdown of a cohabiting relationship, rather than widowhood (Roll, 1992), and that the most rapidly expanding route to lone parenthood is for never-married women (Haskey, 1993, p. 29).

*Family and household size and composition*

Data collected about private households, following the criteria recommended by the United Nations, make it possible to track family size and composition over time and across countries. As well as providing information about changes in family size, data collated by Eurostat distinguish between family and non-family households and different family types, including couples with and without children.

As shown in Figure 1.6, between the 1980/81 and 1990/91 censuses, the average size of households had declined everywhere except Germany. The steep fall in fertility rates in the south European countries had not yet resulted in their household size falling to the level reached in the northern member states. The reduction in cohabitation between several generations, which had contributed to the decline in household size also helps to explain the increase throughout the Union in the number of one-person households during the 1980s. Data from the 1990/91 censuses showed almost 70 per cent of private households comprised at least one family, but the proportion of one-person households ranged from below 14 per cent in Portugal and Spain to almost 40 per cent in Sweden. Denmark, Germany and Sweden, which already showed the highest proportion of one-person households at the beginning of the 1980s, saw their proportion reach more than a third of all households but, as indicated above, the rank order may be distorted due to differences in definitions.

Eurostat data for couples without children do not distinguish between couples whose offspring have left home and those who have not yet had children but are expecting to do so, or couples who have never had children. Although they do record the number of divorces and remarriages, national data are not available across the Union to enable analysts to begin to unravel the structure of reconstituted families or the transitions from one family or household type to another. Differences between countries in definitions of family units and, consequently, in the way that

*Figure 1.6*  **Private households in EU member states (1980/81–1990/91)**

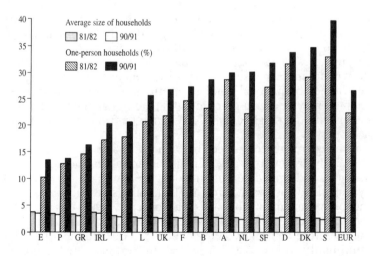

*Sources*: Council of Europe (1990), tables 3.1, 3.2a; Eurostat (1995b), tables 2, 5.

*Note*: Federal Republic of Germany for 1981/82 figures.

statistics are collected – not all countries record consensual unions or the relationship between adults and children living together – mean that comparisons cannot be made for reconstituted families. In the new form of lone parenthood that has been developing, the second biological parent is still alive but living apart from his or her children and, like the parent living alone with children, can create a new or reconstituted family unit. Survey data for France, collected in 1990, indicated that some 750,000 children aged under nineteen were living in families composed of one of their parents and a stepparent, or 5.5 per cent of children in that age group, and that 660,000 families could be described as reconstituted (Desplanques, 1993, pp. 82, 86). Data from the GHS in the United Kingdom suggested that 8 per cent of families with dependent children contained one or more step-children (Bridgwood and Savage, 1993, p. 14). Information collected for Eurostat on Finland indicates that 7 per cent of all families with children may be 'reconstituted'. The phenomenon is not therefore negligible and deserves to be more widely analysed.

## Statistical comparisons of family and household structures

The material examined in this chapter suggests that cross-national comparisons of statistical data on families and households need to be handled with extreme caution for several reasons: firstly, the statistical apparatus used for collecting and analysing data has often been constructed differently from one country to another in accordance with national conventions; secondly, social statistics are drawn up in response to a specific demand, which may be determined by national political priorities; thirdly, the categories adopted may be based on criteria that are not applied uniformly, either within a single country over time or from one country to another.

Although reference has been made in this chapter to definitions of the family drawn up by international organisations, no universally accepted and agreed definition would seem to have been applied systematically across the Union. The family is not, in any event, a monolithic and immutable statistical concept. Rather, it is a generic term concealing a plurality of family forms. Statistical definitions are therefore constantly being called into question and must be continually revised and adapted in response to changing circumstances.

Whereas registers can be used to record formal events in family life (births and deaths, marriages and divorces), consensual unions, lone parenthood, reconstituted families and one-person households are unstable situations, which are difficult to identify and track over long time intervals. Yet, they are the family and household relationships which may create some of the heaviest demands on policy makers. Statisticians have therefore been required to find new ways of defining and measuring them. The high rates recorded in some countries may, like crime figures, reflect the refinement of data collection techniques as well as the willingness of individuals to admit to a relationship previously considered socially unacceptable.

Several examples have been given in this chapter of discrepancies that can arise from one country to another in definitions of families and households: the use of the conjugal family concept may or may not include unmarried cohabiting couples; the household may be defined in terms of a common dwelling or shared housekeeping; censuses may record *de jure* or *de facto* situations; the age category attributed to dependent children may vary from one country to another and from one census to another. Even when the same questions are asked and data are supposedly harmonised, similar findings may reflect quite different realities. Overall figures for marriage and divorce, consensual unions, lone parenthood, extramarital births and household size conceal divergent underlying patterns: unmarried cohabitation may be a prelude to marriage or represent a more enduring arrangement; the growth in the number of people recorded as living alone may be due to more young people leaving the parental home before getting married; it may reflect the number of divorced men temporarily living alone, or it may be explained by the increasing number of older people living by themselves. In most countries, a variety of factors will lie behind the statistics, but the way they combine to produce particular configurations will be determined by national statistical conventions and other contextual factors.

Users of statistical measures of families and households for comparative purposes therefore need to remain alert to possible errors of interpretation that can arise if conceptual and contextual differences are ignored.

CHAPTER 2

# Institutional definitions of the family

For many centuries governments, at national and local level, have collected information about the characteristics and behaviour of their populations for administrative purposes. In seventeenth-century France, for example, the monarch required regular reports on the population in the provinces as a basis for levying taxes and ensuring the efficient operation of the apparatus of the state. In the second half of the same century, the fragmented German Empire needed demographic information to help it redefine the rights and duties of individuals within rival micro-states. During the same period in England, in the face of opposition to nationwide censuses, the state was using parish registers as a means of identifying and recording population size and growth and the relationships within households for administrative ends (Desrosières, 1993, pp. 26–59). Since the Second World War, the development of universal social protection systems in Western Europe has focused attention on the needs of individuals, and more especially of families, making accurate and up-to-date socio-demographic indicators of family formation and structure even more necessary as instruments for policy formulation and implementation. Legal systems must be able to identify family relationships for the purposes of establishing the rights of individual members, as for example in the case of inheritance or custody and maintenance following divorce. The rules to be observed in raising taxes may require government officials to determine the relationship between cohabiting couples or the paternity of children in reconstituted families. Eligibility for social security benefits and access to social services may also depend upon legally defined family relationships.

In the process of gathering information, the state inevitably encroaches on the personal lives of individuals and infringes their privacy. Article 8 of the Council of Europe's European Convention for the Protection of Human Rights and Fundamental Freedoms, drawn up in 1950, sought to impose limits on state intervention in family affairs by stipulating that:

1.  Everyone has the right to respect of his [*sic*] private and family life, his home and his correspondence.

2. There shall be no interference by a public authority with the exercise of this right except such as is in accordance with the law and is necessary in a democratic society in the interests of national security, public safety or the economic well-being of the country, for the prevention of disorder or crime, for the protection of health or morals, or for the protection of the rights and freedom of others.

(The European Convention on Human Rights, signed in Rome on 4 November 1950)

Some EU member states, for example Ireland or the United Kingdom, interpret Article 8 as meaning that the state should not interfere in family matters and have used it to justify their own formal non-interventionist stance. Others, such as France or the Netherlands, have found that their constitutions and national legislation, which legitimate state intervention in family affairs, bring them into conflict with the European Convention because it implies that unwarranted interference by the state or by other individuals is not acceptable (Meulders-Klein, 1993, pp. 113, 127, 138–9).

The concept of privacy as embodied in the Convention is a potential source of disagreement in that it juxtaposes two sets of rights that are not necessarily compatible: those of the individual and those of the family unit. While Article 8 emphasises individual rights, Article 12 empowers states to exercise control over marriage and family formation by giving them discretion to find ways of achieving a balance between the interests of individuals and those of the family as a unit: 'Men and women of marriageable age have the right to marry and to found a family, according to the national laws governing the exercise of this right.' Cases brought before the courts have clarified the obligation of states towards family members, for example by ensuring legal protection for children born in and out of wedlock, but it has not confirmed the existence of a right to marriage or to divorce for two persons of the same sex (Meulders-Klein, 1992, pp. 774–5). The issue of the relationship between public (state) and private (family and individual) rights, obligations and responsibilities is central to an understanding of the institutionalisation of the family and is a recurring theme in subsequent chapters, particularly within the context of the debate over public and private provision of services.

Chapter 1 showed how statistics are compiled and analysed at the behest of institutional users and how statistical representations of families and households are determined in no small measure by national conventions and by political priorities and ideologies. In this chapter, an attempt is made to illustrate the ways in which the definitions used for administrative purposes can also be influenced both by national cultural traditions and supranational organisations, resulting in different practices from one EU member state to another. In the first section, the constitutional and institutional status of the family is examined across the Union, followed by an analysis of definitions of family relationships within national frameworks, particularly with reference to the legal obligations and responsibilities of family members towards one another. The account taken of family structure in tax law and the concept of the 'benefit' family as the recipient of welfare are examined in Chapter 3 within the wider context of public policies directed towards families. The intention in both these chapters is not to produce a country-by-country catalogue of the main characteristics in each member state for all the aspects being examined, as in the reports of the European Observatory on National Family Policies or European-wide studies like that carried out in the early 1990s for the German Bundesministerium für Familie und Senioren (Neubauer *et al.*, 1993). Rather, clusters of countries are identified which display similar patterns in their legislative frameworks, and cases are highlighted that are of particular interest from a comparative perspective.

## The constitutional status of families

The family has served as a focal point for social protection and is generally held to be a – if not the – core social institution in most EU member states. Whereas in statistics, the household is the main unit of measurement, the family group is more often the reference point for legislation. Several EU member states commit themselves in their constitutions to ensuring the protection of families. In this section, constitutional frameworks for dealing with family affairs are examined as a means of illustrating how different countries have conceptualised the family in institutional terms.

In most member states, the normative institutional framework of the family is embodied in the national constitution. In Finland, France, Germany, Greece, Ireland, Italy, Luxembourg, Portugal and Spain, the constitution recognises the family as a social institution and undertakes to afford it protection. The ways in which the family is conceptualised in the constitution differ, however, from one country to another. In some cases, as exemplified by Finland, Greece, France and Portugal, the national constitution affords an enabling and supportive framework for family law; in other cases, as for example in Germany or Luxembourg, the constitution may act as a source of rigidity, focusing attention on the legitimate family as sanctioned by marriage; or the constitution may constrain action on the grounds that the state should protect the family unit against outside intrusion, as in Ireland; some countries have shifted from a position where, in periods of oppression, the constitution provided a strict normative framework, as in Italy and Spain, to a situation where it is used to justify intervention by the state only when the 'proper' channels for action – the family itself or the private market – are unable to respond adequately.

The Portuguese constitution (Article 67) probably goes further than any other EU member state in conceptualising the family as a fundamental social institution deserving support from the state. The family is not simply a legal concept. Rather, it is considered as a social unit and, as such, has the right to protection both by the state and society (Amaro, 1994b, pp. 256–7). The Greek constitution also provides a supportive structure for the family unit. As early as 1926 the state undertook to afford protection to the family and, in the 1975 constitution (Article 21, paragraph 1), it is described as the 'foundation stone for the preservation and the advancement of the nation'. The state has committed itself to protecting the family, marriage, motherhood and childhood (Moussourou, 1994, pp. 87–8). In the 1946 constitution in France, the nation undertook to ensure that individuals and families were provided with the conditions needed for their development, justifying state intervention in support of the family unit and recognising it as an important social institution.

In several countries, the constitution has served to conceptualise the legitimate family founded on marriage. Article 6 of the Basic Law (*Grundgesetz*), established in the Federal Republic of Germany in 1949, and later constitutional regulations, such as section 1 of Article 3GG, state that marriage and the family are to be protected and promoted by the state (Wingen and Stutzer, 1994, p. 57). Although, under Article 11 of the 1868 constitution in Luxembourg, the state is designated as guarantor of the rights of individuals and the family, in civil law the narrower concept of the legitimate family modelled on the state has been prominent in legislation designed to protect family members (Neyens, 1994, pp. 200, 205).

The importance of the legitimate family was recognised in the Irish constitution of 1937, when the state undertook to 'guard with special care the institution of marriage' (Article 41.3.1). Subsequently, in 1966 the Supreme Court interpreted this wording to mean that the family is founded on marriage. The apparent commitment of the state was, however, tempered by the fact that the constitution regards the family as 'possessing inalienable and imprescriptible rights antecedent and superior to all positive law', taken to mean that the private nature of the family is sacrosanct, and justifying the non-intervention of the state in anything that can be regarded as the prerogative of families themselves. Court cases have led to the conclusion that the emphasis on the rights of the family, as enshrined in the constitution, may give greater value to the rights of parents over those of children to the detriment of the latter. The constitution also provides a normative framework for the division of labour within households by stating that 'mothers should not be obliged by economic necessity to engage in labour to the neglect of their duties in the home' (Article 41.2.2). Controversial cases have been used to challenge established norms and test the limits of the powers of the state by bringing them before the courts, as for example over abortion, which is discussed further below (Kiely and Richardson, 1994, pp. 151, 157, 164–5, 171–2).

Both Italy and Spain experienced Fascist regimes during which the family was conceptualised as a patriarchal unit. Subsequent legislation can, to some extent, be considered as a reaction to authoritarianism. Article 29 of the 1947 constitution in Italy recognised the rights of the family as a fundamental social unit founded on marriage, with the express intention of upholding family unity, but dependent on the moral and legal equality of spouses. Under the influence of the Catholic Church, however, the constitution reflected the view that women were primarily wives and mothers. Constitutional rights were ensured only for legitimate families, and Article 37 laid down the responsibility of the state to protect women as workers so as 'to enable them to fulfil their essential family function' (Bimbi, 1993, pp. 147–8). During the period of oppression under the Franco regime, the constitution served as a basis for supporting a hierarchical family, a concept which was rejected in post-authoritarian Spain. The 1978 constitution pledged the state to provide social, economic and legal protection to the family but has not been interpreted rigidly (Valiente, 1995).

These examples show how national constitutions have often set the parameters for legislation with respect to the rights and duties of family members. In some cases, the legitimate family has been defined by the institution of marriage, and the state has been assigned far-reaching powers that may bring it into conflict with the European Convention and impede the process of legislative reform. In others the constitution has been less prescriptive. The representation of the family in national constitutions may, however, be merely symbolic, since constitutional principles are not always legally binding; only in Germany do the constitutional courts have far-reaching powers. It is therefore important to take account of the ways in which the principles embodied in constitutions are translated into civil law and to consider the extent to which laws are enforced in individual countries across the Union.

## The family in law

While the family has been clearly identified in the constitutions of most member states as a target for state protection, civil law has established the legal rights and duties of family members. Over the postwar period, legal frameworks have been adapted to take account of changes in family forms: progressively, EU member states have introduced legislation on the rights of children born in and out of wedlock and on parental authority, reflecting changing attitudes and behaviour. Laws have been adapted in most countries to allow divorce, contraception, abortion and medically assisted reproduction and the legal recognition of consensual unions and extramarital births.

Legal systems are the product of a combination of factors, reflecting different national philosophical and religious traditions, and the pace and timing of social processes (Assier-Andrieu and Commaille, 1995). Although a particular piece of legislation may be interpreted as a response to a situation that is common to all member states, the debates surrounding reforms and the problems encountered by policy makers in formulating, enacting and implementing legislation provide insights into the complexities of the legal frameworks established at national level to deal with family affairs. In this section, the ways in which the family is conceptualised in law by EU member states are examined with reference to the legislation governing the different stages of family formation and breakdown.

### *Marriage and divorce*

Across the Union, legislation has progressively been adapted to reflect the secularisation of marriage, public demand for the recognition of the breakdown of marriage and for divorce to be available on the grounds of mutual consent. Change has not taken place either at the same rate or to the same extent from one country to another: for example, when marriage is presented in the constitution of a country as the defining criterion for the existence of a family, and constitutional principles have been enshrined in legislation, it may be more difficult to introduce reform on divorce, consensual unions or the rights of children born outside wedlock.

Practices differ across the Union with regard to the form that marriage may take and the legal age of marriage. In all the founder member states of the European Economic Community except Italy (Belgium, France, Germany, Luxembourg and the Netherlands), civil marriage is compulsory (Eurostat, 1994a, table 1). The state sets the age at which marriage can take place. In most cases, the legal age of marriage is eighteen for men and women; but in France women can marry legally and without parental consent from the age of fifteen.

In the Nordic, Anglo-Saxon and south European countries that joined the European Union in later years (Denmark, Finland, Greece, Ireland, Portugal, Spain, Sweden and the United Kingdom) and also in Italy, marriage may be celebrated either in a church or in a registry office, or equivalent, but must be recorded in civil registers. The secularisation of marriage in Greece is relatively recent. From 1982 (Law 1250/1982, Article 1), civil marriage was made equally binding as a religious ceremony, thereby breaking with a tradition dating back to the ninth century (Moussourou, 1994, p. 89). The legal age of marriage in these countries is again generally eighteen for both men and women, although a younger age may be possible with parental consent.

Court cases have demonstrated that the European Convention has been more concerned with the bonds linking couples and their children (marriage, filiation) than with the failure of marriage and the arrangements within consensual unions (Meulders-Klein, 1992, p. 775). The extent to which the institution of marriage is binding and enduring – till death do us part – has, however, long been contested in the courts. The postwar period has been characterised by the gradual acceptance of a more lenient stance with regard to the grounds for divorce. The Nordic states tended to lead the way in changing their laws on divorce, making it easier to obtain and removing the need to demonstrate the guilt of one or other of the parties. In Denmark and Sweden, for example, divorce and settlement can be obtained by decree in cases of mutual consent. Under the new marriage code which came into force in 1988 in Sweden, the division of property can take place as soon as the divorce petition is filed. The Divorce Reform Act of 1969 in the United Kingdom virtually removed the notion of marital offence, and divorce by mutual consent was introduced in France in 1975.

Countries with a strong Catholic lobby, or where the constitution identifies marriage as a defining criterion for family life, have had to overcome strong opposition to reform of the law on divorce. In Belgium and Luxembourg, grounds for divorce include mutual consent and a separation of more than five years, and of three years in Germany. Although legal separation may be obtained by mutual consent in the Netherlands, the grounds for divorce have continued to be more restrictive. Among the south European countries, after a decade of parliamentary debate, Italy introduced divorce in 1970 (Act no. 898/1970) in cases of irretrievable breakdown of marriage. The reform of family law in 1975 (Act no. 151/1975) allowed judicial separation by mutual consent, and this became a route more often taken by couples in preference to formal divorce (Sgritta and Zanatta, 1994, pp. 177–8). In Spain, where divorce had been illegal since the 1930s, the law was reformed in 1981 (Fernández Cordón, 1994, p. 106). In Portugal, divorce was banned for Catholic marriages between 1940 and 1975 (Amaro, 1994b, p. 255). Since the state undertakes to protect marriage in the Greek constitution and in family law, divorce was difficult to institute, but by the mid-1990s couples could divorce by mutual consent and on the grounds of mutual incompatibility (Moussourou, 1994, pp. 89–90). The sanctity of marriage was recognised in the 1937 constitution in Ireland, which was the only EU member state not to have legalised divorce by the early 1990s. Legislation was introduced in 1989 to allow a non-adversarial judicial separation (Burke, 1991, pp. 34–6), but the law did not allow divorcees to remarry. Couples who lived together outside marriage were therefore excluded from the constitutional definition of the family (Kiely and Richardson, 1994, p. 163). In a referendum in 1986, 63.5 per cent of the Irish people who voted had wanted to uphold the ban on divorce, while a referendum in 1995 produced a narrow majority in favour of lifting the ban.

## Consensual unions

The case of unmarried cohabiting couples illustrates how social acceptability may affect the way concepts develop and change in different national and temporal contexts. As shown by the statistics on consensual unions, the north European countries were the first to record rising levels of extramarital cohabitation, and this was reflected in their legislation.

The rights of unmarried couples were first recognised formally in the 1970s in Denmark and Sweden, which were soon followed by France. By the late 1980s, unmarried cohabiting couples in these countries, and also in Italy, could officially register their partnership, implying that they could be considered to be living together as man and wife for purposes such as opening a joint bank account or being eligible for social housing. Although unmarried cohabiting couples are not automatically placed under legal obligations towards one another, case law has taken account of institutional changes, and legal systems have gradually recognised the existence of *de facto* relationships, for example with regard to inheritance, the division of jointly acquired property on separation, or paternity of children born outside wedlock, parental authority (see below) and social security entitlements (see Chapter 3).

Sweden affords a good example of the practices gradually being adopted in other countries concerning consensual unions. When the Swedish Marriage Code was initially revised in 1973, it was decided that legislation should be neutral towards different forms of cohabitation. As Kathleen Kiernan and Valerie Estaugh (1993,

p. 65) point out, the potential conflict inherent in the principle of neutrality was resolved by formulating legislation that could be applied to all couples, irrespective of their marital status, thereby avoiding influencing decisions about whether or not to marry. Legislation introduced in 1988 under the marriage code gave cohabitees the right to divide jointly owned property between them or to conclude an agreement to maintain separate property (Ministry of Health and Social Affairs, 1995, p. 23).

English law is less liberal towards consensual unions and does not give cohabitees the same rights and responsibilities towards one another as spouses (Standley, 1993, p. 283). When unmarried cohabiting couples separate, property disputes cannot be settled through the same channels as those used for married couples who divorce, although solicitors may draw up cohabitation contracts (Standley, 1993, p. 289). The rights of cohabitees have to be established on the basis of property law principles which depend upon how the property was acquired and whether it was jointly owned, with the result that cohabitants may be in a more vulnerable situation than married couples if the relationship breaks down (Kiernan and Estaugh, 1993, pp. 35–8).

Although proposals for the institutional recognition of consensual unions have been formally opposed in Italy by the Catholic Church, which continues to uphold its conception of the family as a heterosexual union founded on marriage, *de facto* unmarried couples can register their union and can make use of services, such as family counselling (Sgritta and Zanatta, 1994, p. 185). The Spanish Civil Code recognises only married couples, whereas the constitution accepts a wider definition, resulting in legal problems as, for example, in the case of separation of unmarried couples with children. At the regional level in Spain, some local authorities have begun to establish registers of cohabiting couples, including homosexual couples, as proof of cohabitation (Fernández Cordón, 1994, pp. 110–11). While consensual unions are recognised in Portugal, cohabiting couples are not subject to the same legal obligations towards one another as married couples (Wall, 1995).

In some countries, consensual unions have not been formally accepted. In Germany, where the constitution places emphasis on marriage, cohabiting couples are not entitled to protection from the state and have to make their own contractual arrangements for dealing with property and other matters that are covered by law for married couples. In Luxembourg, where only marital unions are recognised, no public debate on the subject has taken place. In Greece, family law recognises only marital relationships as forming a family. In Ireland, consensual unions are not given recognition in the constitution and have not benefited from the legal rights extended to married couples (Dumon, 1993, pp. 149–60).

While most EU member states have made provision for heterosexual consensual unions, law reform to recognise homosexual cohabitees has encountered much greater resistance. In France, official recognition of consensual unions explicitly excluded homosexual couples, whereas the Act on Registered Partnerships in Denmark, passed in 1989, allowed two persons of the same sex to register their union and obtain most of the same rights as married couples, with the exception of adoption and joint custody. While the bill attracted considerable publicity, it met with relatively little opposition. In Sweden, legislation on heterosexual cohabitees has also been extended to homosexual couples to ensure they have legal protection with regard to property (Bengtson, 1988, p. 8). In the Netherlands, both heterosexual and homosexual cohabiting couples can register their partnerships, placing Dutch legislation among the most progressive in the Union: same sex partners, like unmarried couples can enter into a cohabitation contract covering property rights and taxation (Collins, 1992, pp. 184–5).

*Procreation*

With the development of more effective means of contraception, which can be used at the woman's initiative, the rapid increase in the number of extramarital births since the 1970s (see Figure 1.3) and the availability of new technologies for treating infertility, many governments have reviewed their legislation on contraception, the right to terminate pregnancy and on medically assisted reproduction. The protracted debates and negotiations leading up to legislation on questions concerning procreation are indicative of the strength of feeling among the many interest groups involved and the deeply rooted cultural and ideological traditions within which these issues have to be located: the medical profession, scientists, industrialists, the church, lawyers, civil servants, feminist groups and family lobbies have all been intent on defending their own often conflicting views (Assier-Andrieu and Commaille, 1995).

In addition to fundamental ethical questions, abortion law reform has raised issues concerning the rights of the father of an unborn child. For example, in 1980 the Council of State in France refused a husband's claim for damages against a hospital for carrying out an abortion on his wife without consulting him (Meulders-Klein, 1992, p. 778). Cases brought before the courts in several EU member states since the 1970s have established the principle that women alone have the right to decide to terminate pregnancy (Meulders-Klein, 1993, p. 113). Notwithstanding the legal wrangling, most countries have introduced legislation on the termination of pregnancy. In general, pregnancy may be terminated up to the twelfth week (tenth in France) on social or medical grounds, although the time limit is relaxed in situations where the mother's life is endangered. Legislation on abortion dates back to 1967 in the United Kingdom and 1973 in Denmark. Abortion became legal in 1978 in Italy on very broad grounds. The Netherlands introduced legislation to regulate abortion in 1984, and it was legalised in Spain in 1985 and in Greece in 1986. In Portugal, the law on abortion has remained quite strict, although the termination of pregnancy was partially decriminalised in 1984.

In the Federal Republic of Germany, abortion law was liberalised in 1974, but then the reform was overturned in 1975, leaving West Germany with much more restrictive legislation on the termination of pregnancy than the German Democratic Republic (GDR). The issue was reviewed by section 4 of Article 31 of the German Treaty of Re-unification, covering the protection of the unborn child. A law was adopted in 1992 by the German parliament, within the context of the promotion of a child-friendly society, providing for assistance in pregnancy conflicts and the regulation of the termination of pregnancy (Wingen and Stutzer, 1994, p. 67), but its stipulations were not enacted and were declared unconstitutional in 1993. The termination of pregnancy therefore remained illegal, although it was not punishable provided certain conditions were met, a position confirmed by the Bundestag in 1995 for abortions carried out in the first three months of pregnancy.

In other cases, the prohibition on abortion has been upheld. In Belgium, a proposal to amend the Penal Code in 1990 was opposed by the King, an unprecedented event in the country's history. Abortion is therefore still a punishable offence, unless the mother is in danger and the abortion is conducted in accordance with strict conditions (Dumon, 1993, p.175). In Ireland, the ban on abortion was restated in a referendum in 1992, although the right of women to travel abroad to have an abortion was recognised (Kiely and Richardson, 1994, p. 172).

While abortion law reform has long been a topic of debate, not all countries have examined the ethical issues raised by technologies enabling medically assisted reproduction. Most have been reluctant to legislate on questions concerning lone mothers or homosexual couples wanting to have children. While EU member states accept that legal restrictions should be placed on the age at which young people can marry or have sexual relationships and that legal constraints should apply to abortion, the debate over medically assisted reproduction and surrogacy had not resulted in a strong body of legislation in most countries by the mid-1990s: surrogate motherhood was, for example, banned in France and Germany, whereas in Spain, which recognised medically assisted reproduction in law in 1991, it was allowed except on a commercial basis (Fernández Cordón, 1994, p. 111). In the United Kingdom, the Human Fertilisation and Embryology Act of 1990 set out the conditions under which the use of medically assisted techniques and surrogacy were legal, and legislation had been enacted in Germany. Greece had not legislated in this area, the issue was under discussion in Italy, and professional bodies had made recommendations in Denmark and Portugal (Berthod-Wurmser, 1994, p. 267).

As with abortion or legislation on the rights of unmarried couples and their children, the subject raises questions about the boundaries of state intervention in line with the principle that undue interference by the state in the private lives of individuals cannot be justified. In cases where the national constitution pledges the state to protect the family, the issue of medically assisted procreation, involving artificial insemination by an anonymous donor or surrogate motherhood, has posed important questions about the legal definitions of family relationships, resulting in a potential conflict of interests between individuals and the family group. In Belgium, for example, a court ruled in 1988 that the refusal to have a child despite the insistence of the spouse constituted grounds for divorce (Meulders-Klein, 1992, p. 778). Spain and the United Kingdom have been less restrictive about access to medically assisted reproduction in the name of personal freedom, while ensuring that donors remain anonymous. French and German legislation has been intent on protecting family stability in the interests of the child and has therefore imposed conditions on access. Despite the absence of a legal ban in Germany, access is restricted by the fact that treatment is not covered by social insurance and, while donors can receive payment, their anonymity is not guaranteed (Berthod-Wurmser, 1994, pp. 269–73).

### Paternity and the rights of children

Statistics may provide only a crude picture of family relationships since information collected in censuses and surveys is often unreliable for the reasons explained in Chapter 1. For administrative and legal purposes (parental responsibility, inheritance), more accurate information is often needed on parentage so that biological parents can be identified. In line with an agreement reached at European level in 1975, national governments have gradually been abolishing discrimination between children born in and out of wedlock, and regulations regarding 'illegitimate' children have been adapted to conform to those for legitimate children as far as care, maintenance and inheritance are concerned.

The European Convention on the Legal Status of Children Born out of Wedlock, signed in Strasbourg in 1975, redefined the family by recognising the rights of extramarital children. The Convention stipulated that the fact of the birth of the child should be recognised as proof of maternal affiliation (Article 2) and that paternal affiliation should be 'evidenced or established by voluntary recognition or by judicial decision' (Article 3). Legal obligations to maintain children born outside wedlock were to be the same as for children born to a married couple (Article 6), parental authority could not be attributed to the father alone if affiliation was established for both parents (Article 7), and the child's rights of succession were to be the same as for children born in wedlock (Article 9).

In EU member states, maternity can almost always be established by recognition or by legal proceedings, but paternity is much more problematic. Children born within wedlock are presumed to have been fathered by the husband. In most EU member states – Belgium and the Netherlands are exceptions – the presumption of paternity may, however, be contested or may not apply in cases of legal separation and divorce or when the parents are living apart and the child is registered solely in the mother's name (Meulders-Klein, 1993, pp. 117–18).

Germany, Sweden and the United Kingdom had acknowledged the rights of inheritance of children born out of wedlock as early as 1969. In France, children born in and out of wedlock have enjoyed the same legal rights since 1972 (Commaille, 1994a, p. 139). The emphasis placed by the constitution in Italy on marriage meant that legitimate children were treated more favourably than children born out of wedlock. The reformed family law of 1975 (Act no. 151/1975) granted children born outside wedlock the same rights as legitimate children in cases where paternity is recognised and, in the early 1990s, Italy was considering introducing legislation to enable single people to adopt children, raising the issue of the rights of children to have two parents (Sgritta and Zanatta, 1994, pp. 184–5). In Greece, it was not until 1983 that children born in and out of wedlock were granted equal rights (Moussourou, 1994, p. 89). In Luxembourg, the status of children born outside wedlock was brought into line with that of legitimate children by legislation only in 1993 (Neyens, 1994, p. 215).

Since the woman can take the initiative in contraception and abortion, logically she has the right to procreate a fatherless child. Practices regarding the attribution of paternity in unmarried couples differ markedly, however, from one member state to another. Because paternity outside marriage cannot be by presumption, it has to be established by voluntary recognition or legal decision, involving procedures that many women may wish to avoid.

Marie-Thérèse Meulders-Klein (1993, pp. 122–33) has identified different models for the EU member states in the establishment of paternity outside marriage. Both France and Belgium (until 1987 in the latter case) have made paternal recognition a discretionary right of the father, whereas the Nordic countries and Germany have pursued the father, irrespective of the will of the mother, on the grounds that the biological father has a duty to feed the child. In Germany, the child has a constitutional right to know its origins. Paternity can therefore be established by recognition or legal decision if one party wishes to do so, and the necessary measures, including biological tests, are then taken to identify the father. Elsewhere, the most widespread practice is to recognise paternity subject to conditions that include the consent or right of veto of the mother or the child. In the United Kingdom, for example, the naming of the father on a birth certificate does not establish paternity. Rather, it has to be proven through civil proceedings, as in the case of maintenance claims or, under the Children Act of 1989, through a declaration of parentage at the request of the child. In the early 1990s, the Netherlands represented an extreme case where no attempt was made to establish paternity, and paternal recognition was void during the mother's lifetime unless she gave her written consent (Meulders-Klein, 1992, p. 784). If the biological father can prove paternity, however, the mother's consent is no longer needed to establish his rights (de Hoog *et al.*, 1993, p. 37).

## Parental authority and responsibility

The rights of children to have parents are associated with the duties or responsibilities of parents towards their offspring. After the debates of the 1960s and 1970s on parental authority, important policy issues for EU member states from the 1980s were the rights of biological fathers to the custody of their children after divorce or separation and their financial responsibility for their children's upbringing.

Over the same period, the concept of paternal rights and authority was being replaced by the notion of parental responsibility. Until the 1960s in most EU member states, legally the rights of mothers and their children were strictly subordinated to those of the husband/father. Progressively, legal frameworks have been adapted to reflect the fact that the husband is no longer the undisputed head of the family, and its sole or main breadwinner, and that parents have responsibilities as well as rights. Parental responsibility for children has increasingly been shared between married partners. By the mid-1990s, with the exception of Luxembourg, married men and women in EU member states were jointly responsible for managing family affairs. The civil code in Luxembourg continued to enshrine the power of the father as the head of the family unit, as founded by marriage in the nineteenth century, following the French Napoleonic model (Neyens, 1994, p. 200). Elsewhere in the Union, the legal subordination of women and children had gradually been removed, and the exclusive right of men to paternal authority had been replaced by the principle of parental authority.

The situation after divorce and in consensual unions was less clear cut. In the case of separation or divorce, a trend can be discerned across the Union, although the rate and extent of change vary from one member state to another. The balance tipped firstly in favour of the mother as the person presumed to be best able to look after the child. It then shifted towards the concept of joint custody (introduced in 1987 in France for example) and alternating custody. In some cases, national law had been challenged, as for example in the Netherlands where, until 1984, one parent could be appointed as the legal guardian on divorce. In Germany, parental authority had long been awarded to the mother alone on divorce, and it has been left to her to decide whether the father should have the right to maintain contact with the child. Family courts could award joint custody in cases where both parents agreed, although in practice courts were reluctant to do so (Meulders-Klein, 1993, pp. 136–8). In Spain, provision has been made for judges to choose who should have legal custody of the children after divorce. Previously, custody was automatically given to the mother (Fernández Cordón, 1994, p. 111). The 1989 Children Act introduced the concept of parental responsibility in the United Kingdom but allowed for it to be shared with another person. These powers were retained after separation. In France, from 1993, parental control after legal separation or divorce was jointly exercised unless considered contrary to the child's best interests (Meulders-Klein, 1993, p. 135).

Although the principle of equality was becoming widely established for the sharing of parental authority in marriage, the mother continued to be more likely to have legal custody of children after divorce, and maintenance was frequently a contentious issue. The way that maintenance orders have been treated by the courts illustrates the tensions between public and private solidarity (Commaille, 1994a, p. 133). A law (*loi de soutien familial*) instituted in 1984 in France on maintenance after divorce made provision for the Caisse Nationale des Allocations Familiales (CNAF) to intervene to recover unpaid alimony, while the French Civil Code continued to recognise only the principle of individual responsibility for maintenance. In the absence of divorce law in Ireland, the need existed nevertheless for legislation to deal with separation: the 1989 Judicial Separation Act allowed for the making of orders for the division of property, maintenance and care and custody of children. In the United Kingdom, the 1991 Child Support Act took the concept of parental responsibility a stage further, by stipulating that the absent (biological) father should be obliged to pay maintenance for his children even in cases where a clean break had been agreed.

In most EU member states, a step-parent is under no direct legal obligation to provide for step-children, although cases may arise where maintenance payments for children can be reduced if a mother who has custody remarries. In the Netherlands, married step-parents are under a legal obligation to provide for their step-children, and in Germany, by remarrying, the step-parent is considered to be under a moral contract to ensure the upkeep of step-children (Sosson, 1993, pp. 304–6).

While the interests of children born in wedlock may be considered to be best served by parents sharing responsibility, the situation for unmarried parents is less certain. France provides an example of progressive changes in the law. Until 1970, legal paternity automatically resulted in paternal authority being granted to the father. Since then, the law has been reformed and, by the early 1990s, unmarried parents could exercise parental authority jointly if they both recognised the child before its first birthday and were cohabiting at the time. Otherwise, the mother exercises parental authority, as is the case *de facto* in most other countries, on the assumption that she will be bringing up the child. In the United Kingdom, although an unmarried father does not automatically acquire responsibility for his children, both parents have maintenance obligations towards their offspring. In Portugal, joint authority may be exercised if the father lives with the mother and both parents together make a declaration to that effect. No provision is made for the joint exercise of parental authority for unmarried parents in Germany. The Netherlands treat divorced and unmarried parents differently by granting shared parental authority to unmarried parents provided they jointly declare the child. In Belgium, Italy and Spain, little if any distinction is made between married and unmarried parents in this respect, and the rules depend on whether or not they are living together. In Finland and Sweden, however, joint parental authority may be awarded even if the parents are not cohabiting (Meulders-Klein, 1993, pp. 142–8).

In line with changes occurring across the Union allowing the joint exercise of parental authority, emphasis has thus been placed increasingly on the liability of both biological parents to maintain their children, whether they are married or not, thereby reinforcing an alternative form of institutionalised relationship between parents and their children.

## Gender equality

The conception of the family in law that was dominant in Western Europe until the middle of the twentieth century was centred on the father as head of household. Under growing pressure from women's lobbies, changes have gradually been introduced at both European and national levels to recognise the demand for greater gender equality at work and within the home, including a legal obligation on married partners to maintain one another. These developments have been taken further in some countries than in others, as in the Nordic states where emphasis in public policy is on equality between couples and the interests of children. Gender equality may be reflected in the sharing of parental authority and responsibility between parents, as described above, it may be recognised in the legal arrangements for control of the household and the matrimonial division of property, and it may be symbolised by the right of women to retain their maiden name on marriage and to choose their children's surname.

The principle of equal treatment for men and women was enshrined in European Community law in 1976. Council Directive 76/207/EEC (*Official Journal of the European Communities* L 39/40, 14.2.76) stipulated that there should be no discrimination on the grounds of sex, particularly with reference to marital or family status. This principle was already incorporated in German Basic Law, under Articles 3 (2) and (3) and 33 (2), in the French constitution of 1946 and the United Kingdom's Sex Discrimination Act of 1975. The principle of equal rights for men and women is also contained in the Finnish and Swedish constitutions. The Greek constitution of 1975 upheld the equal pay principle, but the wider concept of gender equality within the family and the removal of the automatic attribution to the man of the title 'head of household' were not institutionalised until the Family Law of 1983, which confirmed the rights and duties of spouses to one another (Moussourou, 1994, p. 88).

In Fascist Italy of the 1930s, the place of women was distinctly in the home, a principle enshrined in law (decree of 1938). The interests of women and children were strictly subordinated to those of the husband or father as head of the household. The 1975 reform of family law (Act no. 151/1975) provided for equal rights and duties between partners within marriage (Sgritta and Zanatta, 1994, pp. 177–8). In Portugal, the husband or father was still recognised as head of household and was held responsible for all decisions affecting the family until the mid-1970s. Amendments to the Civil Code in 1977 introduced equality between spouses, although with some limitations (Amaro, 1994b, p. 256). The Spanish Civil Code of 1978 guaranteed equality between men and women in marriage and with regard to children, so that wives are no longer bound to share their husband's residence, and husbands are no longer the sole providers for the family (Fernández Cordón, 1994, pp. 110–12). Equality between men and women has progressively been recognised in matrimonial regimes. Married partners generally retain the right to ownership of property acquired before marriage, but different practices apply for property acquired jointly. In the United Kingdom, where there is no doctrine of community of property, the division of personal property is maintained within marriage. In Belgium, a distinction is made between the personal property of spouses and property acquired jointly when married. In Luxembourg and the Netherlands, marriage involves joint ownership of property acquired before and during marriage, unless the partners have drawn up a marriage contract. A system of deferred community of property operates in Denmark, Germany and Sweden, but on separation property is shared equally between the partners. In Greece, France, Italy, Portugal and Spain, marriage partners can choose joint or separate ownership of property acquired during marriage (de Gastines and Sylvestre, 1992, pp. 674–81).

Laws governing the rights of individuals to choose their own surnames and those of their children provide a further illustration of the ways in which relationships within families are institutionalised in EU member states. In some countries, the hierarchical relationship within families is still recognised in law on family names, while in others spouses have much greater freedom of choice. Despite legal reforms introducing greater gender equality, once paternity is recognised in Portugal, for example, the father's surname is given precedence over that of the mother (Amaro, 1994b, p. 266). In France, for administrative purposes women keep their maiden name on marriage, and children can be registered in their parents' joint name, but the father's is the official name transmitted to children (Valetas, 1992, p. 29). In the case of unmarried mothers, the children take the name of whichever parent recognises them first but, if parents register them jointly, the father's name prevails. In Greece, women may keep their maiden name on marriage, and parents can decide on the child's surname together (Moussourou, 1994, p. 89).

In Germany, since April 1994 a law has been in force on family names, giving parents a choice. On marriage, a couple can decide whether they want to adopt the husband's or wife's name. The partner whose name is not chosen can affix it to the common name, and the children are given the parents' married name. If no common name has been adopted, then the parents can give their children either the father's or the mother's name (Wingen and Stutzer, 1994, p. 69). In the United Kingdom, by convention, a child usually takes the father's surname, but parents are free to choose any surname for the child.

## The public or private family

Progressively over the post-war period, all EU member states have been adopting a more egalitarian and liberal approach towards the family as an institution, and this is reflected in legislative reforms on divorce or the status of individual family members. In doing so, the state has been encroaching further into family life, for example by regulating the conditions under which contraception and abortion take place, or by instituting rights for the children of unmarried couples or divorcees and equality legislation. One justification for such intervention can be found in the need to establish rules for governing families in a context of rapidly changing social values (Commaille, 1994b, p. 42). State intervention may also be justified by the need to protect members of the family unit from one another (child abuse), or to oblige them to fulfil their responsibilities to one another (the absent father), while also carrying out what may be a constitutional duty towards the family as a basic social institution. Family law presents the legislator with a dilemma: how to reconcile the interests of individuals with those of both the family unit and society at large, and in so doing whether to seek, at all costs, to preserve the legitimate family or to give priority to the interests of individual members, and more especially children, as set out in the 1989 United Nation's Convention on the Rights of the Child, which EU member states have ratified.

Within the Union, the Nordic countries generally gave the lead in introducing more 'democratic' laws and practices, focusing on equality issues and the interests of children rather than the legitimate family unit. France, the United Kingdom and some of the other countries at the geographical centre of the Union have followed a similar route, except if they encountered strong opposition from the church or conservative political forces. Consensual unions and extramarital births have, for example, been more readily recognised in Denmark, France, Sweden and the United Kingdom than in Germany, Ireland, Luxembourg and the south European countries, where hierarchical (patriarchal) systems for the allocation of rights have also been progressively dismantled.

In some cases, the framework provided by national constitutions has lent support to the maintenance of traditional conceptions of the legitimate family founded on marriage, while in others it has provided an incentive to reconsider what is in the best interests of family members, in the name of equality and equity. Marie-Thérèse

Meulders-Klein (1993, p. 149) has argued that, in the child's best interests, 'Biological parentage of a child should, under normal circumstances, go hand in hand with social and legal parentage.' Joint responsibility of the child's biological parents should, she suggests, be reinforced by the legal and social systems. While the joint responsibility of the biological parents for their children in both marriage and, generally speaking, consensual unions has been widely accepted, not all countries have reacted in the same way to the concept of shared parentage, particularly after divorce or separation, and the obligation on the absent parent to provide maintenance after separation has met with strong opposition in some EU member states.

In many countries, particularly in Northern Europe, the interests of individuals rather than institutionalised family units have been implicit in the liberalisation of legal definitions of the family, giving formal recognition to a plurality of family forms and a diversity of practices. Long-standing national conventions have been called into question, and the debate has been sharpened over the justification for state intervention in areas of family solidarity. Many of the changes described in this chapter have taken place over a short space of time – 20 to 30 years – and reflect important shifts in behaviour and attitudes. Although the outcomes may look similar, they can only be properly understood with reference to the complex processes under which reforms have been negotiated. Often attempts to introduce new legislation have revealed deep-seated conflicts over fundamental principles concerning, on the one hand, the legitimacy of state intervention to protect the family as a basic social institution and, on the other, the objective of safeguarding individual human rights, which are ultimately the focus of family and private law.

CHAPTER 3

# Public policy definitions of the family

Statistical and legal definitions of families are shaped by political forces and are largely determined by the needs of institutional users. They are therefore dependent on national conventions and cultural traditions. As both producers and users of statistical data, policy makers are responsible for formulating definitions of families and households which can be applied in the administration of public services. They must also be responsive to shifts in socio-economic behaviour and to the demands of pressure groups. Because of the number and variety of influences to which they are subjected, public policy definitions of the family may differ substantially not only from one national context to another but also with changes in the political affiliations of the governments in power.

Several institutions are interested in defining the family for administrative purposes, whether it be at central, regional or local government level. Where the state is recognised in a national constitution as having a duty to protect families, governments might be expected to establish appropriate administrative structures enabling them to formulate and implement support measures for families as defined in law.

In this chapter, attention is given to the conceptual issues underlying the policy-making process and to the political forces influencing decisions. The way the family is conceptualised by different social actors is first considered across member states, as reflected in public administration, and national and local associations representing families. The resulting national definitions of the family applied in tax law and social welfare systems are then examined and compared across the countries in the Union, and an attempt is made to track the development of the family as a benefit category from one EU member state to another. Specific instances of changes to benefit categories, as a result of the increase in the number of lone-parent families, consensual unions and reconstituted families, are examined to illustrate national differences in the processes and practices that have developed over the postwar period. Particular reference is made to the concept of individualisation within both tax and benefit systems.

## Public policy actors

According to the principle of subsidiarity, in the European context the Council of Ministers should intervene only if member states are unable to initiate appropriate action at national level. The Commission has developed the principle further, recommending that decisions should be taken 'as closely as possible to the citizen himself' (SEC(92) 1990 final, 27 October 1992, p. 1), since 'the powers that a State or a federation of States wields in the common interest are only those which individuals, families, companies and local or regional authorities cannot exercise in isolation' (SEC(92) 1990 final, Annex, p. 1). The implication is that individuals and families have primary responsibility for their own well-being and that of their immediate relations. The minimalist view would be that the state should do no more than provide a safety net, as in the residual model of welfare described in the 1960s by Richard Titmuss (1974, pp. 30–1). When external action is necessary and justified, the preference would be for local rather than national communities to provide support. As Paul Spicker (1991, pp. 5–6) has argued, a tension can exist between the principles of subsidiarity and solidarity. Unless interpreted in terms of a hierarchy of responsibilities, embedded in widely accepted social norms, solidarity can imply the collective provision of welfare which may be in conflict with informal support structures.

In this section, the policy-making context is examined and compared at national and local government level, extending to an analysis of the impact of pressure groups, with a view to assessing whether and how different policy actors conceptualise responsibility for families.

### *Support for public policy in national constitutions*

In the previous chapter, the national constitutions of several EU member states were shown to provide a supportive framework for families, legitimating state intervention in family life. In the south European countries, in particular, the constitution not only identifies the family as an important social institution, it also sets out the duties of the state towards families. In Portugal, the 1976 constitution established concrete measures which the state pledged itself to implement in order to protect the family and respond to its needs. Legitimate action by the state covers the promotion of social and economic independence of family nuclei, provision for mothers and young children and for their education, family planning and tax relief (Amaro, 1994b, pp. 256–7). The Greek constitution makes explicit reference to the duty of the state to provide for the special needs of large families, young people, war widows and orphans and other categories of the population at risk, and it also enshrines the principle of gender equality (Article 4) (Moussourou, 1994, pp. 87–8).

Reference is made in the Italian constitution to the commitment of the state to intervene to promote the family and to assist it in carrying out its tasks, especially in the case of large families (Articles 29 and 31). The definition of the family provided in the Italian constitution has, however, been increasingly called into question and is no longer considered adequate or appropriate to deal with the plurality of family forms that have developed over the postwar period as a result of demographic and technological change (Del Re, 1995, pp. 68–72).

Elsewhere, the support for families, as registered in national constitutions, does not translate directly into a political agenda, although the constitution may establish the parameters of the normative family and thereby influence the way the family is conceptualised in tax law and benefit systems.

## The family in central administration

References to the family in national constitutions have not necessarily been accompanied in EU member states by designated ministerial appointments with responsibility for family affairs. Very few countries – only France, Germany and Luxembourg – have been at all consistent in appointing ministers in this area. In most cases, the attitudes of governments have been ambivalent: they have tended to fluctuate between recognition of the need to support the family as a social institution, either at national level as in Portugal or at regional level as in Belgium and Spain, and a reluctance, as in Ireland, Italy, the Netherlands or the United Kingdom, to interfere directly in family life.

### Responsibility for family policy

In the early 1990s, Germany was one of the few EU member states with a designated Ministry for the Family, but this was not its sole remit. It was also charged with looking after the interests of older people. The Federal Republic of Germany (FRG) has a long history of recognition of family affairs at ministerial level. Since 1953, Germany has had a Federal Ministry for Family Affairs, working closely with other ministries over questions such as housing, social security, labour and tax law (Wingen and Stutzer, 1994, pp. 58–60). Luxembourg is another country which has consistently given a high profile to family matters by maintaining an autonomous Ministry for the Family since 1951. As in Germany, its remit has been extended to cover other areas, such as education, population, equal opportunities and solidarity (Neyens, 1994, pp. 205–7). Most French governments since the late 1970s have appointed a minister, or junior minister, with responsibility for family affairs, reflecting the importance the state has attributed to the family as a fundamental social institution. Austria also had a Ministry for the Family in the early 1990s. The only other country to have had a designated ministerial position for family affairs in the mid-1990s was Italy. At the beginning of the 1990s, responsibility for family policy came under the Ministry of Labour and Social Welfare. Then in 1994, the International Year of the Family, the Berlusconi government created a Ministry without portfolio for Family and Social Solidarity to advise the government on family matters (Del Re, 1995, p. 69).

A few countries have in the past made ministerial appointments in this area, even when the national constitution did not commit the state to protecting family interests. Although Portugal gives a high profile to the family in its constitution and operated a government department responsible for this area of policy between 1980 and 1983, the Portuguese no longer had a designated ministry for family affairs in the mid-1990s. Instead, they had transferred responsibility to a unit consisting of an Interministerial Family Commission, a Family Affairs Council and a Directorate-General for the Family, with the brief of ensuring the co-ordination of measures supporting families in conjunction with representatives of families, but without encroaching on family autonomy (Amaro, 1994b, p. 257). Under Franco, Spain had been a highly centralised state, where family policy was dictated by an authoritarian regime. The prominence given to the family in the Spanish constitution in 1978 was not translated into a ministerial appointment, thereby signalling a lower profile for family affairs (Fernández Cordón, 1994, p. 107). Denmark had a Ministry for Family Affairs only briefly in the 1960s. Since then, attention has been given increasingly to children, a focus confirmed in 1988 by the creation of an Interministerial Committee on Children, involving fourteen ministries charged with preparing an action programme for improving the living conditions of children rather than families (Pruzan, 1994, pp. 35–6).

For different reasons, other member states have not created ministries or government departments to deal with family affairs. While the state in Greece undertakes in the constitution to protect the family, policy makers only began to focus attention on family affairs in the early 1980s, and the Greek government has not chosen to designate a ministry with responsibility for the family. Despite references to the family and marriage in the Irish constitution, Ireland has never had a minister responsible for the family but for reasons different from those explaining the lack of ministerial appointments in the south European member states: Irish governments have deliberately sought to avoid direct and visible intervention in family affairs as a matter of principle (see Chapter 2). The countries which do not incorporate a commitment to the family in their national constitutions generally give a low political profile to family affairs. In Belgium, for example, the family is not recognised by a ministerial position at federal level. Although the Netherlands had a directorate for family policy within the Ministry of Culture, Recreation and Social Work in the 1960s, subsequently family affairs were given a much lower profile, as in Ireland, on the grounds that the state should not interfere with the autonomy of private life, and in recognition of the pluralism of family forms and individual responsibility (Van den Brekel and Van de Kaa, 1994, pp. 225–30). For similar reasons, family affairs were neglected as a policy area in the United Kingdom until the early 1990s, when the Minister for Health was given responsibility for the family, suggesting some recognition of the need to upgrade family matters, a trend reflected in the public rhetoric of members of the government over the same period (Chester, 1994, pp. 292–4).

*Responsibility for administering family affairs*

The administrative structures for dealing with this policy area also differ from one country to another in accordance with the importance attributed to family affairs as an area of legitimate concern for policy makers. Whether or not they are supported by a national constitution and ministerial appointments, all EU member states provide some form of financial assistance for maternity and for children, either as individuals or as members of families. Responsibility for family allowances, as they are generally called in the more family-friendly member states (for example Austria, France and Luxembourg, and the south European member states), or child benefit, the term used in the countries where social protection is more individualised and child centred (in particular Denmark, Finland, Sweden and the United Kingdom), is dispersed across different government departments in combinations that vary from one country to another, reflecting policy priorities.

Only in three countries did family allowances and child benefit fall within the remit of a designated ministry in the mid-1990s: the Ministry for Family Affairs, Public Housing and Solidarity in Luxembourg; the Federal Ministry for Family and Senior Citizens in Germany; and the Ministry for the Family in Austria (Tálos and Wörister, 1994, p. 222; MISSOC, 1995, table I). Elsewhere, they were generally managed by a ministry/department for social welfare, social security or social affairs: Social Security in Belgium and the United Kingdom, Social Welfare in Ireland, Labour and Social Security/Welfare in Italy, Portugal and Spain, Social Affairs, Health and Towns in France, Social Affairs and Employment in the Netherlands, and a Department of Children and Families within the Ministry for Health and Social Affairs in Finland and Sweden. In Greece, family allowances were managed by the Ministry for Labour, and in Denmark the general scheme for child benefit was the responsibility of the Ministry for Taxes and Duties (MISSOC, 1995, table I).

Maternity, the other major area of family affairs with which all governments are directly concerned, is often dealt with by the same ministry as family allowances/child benefit. In some cases, maternity is considered as a separate policy area, grouped with sickness, and sometimes with invalidity and old age. Neither Germany nor Luxembourg considered it as part of the remit of their family ministries in the mid-1990s: in Germany, it was the responsibility of Health and, in Luxembourg, of Social Security. In Greece, where there were only two ministries, maternity came under Health and Social Security and, in Denmark, under the Ministries of Social Affairs and Health.

## From national to local responsibility for family affairs

In line with the concept of subsidiarity, in administrative terms the institutions likely to be able to deal most effectively with family matters, when families themselves are unable to meet their 'responsibilities', are those at local level. The coherence of public policy for families varies considerably from one national context to another and is reflected in the structures available to formulate and implement policy decisions and to monitor their impact. Just as the European Commission draws up social policy guidelines but allows member states discretion for implementing them in accordance with local circumstances, national governments generally formulate policies for implementation at regional or local level, in line with the principle of subsidiarity. Responsibility for family affairs is often shared between the different levels of government. Local government is usually charged with organising services that affect families in their everyday life, such as housing, community care and provision for young children. France, for example, has a specialised non-governmental administrative agency, the Caisse Nationale des Allocations Familiales (CNAF), operating in conjunction with local Caisses d'Allocations Familiales (CAF).

The division of responsibility is particularly evident in federal states. In Belgium, under social security arrangements for employment, the Ministry for Social Security covers family allowances and other provisions that may have an impact on the family, such as sickness, maternity, invalidity and old age. The Communities (Flemish, French and German) have responsibility for family policy and other areas that are of direct concern for family well-being, including care services, health education and social assistance. Responsibility for families therefore tends to be fragmented and subject to variations from one community to another (Meulders-Klein and Versailles, 1994, pp. 13–15). The Federal Government in Germany exercises responsibility for family affairs jointly with the *Länder*. In addition, they have discretion in formulating and implementing their own policies in areas such as childcare. As a result, discrepancies occur in the level of provision from one *Land* to another (Lohkamp-Himmighofen, 1993b, pp. 105–8). In Austria, family policy is administered centrally by the Familienlastenausgleichsfonds (FLAL), while the *Länder* and local authorities have responsibility for social assistance (Tálos and Wörister, 1994, pp. 222–4).

In other countries with less heavily centralised political systems, family policy is an area where local authorities have primary responsibility for implementation and are given wide discretionary powers. In the Netherlands, central government has delegated family affairs to local authorities in line with the principle that family autonomy should be safeguarded. The provision of social services in Denmark has been decentralised so that ever smaller units at the level of district offices are as close as possible to the citizens they are serving. Consequently, local variations are prevalent in childcare, community care and other local services, but they are accepted by the state so long as minimum levels of provision are maintained.

When only a small proportion of resources can be devoted to family policy, as in the south European countries, local authorities play an important role in delivering services. In 1975, local authority services replaced the National Institute for Maternity and Infancy, which had been established in Italy in the 1930s to assist mothers and young children in a context of high infant mortality rates (Sgritta and Zanatta, 1994, p. 174). Since 1978 in Spain, responsibility for implementing social policy and providing social services has been delegated to the seventeen regions (Communidades Autónomas) (Fernández Cordón, 1994, p. 106).

The provision of services for families at local level is also organised without a central coordinating body in Ireland and the United Kingdom. In Ireland, the principle of subsidiarity has been implemented with a strong input from the voluntary sector, following in the tradition established by the religious communities (Kiely and Richardson, 1994, p. 153). In the United Kingdom, implementation of policy is delegated to agencies and local authorities, preventing a coordinated focus on the needs of families as a unit and resulting, it is argued, in overlap and conflict (Chester, 1994, pp. 292–4).

These examples of the ways in which responsibility for family affairs is treated at national and local level suggest that the construction of the family as a fundamental social unit in national constitutions does not necessarily lead to a coherent or effective approach to the administration of family policy. Nor are institutionalisation, centralisation and visibility of the policy-making process necessarily synonymous with effectiveness (see Chapter 9). In some countries, decentralisation and delegation have resulted in efficient services, as in Denmark, while in others, such as Greece, they are associated with fragmented and disparate provision.

*Family support organisations*

In a few cases, recognition of the family unit by national governments has been supported by family associations, which have provided a powerful lobby for protecting the interests of families. In France, for example, strong pressure groups operate in conjunction with government. In others, for example Denmark or the Netherlands, attention has shifted away from the family unit to its individual members, while in Italy, to take another configuration, family organisations may be working to promote the cause of families by way of compensation for the relative indifference of national governments.

France, Germany and Luxembourg are examples of countries that give recognition to family affairs and accept state intervention in the private lives of their citizens. All three countries have well-developed family associations, although those representing family interests in Germany have little political influence. France has a long tradition of family movements, which predate the recognition of the family as an area of social security. Since 1942, the Union Nationale des Associations Familiales (UNAF) has played an important role as a national organisation defending the interests of families. It sets out to protect the well-being of children and the freedom of choice of families, not only by monitoring and evaluating the impact of all policy measures on the family but also by being represented at every level of the decision-making process. The UNAF and its regional branches, Unions Départementales des Associations Familiales (UDAF), have become legitimate and monopolistic institutions representing the collective defence of family interests (Chauvière, 1991, p. 288). They are supported and given recognition in the political decision-making process as strong social partners. In addition, since 1939, the importance attributed in France to demographic and family issues has been recognised officially in the role played by the Haut Comité de la Population, which was set up to monitor demographic trends and advise governments on population policies. In 1984, its brief was formally extended to family affairs, symbolised by the change in title to the Haut Conseil de la Population et de la Famille, presided over by the President of the Republic.

The interests of families in Luxembourg are also supported by non-governmental bodies. Since 1952, Luxembourg has had a Conseil Supérieur de la Famille et de l'Enfance, which brings together family associations to advise government on the family impact of legislation. Families have organised themselves into a powerful action group called Action Familiale et Populaire (Neyens, 1994, pp. 205–7). Although Belgium does not have a central ministry for the family, its family organisations are very influential and have exercised pressure on governments to introduce policy measures in support of families (Meulders-Klein and Versailles, 1994, pp. 18–19). Portugal also has a tradition of sharing responsibility for family affairs: in addition to the Episcopal Conference, which represents the Catholic Church, the National Confederation of Family Associations speaks for family interests (Amaro, 1994a, p. 88).

Family associations exist in other countries, but they do not have the same political power, or receive the same official recognition as in France, Belgium, Luxembourg or Portugal. Although Italy is a strongly centralised state, the weakness of its political structures has meant that regional and local initiatives have developed in support of families and individuals, for example by creating family associations able to comment on the impact of legislation on families, resulting in a forum being set up for family associations in 1992 (Sgritta and Zanatta, 1994, pp. 187–8). In the United Kingdom, voluntary organisations and agencies with an interest in discrete areas of family life have proliferated, but they have not formed a unified family lobby (Chester, 1994, pp. 294–7).

These examples would seem to suggest that, in countries where the state manifests a strong interest in family affairs, other forms of organisational support may also play a prominent role in keeping family issues on the political agenda, even if the policy-making process is not operationalised in the same way and produces different outcomes.

### Defining the family in tax law

Whatever the policy-making structures and the administrative arrangements for dealing with family policy, governments need to identify family relationships and responsibilities for the purposes of determining individual rights to inheritance, settlements after divorce and so forth, as outlined in the previous chapter. Family relationships may also be a factor in deciding the duties of citizens with regard to taxation. The unit of assessment for income tax may differ from one country to another, or in the same country over time, according to changes in the way the family is conceptualised. For the purposes of tax collection, the relevant unit of assessment may be the household, the legally constituted married couple, the unmarried cohabiting couple or the individual. Children may or may not be recognised for tax relief. In this section, similarities and differences are analysed in the practices followed by member states in relation to taxation.

## The income tax unit

In most EU member states, by the early 1990s the basic unit of taxation was the individual or, in some cases, couples could choose between individual or joint taxation. The introduction of separate taxation reflected the increasing importance attributed to the legal rights of individuals, and more especially to women, as described in Chapter 2. In Italy, for example, in 1976 the combined taxation of family incomes, as practised in the early 1970s, was declared illegal by a ruling of the Constitutional Court because it did not take sufficient account of each member of the family (Sgritta and Zanatta, 1994, p. 179). The individualisation of tax liability is also in line with the shift away from the male breadwinner model of the family, where the husband was held responsible for ensuring the economic well-being of his wife and children. By placing emphasis on the production of income, individualised taxation can be considered to provide an inducement for women to enter paid employment and gain control over their earnings, as in Denmark, Finland and Sweden. Most countries that base taxation on individuals do, however, make provision for tax relief for spouses, thereby continuing to recognise that married men and women have some financial responsibility for their partners, as in Austria, Italy, the Netherlands and the United Kingdom. Where the family or household, as in France, Luxembourg and Portugal, or married couple, as in Germany, constitutes the tax unit, the focus is rather on consumption, which may serve to discourage women from becoming wage earners in their own right and perpetuate the hierarchical structure of the traditional conjugal family unit.

Some countries operate a mixed system offering the choice between individual or joint taxation or a combination of the two, as in Belgium, Germany (in cases where spouses are living separately), Greece, Ireland and Spain (Dumon, 1993, p. 43; Millar and Warman, 1996). Among the countries with joint or family taxation, Germany, France and Luxembourg operate a system of 'tax splitting'. Germany provides a good example of tax law which favours married couples where the wife does not go out to work or, if she does, where she earns a low income, since the annual income of both partners is added together, divided in two and taxed as two separate incomes (*Ehegattensplitting*). Luxembourg has maintained joint taxation of spouses since 1913 and has introduced allowances for spouses and children, while also operating *Ehegattensplitting*. France is an example of a country where the tax system is family centred and focuses on the unit of consumption: it recognises the importance to society of the family by giving generous tax relief for children from the first child and at a higher level for three or more children. The taxable income of the whole family is divided into units, or shares (*parts*), according to the number of children. Under the arrangements for dependants' allowances (*quotient familial*), each parent represents one unit and each child a half, except in the case of lone parents where the child counts as a whole unit, and in large families where the third and subsequent children count as whole units.

Italy has already been quoted in this section as a country where separate taxation was introduced on the grounds of equal treatment. In the early 1990s, the Italian government came under pressure to shift towards a more family-centred system. A reform was therefore proposed to enable families to choose between separate taxation or a scheme based on the family unit with relief for children along the lines of the system operating in France (Sgritta and Zanatta, 1994, p. 179).

Belgium provides an interesting example of a situation where the unit of assessment for the purposes of taxation is neither the family nor the individual. The Reform Law of 20 November 1962 had introduced a system whereby the incomes of all family members were counted together, in some cases including children's incomes, under the name of the head of the household. Small allowances were made for family responsibilities, but the system penalised dual-earner married couples and could thus be seen as providing a disincentive for marriage and encouraging separation and divorce. Although the tax reforms of 1988 removed the disaggregation of incomes for dual-earner married couples, the household continued to be identified as the unit of assessment (Meulders-Klein and Versailles, 1994, pp. 25–6).

Whether couples are taxed separately or jointly, the family factor may be taken into account through tax relief or allowances for spouses and children. In the tax splitting system, the recognition of the conjugal relationship is taken to an extreme and is clearly advantageous for women who remain at home, as in Germany. In Luxembourg, as more women entered the labour market in the postwar period, tax relief for spouses was introduced in 1967 to offset the disadvantage for dual-earner married couples (Neyens, 1994, p. 203). When the incomes of husbands and wives are taxed separately, families may be treated differently according to the number of family members with an income. All countries with separate taxation provide tax relief for spouses, but the level is not necessarily sufficient to offset the advantage of dual-earner as compared with single-earner couples.

Practices concerning tax relief for children vary from one extreme, as in Denmark, Ireland, the Netherlands and the United Kingdom, where no tax relief is granted for children, to a situation where, in addition to tax relief, allowances are granted towards childcare costs, as in Belgium, France, Greece and Spain. In the case of Spain, generous tax rebates are made for children, although the largest families may nevertheless be penalised (Fernández Cordón, 1994, pp. 108–9). In Austria, tax allowances for children increase with family size (Tálos and Wörister, 1994, pp. 222–3). Belgian tax law allows for tax relief of up to 80 per cent of the costs incurred by caring for dependent relations and for childcare in approved institutions (Meulders-Klein and Versailles, 1994, p. 26).

### Consensual unions

The legal rights and responsibilities of married and unmarried parents are not always closely matched by provisions in tax law, and the extension of non-marital cohabitation has been recognised to a different extent by tax law from one EU member state to another. In many countries, with the shift from the family to the individual as the basic unit for taxation, the distinction has been removed, or reduced, between married and unmarried households, in effect by bringing the situation of married couples into line with that of unmarried couples, rather than the reverse. Individualised systems of taxation tend to discriminate less between marriage and cohabitation, although disparities have not completely disappeared. In the United Kingdom, for example, individual or independent taxation, introduced in 1990, removed the disadvantage for married couples of being taxed on their joint incomes. Because the married man's allowance was maintained, the married couple does, however, have a financial advantage over unmarried cohabitees. In Ireland, the married couple also has an advantage over unmarried cohabiting couples in that personal allowances cannot be transferred to cohabitees.

In countries where the individual is not the standard unit of assessment, unmarried cohabiting couples may not be treated in the same way as spouses in tax law. The married person's allowance (*quotient conjugal*) in Belgium leaves unmarried couples better off than married couples with a single income (Meulders-Klein and Versailles, 1994, p. 26). In Germany, where non-marital cohabitation is not recognised for the purposes of direct taxation, the effect is the reverse: because cohabitees are not entitled to *Ehegattensplitting*, married couples are likely to pay less income tax than unmarried cohabiting couples, particularly if the wife's earnings are much lower than those of her husband. In France, in the early 1990s, cohabitees had an advantage over married couples in cases where they had one or two children and unequal incomes (Boissières, 1993a, p. 37). Although children could only be offset against one of the partners in unmarried couples, the first child gave entitlement to twice the amount allowed for the first child of a married couple up to a ceiling. A lone parent and his/her children were also considered as a family unit if they were receiving family allowances. Widows or widowers living with the deceased person's children were awarded an additional allowance for married couples, and unmarried or divorced lone parents received an additional half unit (Boissières, 1993b, p. 44).

These examples of the way that couples and families are treated for income tax purposes suggest that tax law is not neutral with regard to the family forms which it supports and may have implications for the decisions couples take about whether or not to marry, whether the wife should stay at home to raise children and about optimal family size.

## The 'benefit family'

Definitions of the 'benefit family' (a term used by Jo Roll, 1991, to describe the family as conceptualised in the British benefit system), and the assumptions on which they are based, are important because they determine the rules for entitlements and can result in discrepancies in the level of payments: as with tax law, eligibility for some benefits may vary depending, for example, upon how relationships within families are conceptualised and whether the partners in an unmarried couple are considered to be 'living together as man and wife'.

Different practices operate across the Union, with the result that the same situation may be treated differently from one country to another. In this section, some of these differences are examined with reference to national definitions of benefit families, particularly as they apply to the non-conventional family types that have become increasingly widespread in the latter part of the twentieth century. The relationship between benefits and employment is touched on only briefly here, since it is explored more fully in Part Two.

## Women as dependants

At the time in the immediate postwar period when most countries in Western Europe were introducing, extending or reorganising their social protection systems to provide more effective cover for all sectors of the population, the 'preferred' model of the family among policy makers was the married couple living together with their children, where the husband was the sole or main breadwinner (Lewis, 1992). Women and children were recipients of welfare in their capacity as dependants. The British system, for example, ensured that, if married women did work outside the home, their earnings were treated differently from those of women who were not married, by exempting them from national insurance contributions and therefore, subsequently, from rights to sick pay or occupational pensions and other employment-related benefits.

At the end of the twentieth century, most women expect to spend a large part of their adult life up to retirement age in paid employment. The male breadwinner model has been substantially modified, but it has not entirely disappeared. Just as most EU member states have shifted towards a system of individual taxation, entitlement to most employment-related benefits has also progressively been transferred from the couple or family unit to individual recipients. Despite European legislation on equal treatment between men and women in social security systems (Council Directive 79/7/EEC of 19 December 1978, *Official Journal of the European Communities* L 6/24, 10.1.79), national legislation does not comply everywhere with EU requirements. The independent rights of part-time workers has, for example, involved the United Kingdom in a number of cases before the European Court of Justice. As in the taxation system, married women may still be treated differently from single women, even if they are living in a consensual union. In most countries, an addition can be claimed to benefits for spouses (Millar and Warman, 1996). In some cases where marriage is the criterion for payment of derived rights, provision has been made to recognise women's unpaid labour for benefits such as pensions, as in Austria, France and Germany, or by allowing them to retire at an earlier age, as in Greece.

The extension of non-marital cohabitation has been recognised to different degrees in social security law. Additions for spouses are not, for example, extended to cohabitees in Greece and

Luxembourg. In France, a cohabitee who is financially dependent on a partner has been identified as a legitimate dependant for social security benefits since 1978. In the United Kingdom, in accordance with the cohabitation rule, no distinction is made between married and unmarried cohabiting couples in identifying the income of the family unit, provided they are living together as man and wife. Cohabitees are not, however, liable to maintain one another. In Germany, only those cohabitees who are considered to be at risk are eligible for social benefits. In the Netherlands, married and unmarried couples have been treated in the same way for benefits since 1987 (Cuelenaere and Van Doorne-Huiskes, 1995).

## Dependent relatives

As for statistical data, the definition of a dependent child applied in assessing entitlement for child benefit varies from one country to another, reflecting differences in policy orientations. In some cases, factors such as family size, the rank of the child or the length of time spent in education, or the needs of children in particular circumstances are taken into account, so that, in benefit terms, not all children have the same value.

Family size produces some interesting examples of the disparities in the assessment of benefits between member states. In the early 1990s in the United Kingdom, child benefit was paid at a higher rate for the first child than for subsequent children, suggesting that the costs incurred by families may be greater for the first child compared with other children. France, by contrast, was the only country not to pay family allowances for the first child. Rates were progressive for larger families in France, Greece, Ireland and Luxembourg, implying that these countries were prepared to adopt size as a criterion for support, whether to encourage large families or to compensate for the additional costs incurred (see Chapter 8).

The age of children is another variable determining entitlements. Portugal imposed the lowest age limit for family allowances by paying benefits for all children up to the age of 15, compared with 16 in Germany, Ireland and the United Kingdom, and 17 in Finland and the Netherlands. Most other countries set the limit at 18, except for Austria with 19. Children who continued in education or training could still be considered as dependants up to the age of 25 in Belgium and Portugal, and 27 in Austria, and Luxembourg. Limits were extended or lifted in several countries for seriously disabled children (Melsted, 1988, p. 5; MISSOC, 1995, table X).

Although family allowances have generally been granted on a universal basis, increasingly most countries have introduced some form of targeting and means-testing to compensate low-income families. The general benefit category of children as recipients of universal allowances is thus being replaced by a category of children in need, or at risk, as in pre-social security times. By the early 1990s, Germany, Greece, Italy, Portugal and Spain had introduced income-related adjustments (MISSOC, 1995, table X).

Targeting of benefits involves an evaluation not only of the resources available, and necessary, to meet individual needs but also an assessment of the extent to which the state should assume responsibility for the welfare of family members. Liability to maintain relatives is not a new concept. In the United Kingdom, for example, the 'liable relative' rules date back to the early seventeenth century with the Poor Law, which required husbands to maintain wives, and parents and children to maintain each other. Grandparents had to maintain grandchildren but not the reverse (Roll, 1991, p. 8).

The extent to which liability for maintaining relatives is formally recognised and determines the limits of state intervention differs across the Union. In the south European countries, family members are under a legal obligation to provide support for one another (Millar and Warman, 1996), and state provision of care is available only if other sources of family support have been exhausted, involving a very wide kinship network in Italy and Portugal. In Austria, France and the Netherlands, relations have a more limited obligation to care which is not strictly enforced, although the state can reclaim social assistance benefits from adult children. Ireland and the United Kingdom do not impose a legal responsibility for caring, and the duties of the state are not clearly defined (Millar and Warman, 1996). In Germany, individuals with the means to do so are legally obliged to assume responsibility not only for their parents but also for unemployed, unmarried children aged under 25 and for their offspring's lone-parent families. In the Scandinavian countries, it is, however, the state which is under an obligation to provide care (see Chapters 7 and 8)

These examples raise the question of the division between the public and private spheres, the conceptualisation of encroachment by the state in family affairs and the place of the private sector, which is examined further in Part Three.

## *Lone parenthood*

Governments in several member states have targeted lone-parent families, thereby indicating that the state is recognising them as a category with special needs. By the mid-1990s, Denmark, Germany, Greece, France, Ireland, Sweden and the United Kingdom paid supplements, in one form or another, for lone-parent families on low incomes (MISSOC, 1995, table X; Tauberman, 1995, p. 23).

Before statistics began recording a steep rise in the incidence of extramarital births, cohabitation and lone parenthood, most countries already had provisions for lone parents as a result of divorce or bereavement, and unmarried mothers were also catered for, primarily in order to ensure that their children would not suffer financially from having only one parent. By taking lone parents, and particularly lone mothers, into account as both a statistical category and social welfare beneficiaries, the *de facto* situation of a growing number of lone parents has been given legitimacy, and they have been identified as a target group for social work and special benefits, usually because of their low incomes (Lefaucheur, 1991). Progressively, statisticians have been required to provide information about lone parenthood because lone-parent families have been recognised as being particularly likely to suffer from poverty and social exclusion and are therefore an important focus of attention for policy makers.

As Jane Lewis (1992, p. 169) has argued, historically single mothers have posed a difficult problem for governments. In some EU member states, lone-parent families are not recognised in administrative documents, while in others the terminology may change according to the benefits concerned. In France, benefits are paid within family policy to *parents isolés*, whereas for taxation purposes reference is made to parents bringing up children alone. Preference is given to terms which emphasise lack of resources or the fact of being alone and in potentially, or temporarily, difficult financial circumstances. In the United Kingdom and Germany, by contrast, lone-parent families are classified as a benefit category eligible to receive income support or social assistance and are thus grouped with the socially excluded. Consequently, quite different proportions of lone-parent families may be deemed to be living in poverty. In the early 1990s, about 20 per cent of lone parents in France were receiving the *revenu minimum d'insertion* (RMI). In Germany, 45 per cent of lone parents were found to have income below the household mean, and as many as two-thirds of lone mothers in the United Kingdom were living below the poverty threshold (Roll, 1992, p. 20; Martin, 1995, p. 50).

These examples show that the attitude of the state towards cohabitation and lone parenthood is ambivalent and problematic. They illustrate the extent to which EU member states are progressively moving towards a situation where individual rights, and particularly those of children, are being given precedence over the rights that accrue to family members as part of a family unit, but they also point to the limitations of individualisation and to the conflicts arising between individual rights and duties.

# Public policy recognition of families

Variations between countries in the way the family is defined and taken into account in legal statutes on parentage, tax law and social security benefits reflect not only the principles underlying national family policies but also differences in the socio-economic and political contexts in which they are implemented.

The examples cited in this chapter of differences in the formal recognition that EU member states give to family matters through their ministerial positions and administrative responsibilities, when read in conjunction with the previous chapter, suggest that a few countries – France, Germany and Luxembourg – recognise the importance of the family as an institution and the duty of the state to afford it protection. Their commitment is translated into institutional structures for formulating and implementing policy. Other states pledge themselves in their constitutions to support the family – Greece, Italy, Ireland, Portugal and Spain – but do not have in place central institutions equipped to carry out family policy making. In Italy and Spain, the family is downplayed because of the disrepute brought upon family policy by authoritarian regimes which imposed a rigid patriarchal family model.

Several states have neither a constitutional nor an institutional commitment to families: some – the Netherlands and the United Kingdom – reject the idea that the state has a duty to interfere in family affairs; others – Denmark, Finland and Sweden – prefer to direct their attention elsewhere. In some cases, the family unit is not overtly identified as a policy area: in Denmark, Finland, the Netherlands and Sweden, individuals, and particularly children, are the focus of policy. In Ireland and the United Kingdom, the family unit has not generally been directly targeted as a policy area because of the concern of governments to avoid interfering in the private lives of individuals.

While tax law represents the interests of adults, and the extension of separate taxation reinforces the concept of individualisation, social security and social assistance schemes have been concerned with the well-being of children as individuals. Attention has focused increasingly on the needs of children and their legal rights to protection, whatever the relationship between their parents, and attempts are being made, as with the Child Support Act of 1991 in the United Kingdom, to ensure that fathers fulfil their responsibilities towards their children after separation. The International Convention on the Rights of the Child, adopted by the General Assembly of the United Nations in 1989, confirmed the joint responsibility of parents for their children, not in response to claims for greater equality between the sexes but rather in support of the needs of children.

Defining families for the purposes of delivering welfare raises issues about official acceptance and recognition of non-standard family patterns or the ability of states to influence family structures by supporting some family forms in preference to others. The state may not recognise non-formalised family relationships where employment-related insurance benefits are concerned, but household resources are sometimes taken into account in assessing eligibility for means-tested benefits, seemingly counteracting the trend towards individualisation and infringing the protection of privacy (Luckhaus, 1994). The examples given in this chapter illustrate how differences in conceptualising and measuring family relationships from one country to another are associated with variations in access to social protection rights. These themes are examined in more detail in subsequent chapters with reference to the family–employment relationship and the wider social policy context.

# CHAPTER 4

# Sociological definitions of the family

The picture of the family that emerges from statistical data, institutional and public policy documents is one of constant and progressive change. While statisticians are expected to record change, institutions and policy makers may be reacting to it or, in some cases, they may use the decision-making process to seek to influence behaviour, whether it be for demographic, egalitarian or authoritarian reasons. For their part, sociologists are interested in tracking, analysing, understanding and explaining changes in family structure and human relationships by locating them within the wider social context. They are therefore looking for definitions which are more flexible than those used by statisticians, policy makers or administrators.

Although statistics suggest that the family nucleus may correspond more closely to the household unit than in the past due to the reduction in family size, as demonstrated in Chapter 1, the family unit has become more difficult to record and monitor because the boundaries are increasingly blurred by the diversity of family forms. In the eighteenth and nineteenth centuries, marital unions were often interrupted after relatively short periods of cohabitation by the death of one of the partners, and it was common for children who survived beyond infancy to experience life with step-parents and step-brothers and sisters (Ariès, 1948; Laslett, 1977). Towards the end of the twentieth century, when marriage has the potential to last for many decades and infant mortality rates are minimal, the breakdown of the conjugal relationship, lone parenthood and the reconstitution of families are more likely to be the result of voluntary separation or divorce, and children are tending to move between the different household and family units formed by their biological parents. The situation has become more complicated and hence more difficult to record, monitor and analyse.

While cohabitation, lone parenthood, reconstituted, blended or re-ordered families are far from being new social phenomena, from the 1960s, they became a focus of sociological interest and of concern for policy makers in Northern Europe because they represented a departure from the trends established in the early postwar period: marriage and childbearing had been occurring at a younger age, and the two-parent married couple with two or more children had come to be considered as the norm. The stereotype and the norm had 'largely coincided' (Willmott and Willmott, 1982, p. 339). Extramarital births, lone parenthood, cohabitation and divorce were seen as deviations from the norm and therefore required special attention. They could be interpreted as indications that the family as an institution was in crisis, a theme addressed by much of the sociological literature on the family in the late twentieth century (for example Nave-Herz and Markefka, 1989, Teil IV; Roussel, 1989; Gittins, 1993).

In the south European countries, as exemplified by Spain, the sociology of the family has remained an under-developed field of study (Iglesias de Ussel and Flaquer, 1993). Studies of cohabitation, lone parenthood and divorce began to develop much later than in other west European countries, and the theme of crisis in the family has not usually been addressed in the sociological literature.

The definitions of the family examined in this chapter reflect different national approaches in sociology to conceptualising and theorising families and the growing recognition of the need to take account of family diversity. In the relatively short space devoted to the subject here, no more than a brief survey can be given of the main trends in the development of the family as a social phenomenon and a subject of sociological interest, by referring to the theoretical frameworks which have proved influential for family sociologists in Western Europe. The main focus of attention is on the relevance of various bodies of theory about the family for different national contexts and on the ways in which they have been developed and adapted by sociologists in response to socio-cultural factors.

## The family as a social phenomenon

The family is widely accepted as a core, or fundamental, social unit, and is portrayed as such in official documents, public opinion surveys and academic research. Just as the commitment of the state to support families has been shown to vary from one national context to another, the level of interest and the sociological importance attributed to family affairs by sociologists and social policy analysts also differ from one country to another. In this section, consideration is given firstly to popular conceptions of families, by examining the responses to questions in European public opinion surveys, before going on to look at the different bodies of academic research and the issues that have been explored by family policy analysts in a variety of cultural settings.

## Popular conceptions of the family

The way in which the family is perceived by public opinion may have a bearing on the legitimacy of statistical, institutional and administrative conceptualisations of the family unit and be reflected in the role played by family associations. It is not possible to gauge with any certainty whether popular conceptions of the family precede or follow statistical and institutional recognition of different family forms or to what extent they are shaped or influenced by political rhetoric. Attitudes towards the institutionalised structure of the family and popular perceptions of its role as a fundamental social institution have clearly been undergoing change over the postwar period, though not to the extent that might have been expected given the marked shifts in behaviour recorded by demographic indicators.

The results of a Eurobarometer survey (Malpas and Lambert, 1993) carried out for the Commission of the European Communities in 1993 showed that attitudes towards the family had changed relatively little since the early 1980s. For 96 per cent of the Europeans questioned the family remained the most important social value. Only in the Netherlands and the former German Democratic Republic (GDR) was it replaced by other values: friends and acquaintances in the Netherlands and work in the GDR. Few respondents were opposed to cohabitation, except in Ireland, where opponents outnumbered supporters. Children continued to be of central importance for the majority of Europeans, particularly in Greece, Italy Portugal and Spain. They were seen as much less important in Ireland, especially, and in the Netherlands, the United Kingdom and Germany (Malpas and Lambert, 1993, tables 3.4, 3.10, 4.3).

Many studies have shown that the popular conception of the family is something much wider than the nuclear family or household, as defined by statisticians or administrators for tax returns or entitlement to benefits. There is abundant evidence demonstrating the enduring nature of the links between the members of extended families, not only in the south European countries but throughout the Union. Contact is maintained by regular telephone calls and visits and the mutual help services they provide, ranging from childcare and caring for elderly relatives to intergenerational financial and moral support (for example Young and Willmott, 1973, for the United Kingdom; Pitrou, 1978, 1992, for France; Köcher, 1993, for Germany; Iglesias de Ussel and Flaquer, 1993, for Spain; Jani-Le Bris, 1993, and Attias-Donfut, 1995, for older people in the European Union).

Periodically, media coverage of extreme cases of juvenile delinquency, as in the early 1990s in the United Kingdom, provokes renewed debate over the possible consequences for society of the breakdown of the family as a primary support group, while public opinion surveys across the Union continue to show that the family, however defined, remains an almost unchallenged central value in most people's lives.

## The family as an object of academic research

Although sociological interest may focus on many of the same issues from one country to another – the dysfunctioning of the institutional family, the diversification of family forms, changing gender relations within families, the rights of children – the emphasis given to any one area is determined to a large extent by the political, ideological, socio-economic and cultural contexts within which these phenomena are located.

Academic researchers are generally dependent on external funding to carry out their research. Their work is therefore likely to reflect the interests of their sponsors. Countries with a strong family policy tradition and a powerful family lobby are more likely to give a high profile to family affairs in their research agenda by commissioning studies of family and household change, as illustrated by the French case, where family studies is a recognised and well-supported area of social research (Pitrou, 1994). In Germany, sociological research on the family is considered as an indispensable tool for policy makers if they are to be able to make informed judgements about the justification and possible impact of policy measures (Wingen and Stutzer, 1994, pp. 80–3).

In Denmark, where family policy as such has not been given high visibility, the impetus has come from a range of social actors, including trade unions, federations of local and regional authorities and government departments, who all commission and fund studies on families matters. Social surveys are seen as an important component in the policy-making process and in bringing about change, as exemplified by policies introducing more flexible worktime and childcare arrangements (Pruzan, 1994, pp. 51–3).

In the south European countries, governments have also shown an interest in sociological research on the family. Portugal has a tradition of policy related academic research on family matters, derived from legal studies of questions such as marriage, filiation, divorce and parental authority. In the 1990s, changes in family organisation and the social consequences of population ageing were research priority areas (Amaro, 1994b, p. 269). The growing interest in the family in the early 1990s in Italy was accompanied by the setting up of advisory committees to the government and the commissioning of reports on the state of the family (Sgritta and Zanatta, 1994, pp. 194–6). In Greece and Spain, which do not have a fully developed family policy, governments nevertheless draw on research findings in drafting policy (Fernández Cordón, 1994, pp. 118–19). In Greece, *ad hoc* committees of academic experts are appointed, as necessary, to advise the government on family law (Moussourou, 1994, pp. 102–3).

Ireland and the United Kingdom are examples of countries where relatively little social research has been commissioned by government on family matters. Studies that have been carried out tend to focus on economic issues, particularly child poverty in the case of Ireland (Kiely and Richardson, 1994, pp. 170–1). Research in the United Kingdom has been described as pragmatic and atomised in that academics are responding to the requirements of policy makers but are not doing so in dedicated centres. Family and family policy research has not been institutionalised, with the result that no 'systematic, cumulative and conceptually or theoretically cohesive body of knowledge' has been gathered together (Chester, 1994, p. 291). The same could probably be said of most EU member states, but there were some indications by the mid-1990s that British research on family matters was set to become more focused under the impact of growing concern among policy makers about the social problems associated with changes in the fabric of families (Utting, 1995).

The United Nations' International Year of the Family in 1994 served as an incentive for a number of countries to fund surveys of family trends and make policy recommendations. The Netherlands Family Council, for example, used the opportunity to assess the current situation and, in particular, to appraise the impact of the individualisation process (de Hoog *et al.*, 1993). In Italy, a White Paper on Family Policy was published, setting out the government's commitment to supporting families as a central social value.

The different national research priorities were illustrated by the contributions to an issue of *Social Europe* (Teirlinck, 1994) prepared by the European Commission's unit for Analysis of and Research on the Social Situation within Directorate-General V on the 'European Union and the Family'. They represented differing national priorities in the mid-1990s, reflecting stages in socio-economic development as well as culturally specific factors.

In some countries, the dominant image conveyed was of the traditional family supported by the state and society: in Portugal, traditional family values were presented as being upheld by the state and the Catholic Church; in Luxembourg, social consensus was said to prevail over the relationship between family and state; the German contribution stressed the importance of the social context of childbearing and childrearing; Belgium was shown to be concerned primarily with institutional reforms and with the reconciliation of work and family life.

In another group of countries, the state was depicted as having loosened its control over the family, or it was seeking to do so: the emphasis in the Netherlands was on reconciling family and social life in a situation where the state was reducing its support for families; the focus in Denmark was on individual rights and equality issues; in France, the balance between individual rights and responsibilities, social solidarity and institutional structures was at the centre of the public/private debate; in the United Kingdom, the boundaries between family obligations and the responsibilities of the state were also important issues. Other countries were grappling with changes in household and family structures, and social values: in Italy, discussion was focused on the recognition of non-traditional family forms and the reconceptualisation of the family; Greece was concentrating attention on the changes in traditional support networks and the role of women, which was also an important issue in Spain; in Ireland, divorce and abortion were on the agenda in a context characterised by the absence of an integrated approach to family affairs.

The examples given in this section indicate that the interest in the family as a social phenomenon recorded in the late twentieth century by public opinion surveys and academic research was not uniform across the Union. While the view was widely held that the family was the most important social value, the degree to which the family as a unit, and more specifically the two-parent child-centred family, should receive public support varied from one national context to another. Whereas, in some cases, new family forms – cohabitation, lone parenthood, reconstituted families – had been widely accepted and were not considered as social problems, in others cases, they were important issues and, in some instances, they were being treated as deviations from the norm, justifying support for policy studies.

## Sociological interest in the family

Sociologists are interested in analysing and describing the complexities of human relationships and changes in family structure over what may often be a relatively short period of time. They are therefore looking for definitions that are flexible and relevant to the issue in hand rather than being comprehensive, unambiguous and straightforward to apply, as is the case for statisticians measuring demographic trends or civil servants required to implement legislation.

Although the theories of some of the founding fathers of sociology – Le Play, Durkheim, Engels, Marx and Weber – all addressed issues concerning the family as a social phenomenon, it was not until the 1950s and 1960s that the family became a focus of wider sociological interest in Western Europe, particularly in the United Kingdom (Young and Willmott, 1957; Harris, 1969, for example). In France, the real take-off for family sociology as an autonomous discipline has been situated in the 1970s (documented by Roussel, 1989; de Singly, 1991). In the Nordic states, feminist researchers in the 1970s were focusing on the structures of power and oppression within the family (Bak, 1989, p. 1), and then in the 1980s on the shift from private dependence to 'public patriarchy' (see Siim, 1993, p. 28). Feminist research also provided the theoretical framework for sociological analysis of family structures in south European countries, particularly from the 1980s and 1990s (see Alberdi, 1979, 1994; Bimbi, 1993; Del Re, 1993; Valiente, 1995, for Italy and Spain).

Sociology of the family was described in the mid-1970s as having a relatively weak theoretical tradition and as lacking a critical tradition (Morgan, 1975, p. 5). In most EU member states, studies of family matters since the 1970s have been commissioned and funded primarily by governments or by agencies concerned with policy issues rather than with advancing sociological theory. The emphasis has therefore tended to be on social problem areas, such as poor families or child abuse, with the intention of feeding the findings into the policy-making process. Commissioned research tends to be applied and opportunistic, focusing of necessity on explanations for current social problems and solutions to them. Because the family as an object of sociological investigation is constantly changing, theories established in a particular place and period, and presented as universal, have subsequently often been discredited by empirical work carried out in different cultural settings. In this section, some of the major trends in sociological theory with regard to the family are briefly surveyed, with particular reference to the impact of functionalism and feminist theory and the critiques surrounding them.

### *From functionalism to crisis management*

In the English-language literature of the 1940s and 1950s, George Peter Murdock (1949) and Talcott Parsons (Parsons and Bales, 1956) were influential in setting the parameters of family sociology in functionalist terms. Murdock's definition of the family, which has been extensively quoted, was strictly normative and was expected to apply in all types of society. Families were defined by four basic functions: common residence; economic cooperation; reproduction; and a socially approved sexual relationship (Murdock, 1949, p. 1). The household unit was normally formed by a married couple and children, and characterised by a sexual division of labour.

In his work, Parsons defined society as a social system. The various institutions and other subsystems emerging in response to social needs were said to be functional or dysfunctional; either enhancing or reducing the functions of the system as a whole. Parsons argued that, as society evolves, the functions of institutions become more specialised and differentiated and they gain a certain degree of autonomy. The nuclear family was functional to industrial society because it increased the mobility of its members. By taking production out of the home, the industrial revolution made the family a more specialised institution, able to concentrate on the socialisation of children, without relying on the support of wider kinship groups.

Critics (for example Harris, 1969, pp. 93–105; Morgan, 1975, pp. 39–48; Gittins, 1993, pp. 60–64) have demonstrated that Murdock's definition of the family was far from being universal, either over time or space. Similarly, Parsons' representation of the family in industrial society was criticised for being concerned essentially with the American middle-class family and for not being applicable in other social contexts. Structural-functionalist analysis has, however, been influential in shaping conceptions of the normative family in postwar European societies and in establishing a reference point against which to assess the effectiveness of particular family forms.

Many family theorists of the 1950s and 1960s, who were looking for universal concepts of the family that could be exploited across societies, focused on the interactions between individuals as required by their different roles in social life (symbolic interactions), thereby highlighting conflictual situations. Advocates of exchange and conflict theory emphasised the gains and losses that are an integral part of relationships between family members, while the developmental cycle approach explored the different stages in the family life cycle in relation to role clusters. Much of the family sociology literature of this period emanated from the United States (reviewed in Christensen, 1964) and is open to some of the same criticisms that were levelled against Parsons, in that the theories were often grounded in culturally specific empirical work and were not necessarily applicable to other societies.

It may be no coincidence, however, that national constitutions in west European countries presented the family as a universal institution needed to carry out functions that ensure the survival of society, or that the monolithic functionalist family corresponds closely to many of the definitions used in public administration for the purposes of levying taxes, identifying beneficiaries for welfare payments and services or defining the deviant family (see Chapter

3). In addition, the heavily normative conceptualisation of the family has been drawn on by social services practitioners because it emphasises the functions of the family as a support system mediating between the individual and society.

While the family was presented as being functional for society, critics of functionalism have also shown that it can be dysfunctional for individuals and a source of conflicts or contradictions (Morgan, 1975, pp. 92–9) which, when taken to an extreme, can lead to the destruction of the family (Cooper, 1972). Writing in the late 1970s and drawing on historical data, Jacques Donzelot (1979) has, for example, demonstrated that families in eighteenth- and nineteenth-century France were far from being functionally effective if left to their own devices, justifying systematic state intervention, such as has been widely practised across Europe during the twentieth century. Many of the functions attributed to the family by functionalists have, in the event, progressively been taken over by the state, with the effect that families have become more specialised institutions, concentrating increasingly on providing emotional support for their members (Roussel, 1989, pp. 75–7).

## The feminist challenge to systems theory

The family arrangement best suited to the functional requirements of industrial society was, according to Parsonian and role theory, premised on sex-role differentiation and specialisation, whereby the wife performed the expressive role of homemaker and the husband the instrumental role of breadwinner. Although Parsons portrayed these roles as different but of equal value, feminists in the 1970s called attention to the subordination, exploitation and oppression of women implicit in their assignment to the privatised world of the home, in contrast to the integration of men into the public sphere (in particular Delphy, 1970, and Michel, 1974, in France; Beechey, 1979, in the United Kingdom).

A large body of theory has developed since the 1970s on gender inequality as derived from capitalist and patriarchal relations (reviewed by Walby, 1986), calling into question the separation of the private and the public domains. The literature on patriarchy has led to the reconceptualisation of domestic labour as productive work and to a renewed interest in the analysis of the gendered division of labour both inside and outside the home, as exemplified in the United Kingdom by Ray Pahl (1984), with the concept of household work strategies, or in France by the work of authors such as Monique Haicault (1984) or the contributors to *Le sexe du travail* (Collectif, 1984), and in Spain by María Durán (1986, 1988). The conceptualisation of the family as a unit of production has afforded a theoretical framework for the analysis of the incorporation of women into men's work and of women's subordination, while also providing a context for analysing the boundaries between the public and private spheres (Finch, 1983). West German feminists have argued for unpaid domestic work to be publicly recognised as socially important and rewarded as such (Ostner, 1993).

Much of the literature on patriarchy, like the functionalist texts it was reacting against, tends to present its theories as being universally applicable to advanced postindustrial societies. In the 1960s, the Swedish sociologist, Edmund Dahlström, had already identified different family and gender ideologies in the democratic capitalist countries of Western Europe, not on the basis of nationally determined characteristics but according to a combination of socio-political and economic criteria. In later work, Dahlström (1989, pp. 32–4) outlined three dominant ideologies, or belief systems, covering family functions, gender relations and human reproduction, providing an analytical framework for classifying capitalist countries, in some ways foreshadowing Gøsta Esping-Andersen's (1990) classification of welfare regimes.

According to Dahlström, countries with strong conservative ideologies favoured the maintenance of existing structures and order, with heavy reliance on private markets. In this context, the traditional family was seen as an important institution requiring protection against state intervention and an expanding public sector. Markets and families were kept free from state coercion and tutelage. Gender asymmetries were seen as being functionally complementary, and gender differentiation as a positive force. Radical gender equality and support for working mothers were questioned, while reproductive work in families was recognised and appreciated.

Dahlström did not identify the countries to which this ideology could be applied. Nor was he explicit about the countries characterised by his liberal-democratic ideology, where free-market forces were seen as the motor of societal development, the traditional authoritarian family as an obstacle to progress and modernisation, and legislation and public policy as the means of attaining gender equality. Both the freedom of families and markets had to be defended against collective encroachments.

In the social-democratic ideology, characteristic of the Nordic states and Germany according to Dahlström, gender equality was a major goal; emancipation from traditional gender roles applied to both men and women. Political, social and economic democracy were being achieved in a context of increasing public control over the productive system and expansion of the public sector, which was expected, in the longer term, to take over family functions.

None of these ideologies corresponded very precisely to what could be identified as the dominant belief systems in the EU member states of the 1990s. Although a conservative (and often Catholic) vanguard may have been defending gender asymmetries in Greece, Ireland, Italy, Luxembourg, Portugal or Spain, the promotion of gender equality, and particularly a more equal sexual division of labour in the home, was a topic of growing interest to feminist sociologists across the Union, often crystallising around the issue of gender and caring (Ungerson, 1990; Leira, 1993; McLaughlin and Glendinning, 1994; Lister, 1995). Feminists could readily defend their argument that unpaid domestic labour was nowhere recognised as being of equal value to paid work outside the home (see also Chapter 6).

*Family diversity*

The normative model of the family derived from the theories of the 1950s and 1960s depended upon the wife staying at home to care for children. Feminist writings have drawn attention to the fact that, by omitting to consider the status of women in studies of social stratification, sociologists have often implied that the social class of the family unit is determined by the husband alone (Walby, 1986, pp. 7–16). While the male breadwinner model might have applied to all but women in economically deprived circumstances and some professionally qualified women in dual-career families in several countries at that time, it was already a much less common arrangement by the 1970s (Rapoport and Rapoport, 1971). Other 'deviant' family forms were also becoming more prevalent and were attracting the interest of family sociologists. Progressively since the early 1970s, sociological research on the family has moved away from the standardisation implicit in the concept of the normative and undifferentiated family to a recognition of the diversity of family forms. The interest shown in diversity is not new. Social historians have provided a wealth of examples of family forms that have coexisted at different times in different places (Flandrin, 1976; Laslett, 1977). In more recent times, the diversity of family arrangements has been illustrated in rural Portugal (Wall, 1992). It can be argued that it is rather the diversity of families which is the norm, and any attempts to impose a uniform definition of the family may be a response to administrative needs for classification rather than a result of sociological observation. The causes of family diversity have, however, changed, particularly since the 1960s. Marriage is no longer the main defining criterion of family relationships or duties.

In order to circumvent the problem of how to deal with family diversity as typified by separated parents with joint custody, ex-spouses still living in the same dwelling or reconstituted families, Jan Trost (1988, p. 301), the Swedish family sociologist, has suggested that new ways should be sought for conceptualising what he has called 'hyphen-families': two-parent families, one-parent families, childless families, families with teenagers, and so forth. He has therefore proposed identifying families as being based on the parent-child or spousal unit, whether or not the members are living together and whether they are married or unmarried. This conceptualisation of family units is useful in that its defining characteristic is the biological bond between parents and children even when they are not living together.

In identifying a parent-child unit as one parent and one child related to each other, Trost (1988, p. 303) recognised that even the terms 'parent' and 'child' may vary in meaning according to whether they are defined by biological, psychological, legal or cultural criteria, which depend on the purpose of the study.

Parent-child units and spousal units can, according to Trost, be combined: a two-parent unit may, for instance, consist of a mother-child unit, a spousal unit and a step-father-child unit, if a new spouse takes over the father role in the cultural sense, as is generally assumed in census statistics, though not in legal definitions. The non-custodial parent in this example would also constitute a parent-child unit, whereas statistical definitions of households would not routinely pick up the relationship with an absent parent. The child would therefore still have two parents.

Trost has applied the concept of the parent-child or spousal unit in the analysis of lone-parent families as a means of overcoming some of the definitional problems in statistical data collection noted in Chapter 1. In doing so, he creates a definition which may be helpful for sociologists but which would make the task of the statistician even more difficult. In addition to suggesting that the issue of age should be dealt with by adopting whatever age limit is most appropriate to the task in hand, Trost criticises definitions of one-parent families that depend on the prolonged absence of one of the parents, and the practice of relabelling them as two-parent families if the custodial parent remarries. Co-residence should not, in his view, be considered as a defining characteristic on the grounds that a parent remains a parent even if he/she does not live together with the child or children. The arrangements for joint custody of children, which was not uncommon in the Nordic states when he was writing in the 1980s, could mean that children spent part of their time with each of their parents, making it difficult to decide which was the one-parent family if statistical definitions were being applied.

Trost's definition of the spousal unit did include the co-residence criterion: a spousal unit consisted of two adults cohabiting, either maritally or non-maritally. He specified, however, that a married man and woman not living together and with no children would be unlikely to be labelled as a family.

This proposal for reconceptualising family relationships reflects the growing sociological interest in analysing family diversity and the need for tools more suited to the task than those developed by statisticians in recording changing family structures. The examples of lone parenthood and reconstituted families have served as focal points for sociological analysis of family forms in the late twentieth century across Europe and are therefore worthy of more detailed consideration in an account of the sociological interest shown in the family in different EU member states.

*Lone parenthood*

The phenomenon of lone parenthood existed in Northern Europe long before national statistics began recording it in census data. In the nineteenth century, divorce and illegitimacy were generally stigmatised and were treated very differently from widowhood. While families headed by a widowed parent were still considered as families, mothers with illegitimate children were not considered as real families, and one-parent families and broken homes were associated with delinquency (Lefaucheur, 1986; Gittins, 1993). Lone parenthood tended to become an important focus of sociological interest at the time when divorce law was liberalised, and larger numbers of families were becoming one-parent units as a result of marital breakdown rather than the death of one of the partners. In Britain, the Divorce Reform Act of 1969 provoked a rapid increase in the number of divorcing parents. The 1970s were characterised by media coverage of single-parent families as the locus of deprivation, instability and insecurity, a picture which tended to be reinforced by the human services professionals. Children of divorced parents were found to fare worse than children with bereaved parents but better than those of young single mothers (Popay *et al.*, 1983, p. 33).

In Germany, lone parenthood has been portrayed as a form of deviance from the norm in a system where rights have been determined either by marriage or by incorporation into the labour market. Since lone mothers, particularly if single, rather than widowed or divorced, are excluded from these two sources of normality, they have been socially neglected (Voegeli, 1991).

The term *famille monoparentale* was imported into France from the Anglo-Saxon world at a time in the mid-1970s when French feminists were campaigning for women living alone with their children to be recognised as real families and as an innovative family form with rights of its own, rather than being categorised as deviant (Lefaucheur and Martin, 1993, p. 31). Feminist interest in lone parenthood also coincided with divorce law reform (1975), a marked change in the factors generating lone parenthood and the introduction of public policy measures to support lone parents. An additional incentive was the momentum gained by post-1968 social movements campaigning for the legalisation of contraception and abortion, women's liberation, the destigmatisation of sexual minorities and radical change in the gendered division of labour (Lefaucheur, 1986, p. 76). While the term *famille monoparentale* was adopted as a category for public policy, sociologists were torn between accepting lone parenthood as an unproblematic family form and a focus on the living conditions and vulnerability of lone-parent families, the effectiveness of family policy and the wider impact of lone parenthood on the socialisation of children (Lefaucheur, 1991).

In other EU member states, lone parenthood has also attracted the interest of family sociologists. In the Nordic states, as illustrated by Trost's proposal, sociologists have attempted to 'normalise' lone parents and their children. Over the postwar period, the south European countries have experienced a phenomenon which was widespread in many other European countries in the nineteenth century: lone parenthood as a result of separation due to emigration. The different situations leading to lone parenthood, the possible effects of lone parenthood on women's employment and in the rural as compared with the urban environment, and the relationship between lone parenthood and delinquency were all issues being examined by Spanish sociologists in the 1980s (Iglesias de Ussel, 1988).

*Reconstituted families*

The increase in the divorce rate associated with divorce law reform in Western Europe was frequently accompanied by a rise in the number of remarriages, thus bringing about 'social reintegration' after periods of lone parenthood. In countries where divorce and remarriage were illegal, as in Ireland in the early 1990s, separation was often followed by cohabitation. The extension of consensual unions, replacing marriage as the locus for childbearing in Northern Europe, was testified by the rapidly growing number of extramarital births in the 1980s and 1990s. Studies of consensual unions and remarriages suggested that they were likely to be less enduring than the more traditional marriages of the 1950s. In all these cases, new family units were being formed, providing substitute parents and often with the potential to produce more offspring. As for lone-parent families, early sociological studies examined the impact on children of living with step-families which fell outside definitions of the normative family and were only slowly being accepted by society (for example Burgoyne and Clark, 1982, in the United Kingdom).

Although the concept of step-families had become a topic of sociological interest in the 1950s in the United States, a different term was needed in the 1970s to take account of the impact of the spread of divorce on family composition and the diversity of step-families. Studies in the 1970s were already highlighting the inadequacies of legal and social concepts that could act as reference points around which to build new relationships in what could easily become dysfunctional and conflictual situations. The concept of 'reconstituted families' was used to describe the family units formed by a second marriage or a consensual union of one or both spouses in a couple that divorced and where children were present (Théry, 1993, p. 10).

Sociological studies of families after divorce in Denmark in the 1980s have referred to the concept of the 'binuclear family' and the effort needed to achieve family solidarity in a unit that might contain outsiders (Koch-Nielsen, 1987, pp. 7–8). The term 'blended family' was used in the 1980s to describe the constellation of parent-child relationships that can arise following the separation of children's biological parents. It depicted the complex situation in which children find themselves as they move in and out and across a series of relationships during their lives. Studies of blended families (*familles (re)composées*) in France have demonstrated that the relationship with the new parent remains difficult to define and manage (Le Gall and Martin, 1990). Work in the early 1990s in the United Kingdom suggested that a negative outcome was inevitable for children in 're-ordered families', as they were being called (Utting, 1995, p. 47). The concept of the 'multiparental' family has also become more meaningful within a sociological perspective because of the emphasis it places on both institutional and biological relationships.

While not giving rise to a strong body of theoretical literature, the return to a sociological focus on family diversity, as exemplified by studies of reconstituted families, has tended to renew interest in different family forms, thereby continuing the ethnographic tradition of family sociology (Segalen, 1981).

**Socially constructed families**

The intention in this chapter was to provide an indication of some of the main themes in the developing sociological literature on families. As with statistical, institutional or legal definitions, the concepts used to describe families are seen to be the combined product of specific geographical, economic and social factors. Their meanings are socially constructed, as exemplified by the terms used at different times and in different cultural contexts to describe a lone-parent or a reconstituted family. The chapter confirms the interest of identifying the point at which, in a given society, a concept is adopted or becomes accepted by statisticians, administrators, sociologists or ordinary people, as illustrated by the conceptual shift from the family in the singular to families in the plural with the recognition of family diversity. The examples presented in the previous section show how the sociology of the family has been developing as a discipline at a time when the family as an object of study has been undergoing transformations requiring analysts to reinvent their concepts and to look for new terms to describe the phenomena being observed if they are not to be interpreted as deviations from the normative family.

The logic underlying the introduction of concepts in specific contexts is shown to be a response to a variety of needs and circumstances. As a result, the same concept may come to denote different phenomena from one national context to another. While Eurobarometer surveys seem to bring confirmation of the enduring attachment of Europeans to the family, what respondents understand by the term may be very different from one social context to another: three family forms were, for example, identified in a village of 1857 inhabitants in rural Portugal in the 1980s (Wall, 1992); Trost's (1988) work suggests a multitude of possible family units. Eurobarometer surveys show marked differences in attitudes and behaviour within societies according to age and gender, but many more variables – social class, ethnicity, living arrangements, religious convictions, political ideologies – are influential in determining the meaning of concepts which relate to each individual's personal experience. Studies in France have shown, for example, that, in reconstituted families, the new parent is more readily seen as a substitute for the non-custodial parent in some social categories than in others (Le Gall and Martin, 1990, pp. 71–101).

While efforts have been made, with limited success, to harmonise and standardise the concepts used in statistical analyses, conceptual equivalence may be even more difficult to achieve in sociological studies of family and household change. The recognition of family diversity is particularly relevant to an analysis of the European context since it implies an understanding of national characteristics and a realisation that family sociology can develop its own theoretical and methodological tools, as argued by Michael Anderson (1971, pp. 7–8) in the early 1970s. In addition, fatherhood and childhood have become the focus of renewed sociological interest and are being reconceptualised to take account of changing family forms across member states (Brannen and O'Brien, 1995). Rather than negating comparative work, the search for a greater understanding of conceptual difference and of the complexities of family forms presents a challenge which is fundamental to sociological enquiry.

# PART TWO

# The Family–Employment Relationship

Although some attention has been devoted to analysing fatherhood and the linkages between men's work and their family lives in the European context (Björnberg, 1992; Danish Ministry of Social Affairs, 1993), the relationship between family and employment is seen by policy makers and social scientists primarily as an issue concerning women. The social order on which the twentieth-century welfare systems were predicated depended upon the concept of women's unpaid domestic production as the natural complement to men's economic production outside the home. The relationship between female economic activity and family life was, however, a topic of interest for policy makers long before social protection became a universal right. The process of industrialisation in nineteenth-century Europe had created harsh working conditions, justifying state intervention to protect women as mothers. Social historians (for example, Tilly and Scott, 1987, for Britain and France) have shown that female labour was essential for the economic survival of working-class families, posing the problem of how to organise the relationship between paid employment outside the home, domestic work and childrearing.

In the postwar period in Western Europe, not many sociologists were interested in the linkages between employment and family life. Two distinct disciplinary fields developed: family sociology and industrial sociology. Until the 1970s, few studies sought to cross the disciplinary divide. Since then, largely under the impetus of second-wave feminism, the literature on the family–employment relationship has become abundant not only within the context of family sociology but also in analyses of workplace segregation and equality of opportunity. The relationship has been analysed from a number of disciplinary perspectives and as a more autonomous disciplinary field, with the aim of identifying the reciprocal influence between female economic activity and family life, and the strategies in operation to make the two areas compatible.

The sociologists' disciplinary boundaries are also relevant to an understanding of the way the family–employment relationship has been treated at European level. Since the establishment of the European Economic Community in 1958, attention has been paid primarily to women as workers. Binding legislation has been introduced to ensure that member states implement equal opportunities policies for women at the workplace. Until the 1970s, little interest was shown at Community level in women as unpaid workers in the home. Since then, reference has been made in Community documents to the need for policies to help families combine employment with family life, thereby placing the family–employment relationship on the social policy agenda and justifying international studies (Peemans-Poullet, 1984).

In the first part of this book, statistical, institutional and sociological definitions of families and households were analysed. The chapters in the second part focus on different disciplinary and national approaches to conceptualising work, employment and unemployment, and the policy strategies for combining work and family life. Although similar trends can again be identified throughout Europe in family structure and employment patterns, important differences remain between member states in the ways in which the relationship between work organisation and family building is managed both by individuals and at national level. The chapters examine how statistical aggregates of different aspects of employment are constructed, how institutions have reacted to changes in family structure and employment patterns, how the relationship has been conceptualised, analysed and integrated into national and EU policy making, and how the expectations and behaviour of family members are adapting to meet new situations.

# CHAPTER 5

# Conceptualising women's and mothers' employment

Statistical indicators of trends in women's labour market participation rates, like those recording family building or household structure, reflect not only different national situations but also variations in definitions and conceptual frameworks. Because of their reproductive role, women do not enter the labour market under the same conditions as men. Nor are the employment patterns, working arrangements and career expectations of women likely to be identical from one EU member state to another. Employment and unemployment, part-time and full-time work, continuous and discontinuous working patterns and occupational status do not have the same meaning across the Union; decisions about labour market activity, whether freely made or imposed, are not based on the same criteria.

In this chapter, national and supranational statistical definitions of the various dimensions of working patterns are first examined as a means of identifying the criteria involved in the conceptualisation and measurement of women's employment. Data mapping trends in employment for women and mothers across the Union are then presented and analysed. In conclusion, an attempt is made to assess the validity and interest of statistical data on employment from an international perspective.

## Statistical definitions of the labour force

At European level, data are collated on labour force participation rates in EU member states using a common definition based on recommendations issued by the International Labour Office (ILO). The first Community Labour Force Survey (CLFS) was carried out in 1960 in the six founder member states. The CLFS has come to be recognised as an authoritative source of comparable data on economic activity across the EU member states. In 1983, a major revision took place to ensure greater comparability of data by following closely the 'labour force' concept defined by the Thirteenth International Conference of Labour Statisticians in

October 1982. The Statistical Office of the European Communities (Eurostat) makes proposals about the content of national labour force surveys (LFS), the list of questions, the common coding of individual replies and the definitions to be applied in analysing the results. Responsibility for the sampling frame, the preparation of questionnaires and the interviewing of households is left to the national statistical agencies carrying out the survey (Eurostat, 1988, p. 8). Every year since 1983, Eurostat has published the results in tabular form, as the *Labour Force Survey*, providing a useful source of descriptive information about trends in employment, job search and education. Some countries, notably France and the United Kingdom, have exploited the Eurostat survey as a vehicle for carrying out much more detailed data collection for use by national governments.

Even though datasets are harmonised, the definitions applied in the CLFS are not unproblematic, because they do not necessarily match the definitions of the various forms of work, employment and unemployment that are widely used for national surveys. Disparities may arise because of the sources used, the way the returns are compiled and the purposes for which data are being collected. In France, for example, several sources based on differing criteria are used to compile statistics on the working population: in addition to detailed LFS, census data are combined with annual employment statistics collected by the Institut National de la Statistique et des Études Économiques (INSÉÉ), either applying ILO definitions or using self-definition. Statistical data on the active population in employment and on the unemployed are collected from a number of sources in Germany in the absence of a dedicated LFS: in addition to information compiled for the micro-census, records are kept of the employed population as registered for insurance contributions. The United Kingdom began conducting LFS in 1973 as a condition of EC membership. Since 1971 it has also collected data on employment in the General Household Survey (GHS) based on a national sample of private households taken from the Postcode Address File.

In this section, CLFS definitions are presented in conjunction with examples of national variants and alternatives to illustrate some of the discrepancies that may arise in data collection and analysis of the labour force across the Union.

## Economic activity and inactivity

The LFS covers the population resident in private households (as defined in Chapter 1) but not those living in collective households, although Denmark uses the family unit rather than individuals and households as the survey unit. The LFS therefore excludes students living in university residences, patients in hospitals, the armed forces (including compulsory military service) and the prison population. The statistical objective of the LFS is to provide descriptive and explanatory data about the working population (generally aged 14 or above), distinguishing between 'persons in employment, unemployed persons and inactive persons' as in the ILO definitions (Eurostat, 1988, p. 10). For the purposes of the survey, the labour force comprises both persons in employment and the unemployed.

Activity rates are calculated by the LFS to represent the labour force as a percentage of the population of working age living in private households. The unemployment rate represents the number of unemployed persons as a percentage of the labour force. The categories most often identified are for the population aged between 14 and 64, which may give rise to inconsistencies for the younger and older age groups, since young people become 'available', and older people cease being 'available', for employment at different ages in member states due to disparities in the length of schooling and training and because retirement age differs from one member state to another. In the mid-1990s, for example, the minimum school-leaving age was 15 in Austria, Belgium, Germany, Greece, Ireland, Luxembourg and Portugal, and 16 elsewhere, except in Italy and Spain where it was 14 (Commission of the European Communities/Eurydice and Cedefop, 1991). Legal retirement age varied from 56 for women in Italy to 67 for both men and women in Denmark (MISSOC, 1995, table VII). A further source of discrepancies can arise when national surveys refer to different age categories. The GHS in the United Kingdom, for example, takes a minimum age of 16 as a criterion for defining the population in employment.

*Employment*

The ILO uses the term 'employment' to refer to all persons in gainful employment or self-employed during the reference period, which is taken to be a specified period of either a week or a day. It is sufficient to have worked for one hour in the reference week to be considered as employed. Payment may be in cash or kind. The definition includes family workers who assist on a regular basis, without direct remuneration, in the running of farms or businesses. Individuals are also counted who were temporarily absent from their employment, for example on holiday or due to illness, as well as those with an assurance of return to work at the end of a contingency (as in the case of lay-offs in Denmark, Greece, Ireland and Portugal), or in receipt of compensation without the obligation to accept other jobs.

National surveys that do not use the ILO definition are likely to be recording a different population, as for example in Germany where data on employment are collected on the basis of returns supplied by employers for workers registered for social insurance. The 'social insurance' definition excludes civil servants, the self-employed, professional workers and family workers. Even when the ILO definition is observed, it may be interpreted differently from one country to another. In France, for example, the armed forces are included in the economically active population (Guillemot, 1993, p. 131). The micro-census used to measure employment in Austria counts all persons who exercise an occupation for at least 12 hours and up to 35 hours a week.

*Unemployed persons*

According to the ILO definition as adopted by the CLFS, the unemployed are persons of a specified age who are without work, currently available for work and actively seeking work. Long-term unemployment is used to describe persons unemployed for more than twelve months. Being without work means they were not in employment as defined above. Being currently available for work means that, if a job was found at the time of the interview, the person could start work within two weeks. Seeking work means that steps must have been taken in a specified recent period – the four weeks preceding the interview – to seek work.

If applied rigorously these definitions prove to be very restrictive. The 'without work' criterion excludes those who are on temporary contracts and short hours (over one hour in the reference week) as well as workers on lay-off. Actively seeking work means that evidence must be given of being registered for employment and responding to job offers. Availability for work implies that arrangements have been made for childcare, if necessary.

Unemployed persons are classified into four categories: job-losers are those who have involuntarily lost their job and immediately began seeking new work; job-leavers are those who have voluntarily left their job and immediately began seeking work; re-entrants are those who are returning to the labour force after a period of inactivity, as defined below; first job-seekers are those who have never worked in a regular job (Eurostat, 1988, p. 11).

Even though the CLFS is supposedly collecting data according to the same definition, the ways in which questions are asked and responses are interpreted in national surveys can produce discrepancies that may not subsequently be remedied in the process of transcoding. In Italy, for example, formal registration is the major defining characteristic of unemployed persons irrespective of whether or not they are actively seeking work, and information is not collected about the job search. German statisticians do not use the criterion of availability in national statistics since they are more interested in the main source of income (work, benefits, dependence on a relative) than the response to questions about the job search (Besson and Comte, 1994, pp. 547–9). In Austria, persons registering with an employment office who are neither in employment nor undergoing training are counted as unemployed (Gross *et al.*, 1994, p. 102)

Apart from collecting data according to the ILO definition of unemployment for the CLFS, most countries compile information based on monthly administrative returns from labour offices or unemployment agencies, which record the number of individuals registered as unemployed and eligible to claim benefits. In the United Kingdom, data derived from administrative returns are described as the 'claimant count', that is the number of people claiming benefit (unemployment benefit, income support or national insurance credits) (Central Statistical Office, 1995, p. 64). Since 1982, unemployment benefit can be claimed without being registered at a job centre. Claiming unemployment benefit is therefore taken as evidence of an active job search for the purposes of the CLFS. Registration as unemployed is, moreover, an important criterion in countries, such as France, that rely heavily on an employment-insurance related welfare system not only to be eligible to claim unemployment benefits but also for entitlement to social insurance cover for health and other contingencies.

As a result of differences in national practices, young people undergoing vocational training or women wanting to return to work after a break may or may not appear in the unemployed category from one country to another, depending upon whether they are eligible to claim benefits and whether eligibility for benefits is a criterion for inclusion as unemployed.

When data on unemployment are transcoded by Eurostat, the results have been found to diverge to a greater or lesser degree from data produced nationally, according to the way in which the guidelines are interpreted and applied: in the case of Germany, for example, the Eurostat figure may be as much as 21 per cent below that for national data on women, rising to 32 per cent for women aged under 25; France follows the ILO definition very closely in identifying job-seekers and availability for employment. The figures show no discrepancy for men and women, and a slight tendency to overestimate the percentage for young women (Besson and Comte, 1994, p. 554). Since Eurostat unemployment rates are used as a measure of need in the distribution of support from European Structural Funds, for instance, representations of national situations can have political and economic implications, and supposedly 'standardised' statistics may be contested.

*Inactive persons*

The ILO concept of inactivity is used to describe all persons who are not classified as employed or unemployed, again with reference to the population in private households aged over 14. No distinction is made between different categories of inactive persons, with the exception of pupils and students.

For the CLFS, questions about education and training, covering a four-week reference period, are addressed to all respondents aged between 14 and 49, and they are coded to show whether education was in a school, university or another training establishment and whether it was under the dual training system in the form of an apprenticeship. Inconsistencies are found in national practices for classifying persons undergoing training as employed or unemployed. In 1983, for example, in the British GHS, young people on youth training programmes were excluded from the labour force, whereas in the following year they were classified according to their own assessment of whether they were working during the reference period. In 1985, they were counted as working if with an employer or as inactive if at college during the reference week. From 1989, they were also considered to be active if at college (Bridgwood and Savage, 1993, p. 81).

## Employment characteristics

For the LFS, information is collected about the number of hours worked and the reasons for any departure from normal working hours, including full-time versus part-time arrangements and permanency of employment.

The distinction between full-time and part-time working is made on the basis of a spontaneous reply from the interviewee. In principle, a person is defined as being part-time when he/she works fewer hours than the norm for a particular job. The actual number of hours defined as the norm may vary from one country to another and from one area of activity to another.

In the Netherlands, since 1983 part-time workers have been defined as family workers, the self-employed working less than 35 hours per week, and employees working less than 31 hours a week, or between 31 and 34 hours if lower than normal for the job. In Greece, part-time work is considered as fewer hours than those provided for in collective agreements for the type of job concerned. In Italy, a person is considered as part time if working less than the hours normally worked in the particular type of employment (Eurostat, 1988, p. 57). In the United Kingdom, until 1983 the part-time category was restricted to employees, and the self-employed were automatically considered to be working full time. For internal purposes in the GHS, persons who work 31 hours or more a week are classified as full time, whereas those working 30 hours or less are part time. Germany has defined part-time working hours as between one and 36, implying a commitment below the normal working hours set by collective bargaining (Blossfeld, 1994, pp. 18–19). In Austria, part-time work is taken to be anything between 12 and 35 hours (Gross *et al.*, 1994, p. 83). Most countries have moved towards self-definition in their own statistics, which may be helpful in terms of international comparability but creates problems for comparisons over time if they previously used a set number of hours.

Employed persons may be defined as being in temporary work if the cessation of employment is determined by objective conditions such as the expiry of a given period, the completion of a task or the return of another employee who has been replaced temporarily. The category includes persons with a seasonal job, those hired out to a third party for a 'work mission' and persons with a specific training contract. Luxembourg has an additional code to cover individuals on probation where a new contract is needed at the end of the probationary period (Eurostat, 1988, p. 57).

## Occupational status

The occupational status and other details about the respondent's main job are collected and analysed for the CLFS using the International Standard Classification of Occupations (ISCO) (ILO, 1968). Recognition is given to the fact that each country may need a classification system adapted to its own situation, for example by providing more detail on particular occupations in one national context compared with another. The CLFS identifies seven main occupational groups: professional, technical and related workers; administrative and managerial workers; clerical and related workers; sales workers; service workers; agricultural and related workers; production, transport, labourers and related workers.

Even at the European level, the ISCO system is not routinely observed. In its surveys, Eurobarometer uses a standardised classification comprising sixteen categories. EU member states have used – and continue to use – a variety of socio-economic or socio-occupational classifications, which are more or less amenable to the ISCO categories. For the 1982 census in France, for example, occupations were reclassified into six broad categories, replacing the previous nine, to take account of major shifts in employment sectors since the 1950s: farmers; craftsmen, shopkeepers, employers; managers and professionals; intermediate non-manual occupations; employees; and industrial workers (Desrosières, 1984). Since the 1991 census, occupational groups have been reclassified in the United Kingdom into seven socio-economic groups: professional, employers and managers, intermediate non-manual, skilled manual and own account non-professional, semi-skilled manual and person service, and unskilled manual.

Data on socio-occupational groups, like those collected on economic activity rates, unemployment and inactivity for the CLFS are subject to the same problems of limited comparability as demographic data because they also reflect national conventions and practices as well as social, economic and political factors that determine the demand for statistics.

## Measuring female economic activity

Standardised Eurostat data as supplied from national LFS are virtually impossible to compare for the periods prior to and since 1983 because of changes in concepts and incomplete coverage of member states. In this section, most of the trend data are therefore restricted to the period following 1983. In addition, harmonised data are generally only available for countries from the dates when they joined the European Community or the European Union. From 1990, CLFS data covered unified Germany and are not therefore directly comparable with statistics for the Federal Republic of Germany prior to that date. Where possible, alternative sources are used in the analysis to provide an indication of trends for the periods not covered by Eurostat but are not incorporated into the figures to avoid giving the impression that they are directly comparable.

### Activity rates for men and women

Figure 5.1 shows that female economic activity rates, as recorded by Eurostat, were increasing in most EU member states between 1984 and 1994, whereas those for men stabilised and, in most cases, fell. The data for the mid-1990s suggest that, although women's economic activity rates were still below those for men in all EU member states, the differences between men and women had narrowed: in the Nordic countries, female activity rates differed from those of men by about 10 points, compared with between 20 and 30 points in most other EU member states.

The overall similarity in the direction of trends, in so far as it can be gauged from the available data, conceals major differences between countries. As with the demographic trends examined in Chapter 1, the extent and pace of change in women's employment rates varied from one country to another: in the later period, the

*Figure 5.1   Eurostat economic activity rates for men and women aged 14/15 and over as a percentage of total population of working age (1984–94)*

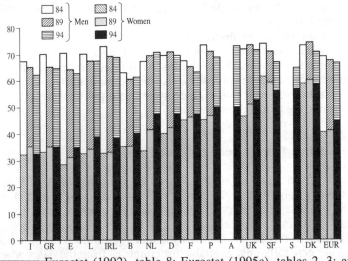

*Sources*: Eurostat (1992), table 8; Eurostat (1995c), tables 2, 3; and data supplied by Eurostat.

*Notes*: Provisional data for 1994 for population aged over 15; 1986 data for Portugal and Spain, 1985 and 1990 for Finland, 1993 for Austria and Ireland.

increase in female activity rates was much greater in Germany and the Netherlands. The Nordic countries retained their lead, however, followed by the United Kingdom, then Austria, Portugal, France, Germany and the Netherlands. The rise in female economic activity rates for Germany may, to some extent, be inflated by the inclusion of the new *Länder* where larger proportions of women were economically active than in the old *Länder*. A large gap continued to separate the Nordic from most of the south European countries and Ireland.

### Trends in female economic activity rates by age

The graphs in Figure 5.2 reflect the significant overall increase in female economic activity rates that began in the early 1970s, as well as changing patterns of female employment, particularly in the 25 to 49 age group. In the 1970s, women tended to be economically active until they reached the age of 25, when they left the labour market permanently, a trend that was still prevalent in some countries in the early 1980s.

By the mid-1990s, four patterns of female economic activity by age could be identified, as illustrated by the graphs. In Ireland, Luxembourg and Spain, female activity rates peaked in the 25 to 29 age category, and then declined as women had their first child. Although Spain was still recording one of the lowest overall activity rates in the mid-1990s, women between the ages of 25 and 49 were entering and remaining in the labour market in much larger numbers. Belgium, Greece, Italy and Portugal also showed an early peak, at a higher level for Belgium and Portugal than for the other two countries. In this case, the peak was followed by a more gradual decline from the age of 35. In Germany, the Netherlands and the United Kingdom, activity rates fell between the ages of 25 and 35 and then picked up again to a greater or lesser degree as women returned to work when their children were older. Relatively high economic activity rates were maintained for women aged 25 to 49 in Denmark, France, Finland and Sweden; the lowest levels were recorded in Greece, Ireland and Spain, with women in Ireland almost 35 points behind Denmark in this age group. Although directly comparable data were not available for Austrian

*Figure 5.2* **Economic activity rates for women by age groups in EU member states (1983–93)**

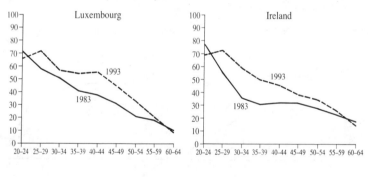

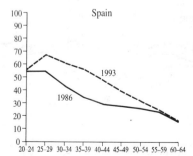

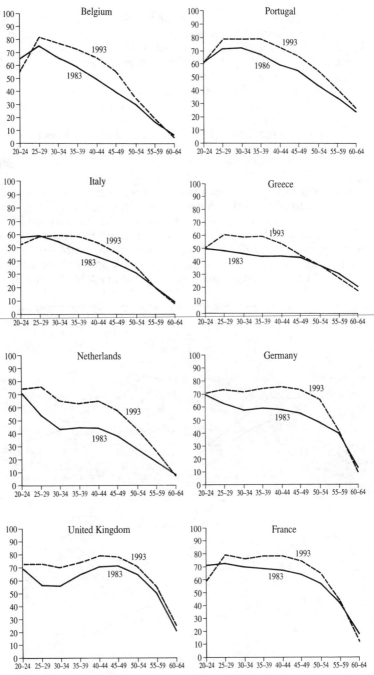

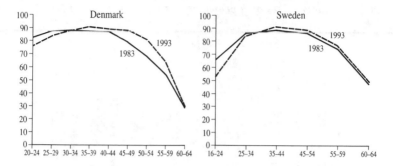

*Sources*: Eurostat (1985), table T03; Eurostat (1995d), table 003; data supplied by Eurostat.

women, their pattern would seem to correspond to that recorded for Belgium.

### Full-time and part-time female activity rates

Overall activity rates conceal important national differences in levels of full-time and part-time work. As shown in Figure 5.3, although more women have been entering and remaining in the labour force, full-time rates are much lower for women than for men, and disparities are more marked in some countries than in others. Although fewer women are economically active in Ireland and the south European countries, those who are in employment more often work full time, and this is particularly so in Greece. Women in Austria, Finland and Luxembourg also display relatively high full-time rates. France and Portugal are the only countries to combine an above average economic activity rate with above average levels of full-time working.

One explanation for the relatively high overall economic activity rates for women in the United Kingdom and the Nordic countries may be the large proportion of women working part time, as shown by Figure 5.4. Almost everywhere, rates of part-time work have been increasing since the early 1980s. By the early 1990s, women accounted for between 61.6 per cent (Greece) and 89.3 per cent (Belgium) of all part-time workers (Eurostat, 1995d, table 049). In 1994, both men and women were more likely to be in part-time work in Denmark, the Netherlands and Sweden than in other EU member states, but high levels of part-time work were also characteristic of women's working patterns in Germany and the United Kingdom. Part-time work was rare in the south

*Figure 5.3    Full-time economic activity rates for men and women in EU member states as a proportion of total employment (1984–94)*

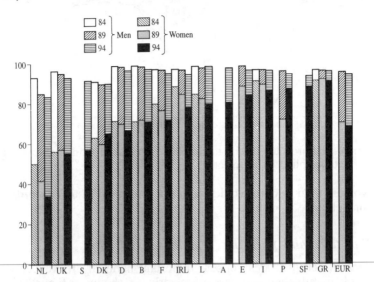

*Figure 5.4    Part-time economic activity rates for men and women in EU member states as a proportion of total employment (1984–94)*

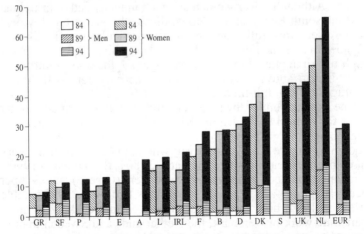

*Sources*: Eurostat (1992), table 28; Eurostat (1995c), tables 2, 3; and data supplied by Eurostat.

*Notes*: Provisional data for 1994; 1993 data for Austria and Ireland; 1985 and 1990 data for Finland.

European member states, including Italy. By the mid-1990s, two-thirds of all economically active women in the Netherlands were engaged in part-time work, compared with nearer to one in ten in Greece, Italy and Portugal. National data for the south European countries probably underestimate the number of part-time workers due to problems of measurement, including, for example, cases where homeworking is not recorded in official employment statistics.

Part-time work does not mean the same number of hours in different member states. Two-thirds or more of the women working part time in Belgium, Ireland, Luxembourg, the Netherlands, Spain and the United Kingdom were employed for fewer than 20 hours a week in the mid-1990s. In Denmark, France, Greece, Italy and Portugal, a third or more of female part-time workers were employed for 25 hours or more and, in Sweden, the vast majority of women with part-time hours were working more than 20 hours per week (Eurostat, 1995d, table 078; Statistics Sweden, 1995, p. 41).

### Activity rates for women with young children

Data supplied for the CLFS covering the twelve EC member states have been cross-tabulated with information about activity rates for women married to a head of household or who are the household head (Rubery and Fagan, 1992, appendix). Some data are available from other sources for Austria and Sweden (Gross *et al.*, 1994, table 35; Statistics Sweden, 1995, p. 50). In the early 1990s, in most countries female economic activity rates were higher for women aged 20 to 59 with one child than for women without children. With the arrival of the second child, rates fell steeply in Austria, Germany and Luxembourg, and, with the third child, in Belgium, France and the United Kingdom.

Belgium, Denmark, France, Portugal and Sweden registered relatively high activity rates for women with children aged under seven, and they were the only EU member states, with Austria, to show activity rates above 50 per cent for women with children aged under two. Italy and the United Kingdom achieved the 50 per cent level for children under seven. Rates for Germany, Greece, Ireland, Luxembourg, the Netherlands and Spain remained below 50 per cent even when the youngest child reached the age of 14.

The impact of children on women's working patterns is considered more fully in Chapter 6. It is sufficient here to note that, at least in statistical terms, women's employment patterns seem to be disrupted to a greater or lesser extent from one member state to another due to the presence of children and their age.

## Unemployment rates

Measurements of unemployment are notoriously unreliable even within countries, yet alone across national borders, not only because of the problems of definition and measurement discussed above but also because of the political implications of high or rising levels of unemployment for governments and public opinion. Politicians are generally seeking to demonstrate that unemployment is under control, and it is therefore in their interest wherever possible to avoid including categories of the population that can be hidden from statisticians, except if they stand to benefit from international subsidies.

The data in Figure 5.5 suggests that unemployment rates did not follow a consistent pattern across EU member states during the period being analysed. Whereas the overall trend was for unemployment to increase, fluctuations were recorded from one country to another, which may, to some extent, be attributable to discrepancies in the measurements used.

A more consistent pattern is found in the unemployment levels by gender: women are more likely than men to be unemployed at the different survey dates. By 1994, with the exception of Finland, Sweden and the United Kingdom, unemployment rates among

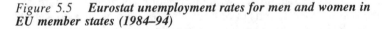

*Figure 5.5   Eurostat unemployment rates for men and women in EU member states (1984–94)*

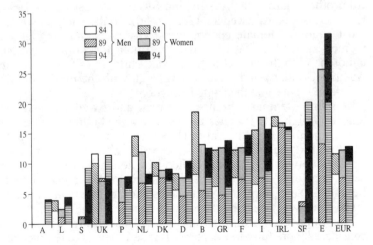

*Sources*: Eurostat (1992), table 38; Eurostat (1995c), tables 2, 3; and data supplied by Eurostat.

*Notes*: Provisional data for 1994; 1993 data for Austria and Ireland.

women were higher than for men. In Greece and Italy, female unemployment rates were double those for men. Eurostat figures most probably underestimate female unemployment since women are also more often than men in less stable forms of work; they move in and out of the labour market at different stages in family life, and they may not be eligible for benefits because of their irregular working patterns. They are more often than men employed on temporary contracts and are therefore more likely to be categorised as non-active (hidden unemployment).

Because a common definition is not used in registering the number of people out of work, the unemployment rates recorded by different sources are inconsistent. For example, when the claimant count is used to define unemployment, the number of women seeking work is likely to be underestimated as they may not be eligible for unemployment-related benefits. The phenomenon of 'discouraged workers', defined as those wanting a job but who are not actively seeking employment because they believe no suitable jobs are available, may apply to both men and women, particularly in the older age groups.

## Occupational segregation

Everywhere women are in lower paid, less secure employment than men. Women have increased their share of clerical jobs, and they tend to be concentrated in the caring professions and public sector employment, where working conditions are more flexible and 'women friendly', but where pay is lower than in the private sector. Occupational segregation, as measured by the division of paid work between what are commonly accepted as men's and women's jobs, has not disappeared, as shown by a study carried out by the European Commission's Network of Experts on the Situation of Women in the Labour Market in the twelve EC member states (Rubery and Fagan, 1993). Again, important variations can be identified from one member state to another. Whereas fewer than 50 per cent of clerical and related jobs in 1990 were occupied by women in Spain, the proportion was over 70 per cent in Denmark, France, Greece, Ireland, Portugal and the United Kingdom. Around 38 per cent of professional jobs were occupied by women in Luxembourg, compared with 64 per cent in Denmark (Rubery and Fagan, 1993, appendix table 1).

Not only do women continue to be concentrated in the least secure and least well-paid sectors of employment, but the growing proportion of women in lower skilled service jobs has also made such low-paid work even more female dominated. The feminisation of public sector work may be associated with a decline in relative pay and prove to be a gender trap (Rubery and Fagan,

1993, pp. 10–20). In some of the EC member states examined, the recession and economic restructuring of the 1980s curtailed expansion of intermediate-level clerical work which might have attracted women. Similar trends have also been recorded for Austria (Gross *et al.*, 1994, table 45) and Sweden (Statistics Sweden, 1995, p. 46). Here too, women are very much over-represented in service and health professions.

**Interpreting statistical data**

Analysis of harmonised LFS data based on agreed definitions at the European level would seem to suggest that female economic activity rates have been increasing since the late 1960s and that women's working patterns have moved closer to those of men, even though women tend more often than men to be employed in part-time jobs and to have less continuous work histories. Differences can be distinguished between countries, which cannot be explained entirely by discrepancies in statistical definitions and the ways in which they are applied. Continuity of employment is greater for women in Denmark, France, Portugal and Sweden in the younger age groups. In Belgium, Germany, the Netherlands and the United Kingdom, women's working patterns are characterised by movement in and out of the workforce in accordance with family commitments. Relatively small proportions of women are economically active in Greece, Ireland, Italy, Luxembourg and Spain. In Greece and Italy, female activity rates are consistently low, whereas in Luxembourg, Spain and, especially, Ireland, they peak in the earlier age categories and then fall steeply and do not recover. Part-time working is much more developed among women (and men) in Denmark, the Netherlands and the United Kingdom, compared with France and Portugal, which were noted for their relatively high proportions of women in full-time employment. The small numbers of women who are economically active in Greece, Ireland, Italy and Spain appear to be working full time; part-time work does not therefore compensate for low female activity rates.

The growing commitment of women to economic activity, as measured by the data presented in this chapter, has been accompanied by rising levels of unemployment, which have overtaken rates for men in almost every EU member state. These relatively high levels are, however, likely to be underestimates, since women are particularly prone to hidden unemployment (Metcalf, 1992). Because of differences in the way unemployment is measured from one EU member state to another, rates may appear to be lower for women than men. In the United Kingdom, which displays a relatively low level of female unemployment, many women may not meet the criteria for being counted as unemployed: they may not be eligible for benefits, either because of their irregular employment histories or because they are not considered to be available for work (Glover, 1994; Letablier and Daune-Richard, 1994). In countries where the provision of childcare facilities is limited (see Chapter 7), women may not declare themselves as 'available for work' since they would have difficulty in making the necessary arrangements for young children. In countries with high levels of informal work that goes unrecorded in official statistics, many women will have no employment protection and will not figure in the statistics for the economically active population, which may help to explain the low economic activity rates for women in Greece and Spain.

The data presented in this chapter, like the demographic indicators examined in Chapter 1, need to be handled with caution. The problems of non-compatibility of criteria identified here, while making comparisons over time and space difficult, if not impossible, are of interest to the analyst of the family–employment relationship from a conceptual point of view for the insights they provide about different national statistical traditions and the culturally determined conventions on which they are based.

# CHAPTER 6

# The relationship between women's paid and unpaid work

The employment of women outside the home is not a phenomenon peculiar to the second half of the twentieth century. The distinguishing feature of the shifts recorded since the 1960s in patterns of female employment and in the nature of women's work is that they have occurred at the same time as major changes in family and household structure, thereby creating the need for new paradigms in the analysis of the family–employment relationship.

Across Western Europe, full-time male employment in manufacturing has progressively been replaced as the dominant form of paid work by more casualised and less secure female employment in a fast growing service sector. The Nordic states, Luxembourg, the Netherlands and the United Kingdom led the way in recording high rates of employment in the services (Eurostat, 1995d, table 035), and the feminisation of public sector clerical jobs has been taken furthest in Denmark, France, Germany, Ireland and the United Kingdom (Rubery and Fagan, 1993, table 2.8). In the 1970s in the wake of the oil crises, while overall levels of employment were falling, women's share of the labour market continued to increase, and the greater continuity of their economic activity was confirmed (see Chapter 5). Although the presence of young children was still associated with lower levels of full-time working for women in the last quarter of the twentieth century, the relationship between employment and family life was also undergoing change as family size declined, and family and household composition were affected by rising divorce rates and the growing number of reconstituted families. The length of time spent caring for young children was consequently reduced, and the legal framework assigning parental authority and setting the institutional boundaries of family responsibilities was revised (see Chapter 2), thus preparing the way for a reconceptualisation of the relationship between family and employment, domestic and economic activity, unpaid and paid work or private and public life, according to the terminology preferred by different commentators.

In the 1950s and 1960s, disciplinary boundaries tended to prevent the family–employment relationship from being a focus of analysis. Sociological interest in the relationship between the two areas was, however, developing into a specific and autonomous field of study during the period when the changes outlined above were occurring. The aim in much of this work in the 1970s and 1980s was to identify and explore the reciprocal influence between female economic activity and family life and the strategies deployed to make the two areas compatible. The socio-economic perspective has been central to a number of comparative analyses (for example Dex and Shaw, 1986; Joshi and Davies, 1992; Dex *et al.*, 1993). Cross-national sociological studies have confirmed the interest of locating the family–employment relationship within broader socio-cultural and political contexts (for example Peemans-Poullet, 1984, Borchorst, 1993, and Hantrais, 1995, for Europe; Pitrou and Gaillard, 1989, for France and Sweden; Hantrais, 1990, for Britain and France; Daune-Richard, 1993, for Britain, France and Sweden). By the early 1990s, the European Commission had given recognition to the family–employment relationship by changing the title of the Childcare Network into Childcare and other Measures to Reconcile Employment and Family Responsibilities and by creating a Network on Families and Work.

The insights gained in previous chapters into national statistical definitions of family and household structure and women's work and employment demonstrate the importance of examining the assumptions underlying national trend data and the interest of attempting to identify and explain national and disciplinary differences in the way the relationship between work and family is conceptualised. In this chapter, sociological approaches to the family–employment relationship are presented as a framework for analysing and explaining national differences revealed by statistics before going on to discuss the household strategies adopted for combining professional and family life from a comparative cross-national perspective.

## Sociological analysis of the family–employment relationship

Analysis of the family–employment relationship is situated at the intersection of two areas of sociological research: the sociology of work and the sociology of the family, each of which has developed its own concepts and frames of reference. The sociological literature was slow to make the link between family life and employment. In the absence of an accepted interdisciplinary field, a distinction was maintained through to the 1970s between family (unpaid domestic production and women) and working life (economic production and men), reflecting the strict disciplinary divisions between family sociologists and industrial sociologists. Isolated studies ventured across the boundaries to focus on 'women's two roles' and to highlight what were described as 'contemporary feminine dilemmas' (Myrdal and Klein, 1956, pp. 135–52), or to analyse women's paid and domestic work.

By the late 1960s, references to the family–employment relationship were appearing in workplace studies (Goldthorpe *et al*, 1968, and Millward, 1968, in the United Kingdom; Mallet, 1969, in France). Whereas for a long time the sociology of the family tended to ignore the issues raised by mothers' work outside the home, the sociology of work saw them as a problem concerned with working conditions which might be resolved by restructuring working hours if employers were intent on attracting female labour.

From the 1970s, feminist researchers were influential in raising the level of sociological interest in the family–employment relationship and in building a substantial body of theoretical and empirical work. Largely under the impetus of second-wave feminism, the literature on the subject has become abundant not only within the context of family sociology, as indicated in Chapter 4, but also in analyses of workplace segregation and equality of opportunity at work. The relationship has been analysed as cutting across a number of disciplinary perspectives and also as a more autonomous disciplinary field mediating between the two areas, with the aim of identifying the reciprocal influence between female economic activity and family life and the strategies operating to make the two areas more compatible.

The developing field of sociology of the family–employment relationship has largely been subsumed by women's studies and gender studies, since women are the primary mediators between the two areas. Women's studies is seen as both interdisciplinary, evolving from traditional academic disciplines, and as an embryonic discipline in its own right, encompassing 'the study of women, men and children, gender relations and sexual divisions in society' (GRACE, 1992, p. 16). In Northern Europe, women's studies largely originated from social science disciplines, and in France and Spain from history, anthropology and cultural studies. In Denmark, the Netherlands and the United Kingdom, women's studies became an established academic discipline in the 1970s. In Belgium, France, Germany (with important regional variations), Greece, Ireland and Spain, it became a topic of scholarly interest mainly in the 1980s, whereas the situation in Italy and Portugal in the early 1990s was still described as underdeveloped (GRACE, 1991, pp. 20–8).

The examples of the Nordic states, France, the United Kingdom Germany and Spain provide an indication of the ways in which the growing sociological interest in the family–employment relationship has been pursued within the Union.

Studies carried out in Sweden have fallen within the ambit of the sociology of work and the sociology of life styles (Ruggie, 1984). Across the Nordic states, emphasis has been placed increasingly on the personal development of children and their well-being (Björnberg, 1992). Considerable attention has been devoted to the women and welfare debate, where the state is frequently depicted as an ally for women, a view contested by many observers (Lewis and Åström, 1991; Leira, 1993; Siim, 1993).

In France, the sociology of women's employment was already emerging as an area of growing interest in the late 1960s. Paid work was presented as distinctly gendered (Sullerot, 1968). From the 1970s, labour market studies began to focus on the discontinuity of women's employment patterns and looked at childrearing as a factor explaining why women temporarily left the labour force (Labourie-Racapé *et al.*, 1977). In the 1980s, feminism gave a new impetus to studies of the family–employment relationship within the context of work on gender relations, the sexual division of household labour, equal opportunities and segregation at work, emphasising discriminatory practices both at work and in the home (Collectif, 1984; Daune-Richard and Devreux, 1992). The feminist literature looked at how women are caught between two forms of patriarchal oppression in domestic and paid work (Delphy, 1984; Daune-Richard, 1988). Family sociology has also explored the theme of patriarchy, presenting the family as a place where the division of labour is determined by a process of negotiation and bargaining and where individual strategies unfold (de Singly, 1987; Barrère-Maurisson, 1992; Commaille, 1993). From 1986, a series of historical, economic, sociological and international studies were launched to examine the implications of the increase in economic activity rates for mothers and the policy measures which might be implemented to make employment and family life more compatible (Renaudat, 1989/90).

In Britain, the gender dimension played a prominent part in both the sociology of work and family sociology. In the 1970s and 1980s, family sociology addressed issues such as the recognition of domestic labour as work and the organisation of household tasks (Oakley, 1974). The sociology of work examined working conditions and flexible worktime arrangements (Martin and Roberts, 1984), and interpreted them in terms of sexual divisions of labour, dependence and exploitation (Barker and Allen, 1976). Analysis of the division of labour in the home centred on the extent to which women's paid work outside the home and formal equality of opportunity were resulting in greater equality in the home. Sociologists were also interested in the ways in which household work strategies were developed to enable couples to combine family life with employment (Pahl, 1984).

West German feminists in the 1970s attempted to break down the barriers between paid and unpaid work, but without identifying employment with independence. They did not accept that women would find emancipation through work and, by the 1980s, were looking for solutions that would give women access to paid work but on different terms from men, while recognising women's unpaid work as socially important and to be rewarded (Ostner, 1993).

In Spain, the transition from women as homemakers to women as mothers and paid workers took place much later than in the north European countries, and the family–employment relationship was only beginning to attract the attention of sociologists in the early 1980s. Under the influence of feminist writers, the focus was on the division of labour in the home, worktime arrangements and the value of domestic work (Martínez, 1992; Tobío, 1994).

The literature exploring the questions raised by the interaction between family and employment has pointed to the need for new concepts, both nationally and internationally, to deal with the issues identified. It is not possible here to review what has become a very large body of literature: a report on research undertaken between 1980 and 1990 in France recorded 141 studies on the topic (Freund, 1991), and a report covering British publications on employment and family life between 1980 and 1994 cited 350 references (Brannen et al., 1994). Rather, in this section some of the major issues that have been explored in sociological analysis of the relationship between paid and unpaid work are examined from different theoretical perspectives, and an attempt is made to indicate their relevance to national contexts.

### Two roles theory

Since the path-breaking work by Alva Myrdal and Viola Klein (1956), the concepts of role conflict, role strain and role overload have developed as an important dimension in sociological analysis of women as mothers and workers. The double burden for women is not peculiar to postwar society, but awareness of it as a social problem worthy of sociological analysis dates from the late 1960s. Social historians have demonstrated that the idealised picture of the division of labour between men, as breadwinners, and women, as homemakers, was far from matching social reality in the nineteenth century: female labour was essential for the economic survival of many families, and the relationship between employment and family life was often dependent on tightly structured arrangements operating through family support networks, enabling women to play a full part in both industrial production and social reproduction (Grieco, 1982; Tilly and Scott, 1987; Gittins, 1993).

Studies across the Union have shown that the rising levels of continuous full-time employment of women in paid work outside the home since the 1970s have not been matched by a commensurate reduction in unpaid labour or a more equal sharing of household tasks (Gershuny and Jones, 1987; Roy, 1990; Bonke, 1993; Tobío, 1994; Nousiainen, 1995). While the possible economic and social benefits for women of working outside the home are widely recognised and documented, the accumulation of roles that are competing for scarce time and other resources and their mutual incompatibility have been shown to result in stress, strain and overload (Morris, 1990, pp. 94–6).

As illustrated by the statistics presented in Chapters 1 and 5, the likelihood of role overload differs from one national context to another. Where women display high rates of full-time economic activity when their children are young and continue in employment even when they have several children, as in Portugal and the Nordic states, role stress might be expected to be greater than in countries where women leave the labour market to look after young children and progressively return on a part-time basis, as in Germany, the Netherlands or the United Kingdom, or do not return at all, as in Ireland, Luxembourg and the south European countries, at least until the mid-1990s (see Figure 5.2).

Individual strategies for making paid and unpaid work compatible are considered below, and collective strategies are examined in the next chapter, but it is worth noting here that the social acceptability of mother's employment outside the home and the willingness of men to contribute to household labour, and hence the ability to cope with the two roles, also vary according to the cultural context and the political climate at a particular time. In countries where women are formally recognised primarily as homemakers, as for example in the national constitutions of Ireland or Italy, paid work outside the home for women may be less readily accepted by some sectors of society than in countries where equality of opportunity is a central social value, as in the Nordic states.

Role stress may result from trying to juxtapose paid and unpaid work, whether from necessity or choice, but it can also arise in cases where women adopt a sequential approach to employment and family life by taking a break from employment to raise children. Even if they have a right to reinstatement, as in the case of parental leave or formal career break schemes (see Chapter 7), the longer term implications for pay, seniority, promotion and insurance-related benefits can be sources of stress and frustration, as demonstrated by French studies focusing on the concept of trajectories or family and career paths (Barrère-Maurisson, 1992), studies of women's work histories in Britain (Dex, 1984), and studies of differences in the time use of men and women in Spain (Izquierdo *et al.*, 1988; Ramos, 1990).

Men may also be subjected to role strain, but much less attention has been paid to men as fathers in the sociological literature on the family–employment relationship. Studies in the 1970s and 1980s of dual-earner couples (Rapoport and Rapoport, 1971) and middle-class families (Edgell, 1980) in the United Kingdom reported, for example, how husbands' jobs took precedence over those of their wives, leaving women to manage family life by accommodating to the occupational systems of their spouses (Finch, 1983). By the 1990s, sociological interest in fatherhood and the compatibility of men's paid and unpaid work roles was beginning to provide evidence in some EU member states, particularly the Nordic countries, that more men were wanting to be involved in family life (Björnberg, 1992; Moss, 1993; O'Brien, 1995), but nowhere to the extent that women were completely relieved of role stress.

### Human capital theory

Labour market theorists have argued that women's family responsibilities explain their choice of occupation by influencing their ability to accumulate human capital. Because of their family commitments, and because they interrupt their careers to raise children, the argument continues, women possess less education, training and work experience. They therefore opt for less demanding jobs in what are labelled as female occupations to maximise returns on their human capital investment. The theory was contested in the 1980s by sociologists on the grounds, among others, that there was no empirical evidence in support of the claim that women choose female-dominated occupations for rational economic reasons (see Walby, 1986, pp. 71–4).

By the early 1990s, women outnumbered men in higher education in Denmark, Greece, Finland, France, Portugal, Spain and Sweden, but the narrowing of differences in levels of educational attainment did not appear to have significantly reduced gender segregation in jobs or pay differentials (Rubery and Fagan, 1993, 1994; Eurostat, 1995f). Even in countries where women have made inroads into male-dominated subjects, such as engineering, their human capital investment does not appear to have paid dividends to the extent that might have been expected if their 'exclusion' could be explained by the absence of appropriate qualifications (Marry, 1989). Studies of women in professional occupations suggest that other factors, including male exclusionary practices, may be preventing appropriately qualified women from attaining higher status positions (Kirkham and Loft, 1993; Hantrais and Walters, 1994).

## Patriarchy and gender differentiation theory

Theories of patriarchy have sought to understand the gendered distribution of paid and unpaid work by linking it with capitalism. Men's control over women's labour both at the workplace and in the home is presented as a manifestation of the oppression of women in capitalist society (as noted in Chapter 4 with reference to feminist critiques of functionalist conceptualisations of the family). Women are excluded from certain jobs or segregated into low-paid insecure jobs and made responsible for unpaid low status work in the home so that they remain dependent on men to support them. According to patriarchy theory, the system is self-perpetuating and is reinforced by the state. In Britain, Sylvia Walby (1986) has argued that the position of women in the labour market is not determined by their position in the family. Rather, it is labour market structures that have confined women to a subordinate role in the household. Gender relations in employment vary over time as does the nature of patriarchal relations at the workplace, with trade unions, employers and the state jointly or individually supporting the exclusion of women from the labour market, as exemplified by the bar on the employment of married women during the interwar depression in the United Kingdom, particularly in better paid white collar jobs (Walby, 1986, pp. 171–2), confining them to lower grade positions, as illustrated by the literature on occupational segregation (Rubery and Fagan, 1993). After being declared illegal in the early 1930s in Spain, marriage bars were reintroduced during the first two decades of Franco's dictatorship and were finally removed only in 1961 (Valiente, 1994).

In France and the United Kingdom, the search for explanations of labour market segregation in terms of the mechanisms producing gender differentiation has drawn attention to the downskilling of jobs and the reduction in pay and prestige that may result from women entering certain occupations in large numbers or from the development of working arrangements considered suitable for women because of their family commitments (Michel, 1978; Delphy, 1984; Beechey and Perkins, 1987). In Italy, it has been argued that insistence by unions on equal rights for part-time workers may have priced women part-timers out of the market, and low wage differentials have made it less advantageous for employers to take on women (Chamberlayne, 1993, p. 176). Teaching and clerical work, and other public sector employment are examples of jobs which were male-dominated at the turn of the century and have progressively been reconstructed as being particularly suitable for women (Davisse, 1983; de Singly and Thélot, 1988; Rubery and Fagan, 1993). Working conditions are considered to be more family friendly, especially in the public sector, in the countries that have gone furthest in introducing flexible working patterns and policies, such as parental insurance to help couples reconcile paid work and domestic work, as in the Nordic states. But these policies may have had the effect of reinforcing gender segregation (Lewis and Åström, 1991; Leira, 1993).

## Household strategies for combining employment and family life

The statistics presented in the previous chapter suggest that an interactive relationship may exist between women's labour market status and their family commitments. Sociological studies have sought to unravel this relationship and find explanations for it, based on some of the theories outlined above. The literature suggests that the family–employment relationship is not fixed over time or space, either at the level of individual work histories or with regard to national trends. Analysis of socio-occupational categories also points to important differences in the way that particular sectors of the population may conceptualise and experience it. In this section, an attempt is made to explore how the relationship between family and employment is managed within different national contexts as families seek to adapt to changing circumstances. The strategies considered are organised in two main categories. Firstly, attention is given to the mechanisms used to adapt family commitments so that women are more readily available for employment outside the home, for example by delaying family building, reducing the number of children and redistributing domestic tasks. Secondly, adaptations in working patterns are examined, including movement in and out of work, reduced working hours, job sharing and casual work. An attempt is made to assess how these adaptations are conceptualised in different national contexts and the extent to which they can be considered as strategies enabling parents to combine paid and unpaid work.

### Adapting family responsibilities

Greater access to more effective methods of birth control from the 1960s, first in the Nordic and Anglo-Saxon states and then much later in the south European countries (see Chapter 2), meant that couples were in a better position to plan parenthood in accordance with their own circumstances and wider socio-economic factors. Improved medical care combined with the rapid economic growth that most countries enjoyed in the 1950s and 1960s meant that, in general, infant mortality rates were reduced to very low levels. The emancipation of women and the labour shortages of the 1960s were all factors contributing to a reconceptualisation of the family and of women's roles within it, particularly in Northern Europe. These trends were accompanied by a reduction in family size and of the time spent raising young children, potentially freeing women for participation in employment outside the home.

*Controlling family building*

With the lifting of the bar on married women's employment and the liberalisation of legislation whereby men could prevent their wives from taking employment, marriage has come to present less of a constraint on women's access to employment outside the home than the presence of young children, although the socio-economic and cultural environment in some countries could be seen as a powerful incentive for couples to adopt the male breadwinner pattern. The tax and parental leave arrangements in Germany (see Chapters 3 and 7), for example, support the married couple where the woman stays at home or earns considerably less than her husband.

Whether women's increased participation in the labour force is a cause or effect of the reduction in birth-rates is a much debated topic (Hantrais, 1992; Pauti, 1992; Commaille, 1993; Hoem, 1993). Cursory scrutiny of the European data suggests that the evidence is not conclusive. Although fertility rates have been falling in all EU member states (see Chapter 1), and female economic activity rates have everywhere been rising (see Chapter 5), the two trends do not necessarily closely coincide in each country. Economic activity rates of women in Portugal were, for example, rising steeply at the same time as their birth-rates were falling, whereas Greek women did not significantly increase their economic activity rates as they reduced their levels of fertility. The particularly marked fall in the birth-rate in Spain in the 1990s could be interpreted as a sign that Spanish women were deciding to forgo or postpone childraising to enable them to achieve continuity of employment. In Denmark, Finland, France, Sweden and the United Kingdom, the reduction in family size has been less marked than in other EU member states, despite above average levels of female economic activity. In some cases, it had begun to rise at a time when levels of female labour market participation had reached a particularly high point, as in Sweden in the mid-1990s.

In line with human capital theory, data on well-qualified women in some countries (France, Germany and the United Kingdom) suggest that they may decide to remain childless or delay the arrival of the first child because they are investing in an employment career and are aware of the high opportunity costs involved (Desplanques, 1987; de Singly, 1987; Hantrais, 1990; Ostner, 1993). Elsewhere, a different process may be operating, as for example in Sweden where well-educated women are most likely to combine higher employment rates with larger families (Hoem, 1993, pp. 114–16).

The relationships between family size and employment is discussed further below. Suffice it here to note that women may decide to limit the number of children in order to be able to maximise their labour market participation and minimise the length of time when they are not available for employment, but that they may be less constrained in countries where the working environment and society in general are receptive to the needs of working mothers.

*Redistribution of household labour*

Early studies of household labour (for example Oakley, 1974) pointed to a more equal distribution of domestic tasks as a means of reducing the load women were carrying due to their involvement in paid and unpaid work. As women's economic activity rates have risen, numerous studies have tried to measure the extent to which household labour has been redistributed. While the findings often suggest that younger and better educated couples may practise a more equitable distribution of labour in the home, nowhere does the evidence confirm that domestic roles have become interchangeable so that men devote the same amount of time to household tasks as women, even when they are unemployed (Kamerman, 1980; Brannen and Wilson, 1987; Gershuny and Jones, 1987; Witherspoon, 1989; Herpin, 1990; Morris 1990; Bonke, 1993).

Nor have attitudes towards the employment of mothers outside the home changed to the extent that might have been expected. A Eurobarometer survey (*Eurobarometer*, no. 39.0), reporting on the situation in 1993, showed that three-quarters of the Europeans questioned were of the opinion that mothers with young children should remain at home. This view was held by particularly large proportions of respondents (above the European average) in West Germany, Portugal, Luxembourg and Italy, in that order. Despite a theoretical preference for domestic tasks to be shared between parents, in all countries, irrespective of the employment status of women, mothers were expected to assume the main responsibility for the everyday lives of their children (Malpas and Lambert, 1993, tables 4.7, 4.9, 4.17). As the number of families where both partners are economically active has increased, a not uncommon way of avoiding role overload is for couples to revert, at least temporarily, to a division of labour whereby the male partner is designated as the main breadwinner, while the female partner gives priority to the tasks of homemaker.

Analysis of the caring duties carried out by women demonstrate that they are not only the primary carers for young children but also for older and disabled people. How to support family carers has become a topic of on-going debate at a time when informal care structures have been under strain due to changes in family and employment structures (Ungerson, 1990; Jani-Le Bris, 1993; Lesemann and Martin, 1993; McLaughlin and Glendinning, 1994; Attias-Donfut, 1995). The growth of sociological interest in carers in the English-speaking literature from the 1960s coincided with the shift away from institutional care to so-called 'community care', and the awareness that women would not necessarily be available to take over from the state, unless they were compensated for jeopardising their employment opportunities. The concept of caring has not, however, been developed to the same extent across the Union. In the south European (Latin) languages, including French, the terms 'care, caring and carer' have no direct equivalents. This does not mean that caring duties, obligations or responsibilities do not exist or do not present problems for families in the distribution of household labour. In France and the Nordic countries, the state does recognise a responsibility to support carers, whereas, in Greece, Italy, Portugal and Spain, community care means family care, and relatives, especially women, are expected to assume unquestioningly their natural role as carers (Jani-Le Bris, 1993; Attias-Donfut, 1995; Millar and Warman, 1996).

### Adapting working patterns

Family life can impact on employment in a number of ways according to a variety of socio-economic factors, which may both shape and be influenced by collective and individual representations of roles. The data on economic activity rates for mothers suggest that the presence of young children has an effect on women's employment patterns but in ways which differ from one country to another: women may move in and out of paid work or leave work for good; or they may reduce their commitment to employment by working shorter hours or on a casual basis. Women may be seeking more flexible worktime arrangements or be obliged to accept them as a condition of access to paid work.

*Movement in and out of the labour market*

Childrearing responsibilities are not experienced and conceptualised in the same way across the Union. Compared with other EU member states, by the mid-1990s in France, Portugal and the Nordic states, female working patterns had moved closer to those of men in terms of continuity and full-time employment, indicating that, in some countries, childbearing might be having less of an impact on women's paid work (see Chapter 5).

In most EU member states, women were still following quite different employment patterns from men. In Ireland, Luxembourg and Spain, they tended to leave the workforce, often permanently, as soon as they started a family, as shown in Figure 5.2. In some member states – Belgium, Greece, Italy and Portugal – women also left the workforce but more gradually and as their children grew older. In another group of countries – Germany, the Netherlands and the United Kingdom – women took a break in employment and returned subsequently, and at a relatively high level in the United Kingdom. In Denmark and Sweden, particularly, and in France, the arrival of children did not have such a marked effect on female employment patterns.

The data presented in Chapter 5 suggest that the impact of number and age of children varies from one national context to another. While in the 1960s women everywhere left the labour market when they had young children, by the 1990s in Denmark and Sweden, in particular, and to a lesser extent in Portugal, more women seemed able to maintain high levels of employment whatever the number of children and their ages. In Austria, Germany and Luxembourg, the second child was associated with a marked fall in activity rates. The third child brought about a steep drop in activity rates everywhere except Greece and Luxembourg, where rates were already low. Despite the return to work as children grow older, activity rates in Greece, Ireland, Italy, Luxembourg and Spain remained well below levels elsewhere in the Union. In Austria, Germany, the Netherlands and the United Kingdom, women's employment was affected temporarily by the presence of children, as mothers left the labour market to look after pre-school age offspring but then returned to work as their children began schooling, confirming the pattern identified above.

*Adaptations to worktime arrangements*

The main form of worktime flexibility analysed in the sociological literature from the 1970s concerns part-time work (Nicole, 1984; Beechey and Perkins, 1987; Dale and Glover, 1987; Barrère-Maurisson *et al.*, 1989; Daune-Richard, 1993; Blossfeld, 1994;

Frotiée, 1994). Job sharing, teleworking and flexitime were later innovations generally introduced by individual firms and have not attracted the same attention.

Over and above the problem of finding a common definition and measurement (see Chapter 5), part-time work has been conceptualised differently from one national context to another (see also Chapter 7): part-time working may be an arrangement sought by employers and employees to their mutual advantage, as in the Netherlands and the Nordic states; it may afford a convenient solution in the short term but, in the longer term, it can be to the detriment of the female workforce, as exemplified by the British case; it may be either imposed or 'freely' chosen, as in France; or its status may remain ill-defined, as in Spain.

In the Netherlands, part-time work is conceptualised as a secure form of employment where the hours may be only marginally shorter than for full-time work. High economic activity rates for women in the Nordic states are associated with high part-time rates which are used by women to increase their labour market flexibility without loss of employment rights. In the United Kingdom, short part-time hours may suit employers, since they are exempt from national insurance payments. Women with young children may welcome the opportunity to work very short hours, but in doing so they lose entitlement to employment-related benefits. In France, women in secure public sector employment may choose to reduce their working hours by 20 per cent to be available to look after young children one day a week, but for other women part-time work may be imposed by employers needing a flexible labour force and may involve unsocial hours. It may also serve as a means of sharing out the available work when levels of unemployment are high. In Spain, where part-time rates are relatively low, part-time work is often confused with temporary employment, but it can serve as a way of entering a tight labour market.

When the hours involved are amenable to nursery or school opening times, part-time work may be sought by women (Eurostat, 1995d, table 107) and can afford them a useful means of adapting their work schedules to fit in with arrangements for young children. As illustrated above, the advantages of state regulated part-time working can, however, easily be turned against women, and the sociological literature has amply demonstrated the ways in which flexibility can be used to reinforce a dual labour market.

Flexibility may take other forms which are more characteristic of women's than men's working patterns, involving casual work and unemployment (see Chapter 5). Everywhere, women are found to be in lower paid, less secure employment than men, and the proportion of women in lower skilled service jobs has been rising (Rubery and Fagan, 1993). The greater the commitment of women to full-time employment, the greater may be the likelihood of their being unemployed, as demonstrated by a Franco-British comparison (Letablier and Daune-Richard, 1994). Whether women's childrearing responsibilities are a pretext for assigning them to a secondary labour market or whether women opt for a lesser commitment to economic activity because they want to give priority to their families is a mote point. The interpretation depends upon the way the family–employment relationship has been conceptualised not only in different national contexts but also from different ideological standpoints.

### Re-assessing the relationship between paid and unpaid work

Statistical analyses of the possible impact of children on women's economic activity rates and the effect of paid employment outside the home on family building across Western industrialised nations have pointed to different models which take account of many of the factors referred to in this chapter. Marie-Agnès Barrère-Maurisson and Olivier Marchand (1990) used 60 indicators of the relationship between household structure, labour markets and demographic trends to draw a clear distinction between the south European and Nordic states, with Belgium, France, the Netherlands and the United Kingdom displaying less clearly delineated features. The same authors contrasted traditional family structures and a low level of integration of women in the labour market, as in Ireland and Spain, with the de-institutionalised families and high economic activity rates of the Nordic states.

In another study, Marianne Kempeneers and Éva Lelièvre (1991) identified Belgium, Denmark and France as the countries where women as mothers are most integrated into the labour force. In the south European countries, family life was not seen as incompatible with an occupation for women, since those who do work show a high degree of continuity of employment. West Germany, Ireland, Luxembourg, the Netherlands and the United Kingdom were described as not offering women 'the best environment for combining a career with a rewarding family life' (Kempeneers and Lelièvre, 1991, pp. 136–7). Women in the Netherlands, Denmark and the United Kingdom were more likely to take part-time work when they had young children. Women in the United Kingdom and West Germany more often than in other member states took a break of at least a year when they had children. Women in Ireland and Luxembourg tended to leave the labour force permanently to raise children (Kempeneers and Lelièvre, 1991, table 26).

These findings are, to a large extent, confirmed by the data examined in this chapter. The prolonged economic recession of the

1980s and 1990s in many parts of Europe, job shortages and high and persistent levels of unemployment, in combination with changing family structures, have led to a reassessment of the relationship between paid and unpaid work but, as shown above, attitudes and practices have not changed to the point where men's and women's domestic and economic work have become interchangeable.

Statistical data, combined with the results from sociological and public opinion surveys, suggest that unanticipated changes may have taken place in the allocation of paid as compared with unpaid work. Women have been establishing a firm presence in the labour market at a time when flexible and less secure forms of employment have become more widely available, to the detriment of full-time permanent employment. More flexible labour markets could be a source of opportunities for women, and for parents in general, although, as indicated by the analysis in this chapter, the ways in which flexibility is interpreted and implemented can have quite different impacts for women from one member state to another. In addition, even when advantageous for women, flexible working serves as only one of a number of possible solutions to the problem of combining employment and family life.

# CHAPTER 7

# Policies for women and mothers as paid workers

Although much has been written since the 1970s about the relationship between the paid and unpaid work performed by women, and the topic has long been on the political agenda, relatively little direct action has been taken at either European or national level to implement measures designed to make employment and family life more compatible. From the mid-1970s, the Council of Ministers and the European Commission were expressing their political will to intervene to help couples combine employment and family life, and some national governments were making a firm commitment in policy statements to take appropriate action. In very few cases were these declarations of intent translated into positive measures, whereas policies initiated in other areas may have had more of an impact on the ability of couples to combine employment and family life.

In this chapter, attention is given to the ways in which the relationship between family responsibilities and paid work has been conceptualised at EU and national level and translated both explicitly and indirectly into policy. Three types of policy measures are examined: equal opportunities in access to employment and welfare rights, worktime organisation, including maternity and parental leave, and provision for young children. Policies in these areas are considered in relation, firstly, to European legislation and, then, to different national contexts with reference to the conceptual frameworks from which they are derived.

## The EU policy agenda for women as mothers

The family–employment relationship has been on the European political agenda since the mid-1970s, both explicitly as an area to be targeted in policy and indirectly through measures to protect women as working mothers. In this section, after briefly reviewing the policy statements on the subject made at European level, these two types of action are examined as a framework for subsequent discussion of national policy making.

## Policy statements on the reconciliation of employment and family life

The social policy provisions of the Treaty establishing the European Economic Community (EEC), signed in Rome in 1957, were concerned almost exclusively with workers' rights and working conditions, and did not take account of non-working life (Articles 117–22). Article 2 of the EEC Treaty was, however, invoked nearly 20 years later to justify proposals for EEC action outside the workplace. In addition to setting economic objectives, Article 2 assigned the Community the task of promoting 'an accelerated raising of the standard of living'. Council Resolution of 21 January 1974 establishing a social action programme referred to the need for measures 'to ensure that the family responsibilities of all concerned may be reconciled with their job aspirations' (*Official Journal of the European Communities* C 13, 12.2.74, p. 2). The Council affirmed the view that 'economic expansion was not an end in itself but should result in an improvement of the quality of life as well as of the standard of living' (*OJEC* C 13, 12.2.74, p. 1). In the programme, the Council was expressing the political will to adopt the measures needed to achieve the objective of attaining full and better employment in the Community as a prerequisite for realising the social aims of European union. While action was taken in many of the other areas mentioned in this section of the programme, for example through equality legislation, no concrete measures were formulated specifically with the purpose of reconciling employment and family life.

The theme was not identified again in the same terms until the late 1980s. Meanwhile, in the context of a proposal for the European Community to develop its own family policy, a Resolution from the European Parliament called for 'a gradual reduction of working time to allow the family more time' (*OJEC* C 184, 11.7.83, p. 117). Little immediate progress was made at European level in bringing forward any draft legislation on working time with a view to achieving this objective. The Commission was, however, preparing a policy document addressing a number of related issues. A Communication from the Commission on family policies identified ways of reconciling work and family life and sharing family responsibilities as one of four main areas of common interest across the Community (COM(89) 363 final of 8 August 1989, p. 3). The Commission recognised women's employment as beneficial for the economic system and as a necessity at individual level. It attached particular importance to childcare arrangements and the development of job flexibility as the means of overcoming the difficulties of reconciling work and family life.

The next explicit reference to the Council's intention to take action in the family–employment area was in the Community

Charter of the Fundamental Social Rights of Workers, signed in Strasbourg in November 1989. Under point 16 in a section on equal treatment, member states were enjoined to develop measures 'enabling men and women to reconcile their occupational and family obligations'. The Community Charter was no more than a solemn declaration and did not set out any specific measures, but in point 28 the European Council invited the Commission to submit proposals for appropriate action. In response, Council Resolution of 21 May 1991 on the third medium-term Community action programme on equal opportunities for women and men for the period 1991 to 1995 enjoined member states to implement policies to reduce barriers to women's employment 'through measures designed to reconcile family and occupational responsibilities of both women and men' (*OJEC* C 142, 31.5.91, p. 2). The same document called upon both sides of industry to 'pursue and intensify the social dialogue on the issues of reconciling occupational and family responsibilities and protecting the dignity of women and men at work' (*OJEC* C 142, 31.5.91, p. 3).

The Agreement on Social Policy annexed to the Treaty on European Union, and signed in Maastricht on 7 February 1992 by eleven of the twelve member states, did not develop the proposal for action in this area framed in the Community Charter, as conceivably it might have done. Article 6 of the Agreement was devoted to the equal pay principle, reiterating almost verbatim the terms of Article 119 in the EEC Treaty. As in the original Treaty, no mention was made of women as mothers. A new clause was added, with reference solely to women as workers, affirming that member states should not be prevented from 'maintaining or adopting measures providing for specific advantages in order to make it easier for women to pursue a vocational activity or to prevent or compensate for disadvantages in their professional careers' (paragraph 3). While the Agreement on Social Policy recognised the legitimacy of positive action to help women overcome their disadvantages, it avoided overtly identifying the nature of these disadvantages as arising from their domestic responsibilities.

In the same year, the Council's concern that differences in social security cover from one member state to another might prevent mobility of labour prompted it to publish a recommendation, one of the least binding forms of secondary legislation, on the convergence of social protection objectives and policies (*OJEC* L 245/49, 26.8.92). In a short section on the family, two aims were set out: to contribute to the integration into the workforce of persons who have raised children; to remove obstacles to occupational activity by providing measures to help parents reconcile their family and professional responsibilities. In both cases, the target group was not confined to women and the measures to be taken were not specified, since the purpose of the recommendation was to achieve agreement between member states over objectives.

The White Paper on European social policy published in 1994 confirmed that the Commission intended to pursue its activities in this area within the context of equality of opportunity between women and men (COM(94) 333 of 27 July 1994, pp. 31–4). A subsection in the document was devoted to 'Reconciling employment and household/family life', on the grounds that it was in the interests of society as a whole that working life and family life should be 'more mutually reinforcing' (COM(94) 333, pp. 32–3). The White Paper addressed two key issues: how to manage and support the relationship between working time and time spent caring for children and older people; how to encourage more effective sharing of responsibilities for care between men and women.

Even though the subject was not broached in primary legislation through the treaties, over the years the Community and the Union showed increasing interest in the family–employment relationship. The rhetoric in official documents has evolved, shifting from global and rather anodyne statements about the need for measures to ensure that the family responsibilities 'of all concerned' could be reconciled with job aspirations, as in the 1974 social action programme, to explicit invitations to governments and industry to address the issue in the interests of gender equality, as in the equal opportunities action programmes. More forceful policy statements were included in the White Paper on European social policy encouraging national governments to take positive action to ensure a more equal sharing of parental responsibilities.

### EU policy measures for reconciling employment and family life

By the time the Maastricht Treaty creating the European Union came into force in November 1993, the family–employment relationship had long been on the policy agenda, but relatively little progress had been made at the official level in formulating measures designed to help parents reconcile paid work and family life. The reasons why direct action was difficult to achieve are probably similar to those explaining why more attention was not given to family policy at European level (see Chapter 8): as a European Economic Community, member states were interested in non-labour market issues only in so far as they were likely to have an impact on competition or the mobility of workers. While equality legislation could be justified in the Community context on the grounds that member states accustomed to paying women at lower rates than men were gaining an unfair competitive advantage, the same argument did not apply to women's unpaid work. The legitimacy of intervention at European level to give recognition to the relationship between family and employment was not widely accepted.

When the Maastricht Treaty was implemented, childcare was the only family–employment area where proposals for action brought forward by the Commission had been adopted. The Council Recommendation on childcare was an equal opportunities measure designed to help parents reconcile employment, education and training with family obligations arising from caring for children (*OJEC* L 123/16, 8.5.92). The recommendation covered not only the provision of public and private childcare facilities but also special leave, the environment, structure and organisation of the workplace and the sharing of family, professional and educational responsibilities. Levels of provision were not specified, but the Commission was assigned the task of monitoring the measures taken by member states and reporting back, a task already undertaken since 1986 within the brief of the European Childcare Network, subsequently renamed in 1991 as the European Commission Network on Childcare and other Measures to Reconcile Employment and Family Responsibilities.

The 1994 White Paper on European social policy indicated that the Commission was prepared to go further in ensuring implementation of childcare. It was planning to undertake an 'economic assessment both of the job-creation and reflationary potential of child and dependent-care infrastructures and services', as well as looking into target levels of provision and the possible use of fiscal and financial instruments to improve infrastructures and services before making further proposals (COM(94) 333, p. 33).

Although the Recommendation on childcare contained references to special leave, for more than a decade the Commission had been developing a proposal for a Council Directive concerning parental leave and leave for family reasons (*OJEC* C 333/6, 9.12.83). The version before the Council in 1994 provided for an entitlement to a minimum of three month's leave up to the child's second birthday, either full- or part-time, with a guarantee of reinstatement and insurance cover for sickness, unemployment, invalidity and old age benefits. Parental leave was presented as an entitlement and not an obligation, and payment of an allowance was a possibility rather than a mandatory requirement. The proposal for leave for family reasons contained in the same draft directive covered cases such as the illness of a spouse, death of a close relative, marriage or illness of a child, which were to be counted as paid leave for the purposes of wages, social security contributions and benefits, and pension rights.

In the White Paper on European social policy, the Commission hinted at its frustration over the slow progress made with legislation, declaring its intention to press for the adoption of the directive on parental leave (COM(94) 333, p. 34). In another section of the White Paper, however, the Commission stated it would be prepared to withdraw the proposal if a framework directive was adopted covering the issues of reconciling professional and family life (COM(94) 333, p. 22). Despite the setbacks and the persistent opposition from some member states, the Commission was making clear its own commitment to direct action at European level.

### Indirect measures for reconciling employment and family life

The difficulties experienced by the Commission in its attempts to promote binding legislation designed explicitly to help parents reconcile family responsibilities and employment contrasts with the easier passage given to some of the proposals brought forward in other areas. A number of directives have been adopted at European level which can be interpreted as having an impact on the ability of men and, more especially, women to combine paid and unpaid work, although they were not initiated with this aim in mind and do not refer to it explicitly. Several of the measures proposed for binding legislation on equal opportunities and health and safety at work fall into this category.

### Equal opportunities measures

The intention behind the equal pay principle contained in Article 119 under the social policy section of the 1957 EEC Treaty was to ensure fair and equal competition between member states by preventing any one country from gaining a competitive edge by paying women at lower rates than men. In that it provided a foundation and reference point for subsequent equality legislation, Article 119 may be considered to have contributed indirectly to the development of proposals for combining work and family life.

No important measures were, however, developed in the equal opportunities area until the mid-1970s, when the growing debate on the subject coincided with both second-wave feminism and the rapid expansion of women's labour market participation. The postwar baby boom had by then come to an end and the full effects of the oil crises were not yet being felt. The Community's social action programme of 1974 recognised that economic growth was not benefiting all sectors of the European population, not least women. The focus of attention was therefore broadened to cover access to employment and vocational training and advancement, as well as working conditions, in a series of equal opportunities action programmes and legislation.

Equality between the sexes, as embodied in Council Directive 75/117/EEC on equal pay (*OJEC* L 45/19, 19.2.75) and Council Directive 76/207/EEC on equal treatment for men and women in access to employment, vocational training and promotion (*OJEC* L 39/40, 14.2.76), took some account of the special needs of women who were seeking to combine motherhood with paid work. Equal treatment under the terms of the directives meant that discrimination was prohibited on the grounds of sex by reference, in particular, to marital or family status.

Council Directive 79/7/EEC, which was adopted in 1978 and finally came into force in 1984, addressed 'the principle of equal treatment for men and women in matters of social security' (*OJEC* L 6/2, 10.1.79). It was supplemented in 1986 by two further Directives, 86/378/EEC (*OJEC* L 225/40, 12.8.86) and 86/613/EEC (*OJEC* L 359/56, 19.12.86), which extended the principle of equality of treatment to occupational schemes and self-employed men and women. Although all three directives made an important contribution to equality legislation, the possible effectiveness of the 1978 directive in providing women with individual access to insurance rights was offset by an exclusion clause, enabling member states to exclude from the scope of the directive a number of entitlements, such as recognition of time spent raising children or caring for a spouse. When the implementation of the directive was being examined in the mid-1980s, only Denmark and the Netherlands had not availed themselves of the exclusion clause (Commission report COM(88) 769 final, of 16 December 1985, pp. 32, 102).

The equal treatment directives were founded on the premise that action was needed to ensure women had access to the same employment rights as men, but the restrictions built into them and the apparent reluctance of national governments to make more generous provision indicated that the unpaid domestic work performed by women had still not been fully recognised as a basis for entitlements in their own right.

*Health and safety measures*

Under Article 118a of the Single European Act (SEA), signed in Luxembourg and the Hague in 1986, qualified majority voting was introduced for areas of legislation concerned with the working environment and health and safety at work. Article 118a offered a route that could be used when it might otherwise be difficult to reach consensus, as with Council Directive 92/85/EEC concerning the implementation of measures to encourage improvements in the safety and health of pregnant workers, women workers who have recently given birth and women who are breastfeeding (*OJEC* L 348/1, 28.11.92). The proposal was brought forward as the tenth individual directive within the meaning of Article 16(1) of Framework Directive 89/391/EEC (*OJEC* L 183/1, 29.6.89), ensuring that it received an easier passage than might otherwise have been the case.

Essentially, the directive sought to protect women as working mothers by guaranteeing they were not exposed to health risks, including night work. Under the terms of Directive 92/85/EEC, women were to be eligible to take an uninterrupted period of at least fourteen weeks' maternity leave before and/or after delivery with pay equivalent to at least 80 per cent of previous salary. They could also take leave with pay to attend ante-natal examinations. In addition, they were to be protected from unfair dismissal during maternity leave.

Legislation on equal treatment in matters of social security did not directly address the issue of part-time working conditions, another important area of concern for women seeking to combine family responsibilities and employment, as shown in Chapter 5. From the early 1970s, several attempts had been made to bring forward legislation on working time. A draft directive on voluntary part-time work, first proposed in 1981, was not adopted. Instead, the provisions of the SEA were used to bring forward contentious legislation on working time as health and safety measures. Directive 91/533/EEC on an employer's obligation to inform employees of the conditions applicable to the contract or employment relationship was intended to cover flexible forms of employment such as part-time and distance or teleworking (*OJEC* L 288/32, 18.10.91). Directive 93/104/EC concerning certain aspects of the organisation of working time laid down minimum daily, weekly and yearly rest periods and regulations for night and shift work (*OJEC* L 307/18, 13.12.93). While no explicit link was made in the two directives between worktime arrangements and family life, they represent some progress towards greater recognition of working hours as an important component in the family–employment relationship.

The 1994 White Paper on European social policy showed that the Commission considered legislation on worktime as outstanding business and planned to initiate a new directive on part-time work. It was also examining the possibility of introducing a framework directive covering the issue of how to reconcile professional and family life, together with the question of parental leave, both in response to changing social needs and as a means of facilitating the full integration of women into the labour market (COM(94) 333, p. 22).

## National policies for reconciling family and employment

Since the Council of Ministers is a forum representing the views of national governments, policies formulated at European level clearly reflect the practices and preferences as well as the willingness of governments to compromise if a consensus is to be reached. Although, as in the case of equal pay, the Union may be influenced by existing national legislation, the impetus provided by the Commission, operating independently of national interests, can serve as a strong incentive for change in individual member states, as exemplified by the equal opportunities legislation of the 1970s, which was accompanied by a spate of national legislation (Commission of the European Communities, 1987).

The documents published in the early 1990s on social policy showed that the Council had progressively moved towards a position where agreement was sought over common aims and objectives, leaving individual member states to formulate and enact measures appropriate to their own socio-economic and political circumstances. In the area of social protection, in recognition of national diversity, member states are allowed to determine how their social protection schemes are framed and the arrangements for financing and organising them (*OJEC* L 245, 26.8.92, p. 50).

The legitimacy of the Union's social policy competence has not been accepted without contest, the more so in the case of the social protection rights of non-workers or non-standard workers. Proposals from the Commission for directives on part-time work, parental leave and leave for family reasons in the 1980s were vigorously opposed by some member states to the extent that they were not adopted, as pointed out in the previous section. Directive 92/85/EEC on the protection of pregnant women, women who have recently given birth and women who are breastfeeding, Directive 93/104/EC on certain aspects of the organisation of working time and the Recommendation on childcare (92/241/EEC), which were ultimately approved, left national governments a certain amount of discretion to take whatever action they felt was most appropriate. The resulting minimalist approach means, however, that individual member states can, and frequently do, offer more favourable arrangements.

At national, as at European level, policy decisions and the institutional arrangements flowing from them often represent a compromise between conflicting demands. In the case of the family–employment relationship, the search for common ground falls at the interstices between employment law and family policies, where the interests of employers and family members have to be reconciled. Even the policy objectives agreed at European level may be conceptualised differently from one country to another as a result of different combinations of factors, including the extent and pace of change in behaviour and attitudes towards women as mothers and workers, the wider policy environment, the state of labour markets and national trends in family building and structure. Differences in the conceptualisation of the family–employment relationship from one country to another may, in turn, help to explain variations in reactions to European policy.

In this section, national policies for reconciling employment and family life are examined by carrying out a cross-tabulation of the different levels of state intervention with the patterns that emerged in Chapter 5 from an analysis of the labour market participation rates for women with young children. Since the role of the state as a social policy actor, and more specifically as a family policy actor, is considered in detail in the next chapter, attention is devoted here to the ways in which national governments in EU member states have sought to intervene in the family–employment relationship, focusing more particularly on the visibility and legitimacy of the policy measures introduced.

A number of different approaches can be identified in public policy as it affects the family–employment relationship. Variations are found in scope and purpose and in the ways in which a particular policy measure is conceptualised. Following Marlene Lohkamp-Himmighofen (1993a, pp. 359–60), EU member states can usefully be grouped according to criteria such as the level of state intervention and its objectives, mapped onto patterns of employment for women with children.

In the first group of countries considered below, family and employment are juxtaposed with support from public policy, either as an equality measure or through a commitment to family well-being and to women as mothers. In a second grouping, work and family are ordered sequentially with support from a state more concerned about maintaining the family unit as a social institution than safeguarding the individual rights of its members. A third approach is adopted by countries characterised by a low level of state intervention, which is generally associated with the sequential ordering of employment and family life. In this configuration, market forces or family networks may be substituted for state support, depending on the willingness or otherwise of governments to intervene in the private lives of families and the financial resources they have at their disposal.

## Juxtaposition of family and employment with state support

Among EU member states, two main types of juxtaposition of family and employment can be distinguished according to national policy objectives. In Denmark, Finland and Sweden, where women display high levels of continuous economic activity, albeit often part-time and interrupted by periods of parental leave, governments have intervened actively to help parents combine paid work outside the home with childraising in accordance with egalitarian principles. In France and also Belgium, although patterns of female employment are less continuous in the second case, relatively high full-time continuous economic activity rates have been supported by generous family-centred state provision. Both groups of countries are characterised by the high profile afforded to a wide range of measures designed to help men and women combine family and professional life, while maintaining continuity of employment.

### Juxtaposition as an equality objective

Denmark and Sweden have led the field in Europe in making the reconciliation of working life and family life a central topic in the equality debate (Wilson, 1979; Carlsen and Larsen, 1993, p. 9; Siim, 1993; Björnberg, 1994). The Nordic states have, however, tended to reject special protection for women as mothers in the labour market on the grounds that such provision would create barriers to women's employment and run counter to equality objectives. Although Denmark already had relatively long maternity leave, but a relatively short period of parental leave, the Danes opposed the clauses on maternity leave in the directive on the protection of pregnant women for these reasons, and they considered that no clear equality benefit would be gained by extending the period of leave (Borchorst, 1993, pp. 173, 175). In Denmark, Finland and Sweden, emphasis has been on provisions that apply to men and women in an attempt to encourage a more equal sharing of paid and domestic work. In the Nordic states, generous state provision of childcare, paid parental leave for both men and women, with additional incentives to ensure take-up by men, and favourable part-time working conditions have to be understood as measures supporting women's access to the labour market. They are also evidence that the state, and through it society at large, accepts it has a duty to support children. In Denmark, for example, caring for young children was recognised as a public responsibility early in the twentieth century and as a right for all children, even though priority has tended to be given to the children of parents employed outside the home since the 1960s (Borchorst, 1993, p. 177).

Extensive childcare provision has also been made available in Sweden to assist working parents. Sweden was the first of the EU member states to introduce parental leave for fathers in 1974. The system which has developed is described as being 'unique for its combination of flexibility and high level of payment to parents taking leave' (European Commission Network on Childcare and other Measures to Reconcile Employment and Family Responsibilities, 1994, p. 27). The extremely high take-up rates are evidence that parental leave has become an accepted practice: by the end of the 1980s, 98 per cent of mothers took paid parental leave, on average for 262 days, during the child's first year, and nearly half of fathers were taking some leave, with a preference for shorter periods or part-time arrangements, on average for 43 days. While this record was better than in the other Nordic states and the rest of Europe, it fell short of expectations. Several studies conducted in Denmark and Sweden have shown that men are still reluctant to take parental leave for a variety of reasons. Even though leave is with pay, men generally earn more than women. Other reasons include supposedly negative attitudes at the workplace and factors such as the presumed indispensability of male workers, although it has also been noted that better educated men and women are more likely to share childcare responsibilities (Björnberg, 1994, p. 65). Nevertheless, it can be argued that the reconciliation of family responsibilities and employment has received greater recognition as a workplace issues in the Nordic states than in most other countries in the Union.

Despite these reservations, the overall impact of family-friendly policy measures in the Nordic states would seem to be the creation of an environment in which employment and family life are not considered to be in conflict with one another; rather, they are complementary. Policy appears to be attenuating any negative effects that work might have on the family, with the result that continuity of employment can be maintained as well as the relative autonomy of family members.

## *Juxtaposition as a family support mechanism*

France has a long family policy tradition (see Chapters 3 and 8), which has served to legitimate measures to help women combine employment and family life. Explicit statements have been made about the intention of the state to draw up measures to help parents combine family life and employment. The issue of the compatibility of women's paid work outside the home with conjugal and family life was already raised as a policy concern in the late nineteenth century. The parliamentary debates leading up to the 1892 bill on work inspectors provide an illuminating example of some of the opposing views prevalent at the time and which still resonate more than a century later.

Advocates of state intervention to impose strict controls on the working conditions and working hours of women and children in manufacturing industry argued that long working hours and night shifts separated family members and resulted in moral decadence. Opponents of legislation produced economic and moral counter-arguments in support of the financial contribution that women and children could make to family income, claiming also that, while they were at work, they were being kept out of mischief (Grossin, 1992).

The gradual recognition by the state over the postwar period that women should be supported whether they chose to stay at home and look after their children or whether they engaged in paid work outside the home was made explicit in the early 1970s. While women as homemakers could receive a single-salary or mother-at-home allowance, in 1972 women who went out to work were granted a counterpart in the form of an allowance for childminding costs. These measures were consistent with the importance accorded by French governments to supporting women as mothers in the interests of the nation.

At the time, equality issues had moved up the political agenda as more women entered and remained in paid employment, and the feminist movement gained momentum in the wake of the social and political upheavals of 1968. From the early 1970s, policy makers in France had been alerted to the unequal distribution of domestic and paid labour between men and women and the constraints on women's opportunities because of their childrearing responsibilities (Michel, 1974; Giroud, 1976; Rebérioux, 1982). Legislation in the mid-1970s to help women combine paid work and domestic work, by improving arrangements for leave and restructuring worktime, can be interpreted as measures to promote female emancipation. By the mid-1980s, the balance between employment and family life was high on the policy agenda, partly in the context of the positive action programmes launched by Yvette Roudy in 1983 and partly within the framework of family policy concerns. The brief given to the authors of a report commissioned by the Haut Conseil de la Population et de la Famille (1987) was reminiscent of the 1970s legislation on childminding: the report indicated that parents should not be forced to choose between employment and childrearing, but should, with support from the state and industry, be able to juxtapose work and family life. Measures to enable women to remain in employment while continuing to produce children included generous support for childcare, paid parental leave and flexible work-time arrangements, which put France among the leaders in Europe with the Nordic states for their women-friendly practices. France was distinguished from the Northern member states, however, by its heavier emphasis on the health and well-being of mothers as workers and the expectation that they would continue in full-time paid employment even when their children were very young.

In practice, state support may not be so effective in relieving the pressures on economically active women as in the Nordic countries. Provision for young children in France is among the most generous in the Union, particularly from the age of three, and parental leave is relatively long, extending until the child is three, but payment is provided only from the second child and for women with a previous employment record. A distinction is made between parental leave (*congé parental*) and the childrearing allowance (*allocation parentale d'éducation*, APE). The APE can be interpreted as a temporary arrangement enabling parents to relieve the pressure when children are very young without compromising their professional life (Fagnani, 1994). Compared with the Nordic states, take-up rates are very low (about 40 per cent), suggesting that the financial conditions may be too restrictive to justify a prolonged interruption to employment.

Belgian governments have also been interested in promoting policies to help parents reconcile employment and family life through a combination of measures including part-time work, reduced working hours, career breaks, job sharing and provision of childcare. As in France, the objectives have been broader than those of the Nordic states, focusing on improving the quality of life for people in work, protecting the standard of living of families, achieving greater equality between men and women and safeguarding the rights of individuals after the breakdown of a relationship (Meulders-Klein and Versailles, 1994, pp. 30–1). The level of provision of childcare in Belgium is similar to that in France (Moss, 1990, table 3), but the career break scheme distinguishes Belgium from the other countries in this grouping in that it is not confined to parents wanting to interrupt their careers to raise young children. Take-up is, nevertheless, essentially by women in white-collar public sector employment under the age of 40 (European Commission Network on Childcare and other Measures to Reconcile Employment and Family Responsibilities, 1994, p. 24), suggesting that it is neither attracting the same interest as in the Nordic states, nor meeting the wider objectives.

Even if the primary focus of policy measures varies, Belgium, Denmark, Finland, France and Sweden have in common the fact that the family–employment relationship has been placed on the political agenda and that the measures taken are expressly intended to help parents reconcile their family responsibilities with their job aspirations. Whether the relatively high levels of female employment recorded are a result of government policies or a response to demand is not easy to discern. What is clear, however, is that the state has generally been supportive of women's .economic activity and of their reproductive function and has thereby legitimated employment outside the home of mothers with young children.

## Sequential ordering of family and employment with state support

Five of the countries where the state has adopted a supportive stance towards the family–employment relationship can be described as organising paid work and family life sequentially by redistributing economic resources from productive (paid) workers to reproductive (unpaid parents at home). Austria, Germany, Italy (sometimes grouped with the south European countries, as in Lohkamp-Himmighofen, 1993a), Luxembourg and the Netherlands have all introduced policies that help parents to combine paid work outside the home with childrearing, but on the basis that one or both of the parents, most often the mother, will reduce their economic activity in order to look after young children. Governments are thereby supporting a particular type of family, where the mother generally stays at home to raise young children, returning subsequently, often on a part-time basis, when they reach school age.

Rather than being a responsibility which can, or should, be assumed by the state, as in Denmark or France, in this configuration, care for young children is seen as a duty to be carried out by families, and more specifically by mothers, for its educational value. In this context, public childcare provision is low, compared with the Nordic states, Belgium or France.

The form that state support takes varies within the group of countries displaying the sequential pattern. Only two of the four provide generous support for parents, almost exclusively mothers, who decide to leave the workforce temporarily when they have young children. Employees are eligible to take paid leave in Austria for up to two years. In Germany, all parents, whether they are working or not, can take paid leave for up to three years. The payment (*Erziehungsgeld*) is intended, as its title implies, as a benefit for mothers, or fathers, who decide to stay at home to raise children. Take-up rates among women are very high, as in the Nordic states, and the benefit can be interpreted as a maternal wage (Fagnani, 1992, p. 35).

Luxembourg makes no provision for parental leave, and the arrangement in the Netherlands is for unpaid leave, except in the public sector, resulting in relatively low take-up rates (European Commission Network on Childcare and other Measures to Reconcile Employment and Family Responsibilities, 1994, p. 22). The German and Dutch cases represent two quite different responses to the problem of reconciling employment and family life by organising them sequentially. In Germany, women are recognised as wives and homemakers; they are paid both while they are performing this role and continue to reap the benefits if they subsequently return to work, for example, by being able to accumulate credits towards an occupational pension. The single factor most likely to explain the sequential pattern of employment and childrearing in the Netherlands is the availability of part-time work. Labour shortages in the 1960s forced employers to offer women tailor-made jobs to attract them into the labour market. Part-time work has since developed into a widely accepted form of employment and has been supported by legislation removing discrepancies between full- and part-time contracts, covering employment protection, social security rights and pensions (European Commission, 1994, p. 117). Since men have not adapted their working conditions to the same extent, the outcome in both countries is to reinforce the dual labour market and to confirm that women do not enter employment on the same terms as men.

Italy presents yet another configuration of the sequential model. In the 1970s, it was one of the first EU member states to introduce paid parental leave well in advance of the proposals for a European directive. Public policy in Italy has been influenced by conflicting objectives: the protection of the privacy of the family unit and the essential role of women in the home; a growing commitment to take account of the relationship between public and private life as a source of gender identity. Women entering the labour force have done so on a full-time basis, with generous state support for long periods of paid maternity leave (five months) and widespread provision of nursery schooling for children over the age of three, as well as intra-family solidarity (Saurel-Cubizolles *et al.*, 1993). Support for working women has been justified on the grounds that high quality provision was needed to ensure that women maintain the standard of maternal care expected by Mediterranean cultures (Bimbi, 1993, p. 156). Italian women have received generous protection as workers when identified as mothers, but possibly at the expense of their employment prospects, since employers may be discouraged from offering women secure employment.

### Non-interventionist states

Among the EU member states characterised by low levels of intervention to help parents combine employment and family life, a distinction can be made between countries where governments have deliberately avoided interfering in the private lives of individuals and those where financial constraints and a relatively undeveloped system of social protection have meant that priority has been given to more pressing social problems, despite supportive policy statements. Cutting across this distinction are countries where low levels of state intervention have not prevented women from displaying high economic activity rates, either on a full-time continuous or a part-time interrupted basis.

*Non-interference in family affairs*

The main opponent of European legislation on policies for statutory maternity leave, parental leave, worktime arrangements and childcare has been the United Kingdom, which refused to sign the Community Charter of the Fundamental Social Rights of Workers and the Agreement on Social Policy and sought to block European legislation in these areas. In the 1980s and 1990s, British governments consistently argued against proposals for directives on part-time work, parental leave and state provision of childcare on the grounds that regulations would impinge on the private lives of individuals and also impose a heavy burden on employers. Over the postwar period, the family–employment relationship has largely been seen as a private matter for individuals to manage by themselves or in conjunction with their employers, except in cases of proven hardship: public provision of childcare is considered to be legitimate if the purpose is to protect children in need but not if it is to enable women to engage in paid employment outside the home.

The United Kingdom was the only member state without a universal right to maternity leave for women in paid employment when the directive on the protection of pregnant women was adopted in 1992. It was one of three countries with no arrangements for parental leave, on the grounds that this should be an area for negotiation between employers and employees. Although the origins of the growth in part-time work are not dissimilar to those in the Netherlands, British governments have been reluctant to support improved contractual conditions for part-time workers on the basis that restrictions might price part-timers out of the market.

In the absence of state support, women have nevertheless entered paid employment in large numbers. They have tended, however, to leave the workforce when they have young children and to return part-time, making their own arrangements for childcare, with implications for promotion, access to social security rights and occupational pensions.

The lack of security of women's labour market position in the United Kingdom, in combination with the emphasis on families in need, means that the majority of women combine employment and family life sequentially without support from the state. Although employers may offer arrangements for career breaks, job sharing, part-time working and workplace nurseries, the level of provision does not compensate for the lack of public facilities and guarantees. The targeting of state support on low-income families and families in need may, paradoxically, have resulted in many women not being integrated into the workforce, since the low level of earnings disregard has meant that lone mothers and the spouses of men who are unemployed are likely to be better off financially if they withdraw from the labour market (Morris, 1990). By the early 1990s, efforts were being made to roll back public spending and move away from welfare dependency by reducing labour market disincentives.

Ireland has also rejected the principle of state interference in family life, and, similarly to the United Kingdom, has concentrated on the problems of poor families and equal rights between spouses, rather than the family–employment relationship. Women's economic activity rates have remained well below the European average and their birth-rates well above those of other EU member states, although the proportion of women with children in paid work has been increasing since the 1960s. The issue of reconciling family and working life had reached the policy agenda by the early 1990s, creating a dilemma for policy makers. On the one hand, the Irish constitution enshrines the role of women as homemakers and carers and undertakes to ensure that they are not obliged by economic necessity to engage in paid labour outside the home, while, on the other, equal opportunities legislation has raised the status of women's employment and their expectations. European legislation and support from the European Social Fund may have provided the impetus for the Irish government to begin to develop policies which they might not have done otherwise (Kiely and Richardson, 1994, pp. 168–70).

*Financially constrained state intervention*

The country which stands out among south European member states for its relatively high and continuous full-time female economic activity rates is Portugal. Since the 1970s, Portuguese governments have supported the participation of women in economic life through equal opportunities policies. The Portuguese constitution lays down the principles of equality and non-discrimination not only at work and in education but also between spouses. The positive attitude of the state has not, however, been translated into substantive measures likely to help women combine employment and family life due to limited resources. Public provision of childcare in Portugal is, in the event, among the lowest in the Union, and parental leave is unpaid (Moss, 1990, table 3; European Commission Network on Childcare and other Measures to Reconcile Employment and Family Responsibilities, 1994, p. 56).

Greece and Spain are in a similar situation as regards support for working mothers, although women's economic activity patterns have not reached the same level as in Portugal and are less continuous. Greece included an article in its 1975 constitution establishing equal rights between the sexes. In Spain, radical changes in women's legal status have occurred since the mid-1970s. The Civil Code was amended in 1975 to recognise women's full legal capacity, and the Spanish constitution of 1978 enshrined equality as an essential constituent element of a legally established social and democratic state. Although both countries make provision for parental leave, in neither case is it with pay, and very few children under the age of three are looked after in public facilities. In all three south European member states, family and community networks, rather than the state, continue to provide a major source of support, but without apparently achieving the same outcome in terms of female activity rates.

### Assessing national policies for combining family life and employment

The examples given in this chapter show how the same policy measures may be used to achieve different objectives and how they may result in unintended outcomes. They confirm the interest and importance of exploring the socio-cultural contexts in which policy is embedded and of tracing its historical roots.

When the package of maternity and parental leave, worktime arrangements and childcare is considered, it is clear that some EU member states have gone much further than others in making provision for working parents and in helping to reconcile employment with family life. In some cases, European legislation has provided an incentive or a framework for action, as in Ireland or the south European countries. In others, such as the Nordic states or France, it has served as no more than a baseline, ensuring that less advanced member states do not fall too far behind. Yet others, the United Kingdom most notably, have resisted European interference in an area where direct state intervention is seen as inappropriate.

The motivation among member states for the introduction of measures to help parents reconcile employment and family life has been prompted by different factors. The high profile given to equal opportunities and the needs of children in the Nordic states would seem to be the main explanation for their efforts in this area. Countries such as France and Belgium have been concerned with family building and the well-being of families, while Austria and Germany have focused on preserving the homemaker role of women. The south European countries have espoused equality objectives but without following them through to their logical conclusion in policy terms.

Patterns of employment among women with young children in EU member states would seem to interact with policy in different ways. While equality measures in the Nordic states are accompanied by high female economic activity rates, the status of women's employment has not become equivalent to that of men in terms of pay and occupational status. Continuous employment in France, supported by equality legislation and a strong commitment to the centrality of the family, is more likely to be on a full-time basis, in principle ensuring the same access to social security rights. A not dissimilar pattern of employment is achieved in Portugal without the same level of financial support, while a similar policy environment in Greece and Spain has not produced the same level of female economic activity. Among the member states with relatively high levels of part-time work, in the Netherlands state support may make part-time jobs less discriminatory, whereas in the United Kingdom they are associated with low security and poor promotional prospects.

These various patterns of development impact on women's lives in different ways. In countries such as Germany or the Netherlands, where the sequential arrangement is supported by the state, childraising does not compete for women's worktime to the same extent as it does in Belgium, France and Portugal, or perhaps to a lesser extent in the Nordic states. In the absence of equal sharing of paid and domestic labour, juxtaposition is likely to imply an accumulation of tasks, particularly if women are working full time and take-up of parental leave by men is low.

# PART THREE

# From Social Policies to Family Policies

Just as the construction of statistical and institutional definitions of the family and the family–employment relationship reflect national conventions in EU member states, the policy-making process and the account taken of the family in policy have been shaped by the different socio-cultural traditions determining the social policies formulated and adopted in each country.

Policy objectives and priorities differ from one member state to another. Not all countries are committed to pursuing designated family policies. Nor do they all target families in their social policies. But they do all implement measures that are likely to have an effect on families. The family impact of policies formulated in others areas, whether by governments or by firms, may be as important in bringing about changes in behaviour and in responding to social contingencies as policies specifically intended to promote the well-being of family members.

Previous chapters have shown how definitions of the family vary from one national context to another. Consensus over the definition of family policy is even more difficult to achieve. The chapters in this part of the book examine different approaches to family policy making, with reference to organisational structures and objectives and the instruments used for implementation. The intention is not to present a comprehensive overview of the policy-making framework for families across the Union, as in the detailed and wide-ranging study carried out for the German Bundesministerium für Familie und Senioren in the early 1990s (Neubauer et al., 1993) and in the annual policy reviews for each member state conducted by the European Observatory on National Family Polices on behalf of the European Commission. Emphasis is rather on analysis of the concepts underlying national policies from a comparative perspective.

The third part of the book explores the ways in which family policy has developed both at European level and in individual member states. The conceptual and operational relationship between social policy and family policy is examined, particularly with reference to the possible impact on the family of policies formulated in other areas. The final chapter returns to the wider European context and considers the prospects for a more integrated EU family policy.

# CHAPTER 8

# Family policy making in Europe

In several EU member states, the family has been recognised by the national constitution as a fundamental social institution. In some countries, for instance Germany, Ireland and Luxembourg, the constitution has identified the legitimate family as the married couple, and in others, for example Portugal, it has prescribed the nature of the support and protection that the state should afford to the family. The national constitutions of Ireland and Italy define the family as a private domain with which the state should not interfere. Official representation through government appointments is another indication of the visibility or otherwise of institutional recognition of the state as a legitimate social actor in family affairs; very few EU member states have consistently made appointments to designated ministerial positions with responsibility for family policy. The formal participation of family pressure groups in the political process, as in France, can also be interpreted as a sign that family policy is institutionalised and legitimised. Analysis of the policy-making environment in the first part of the book suggested that the relationship between family and state has been conceptualised and operationalised in different ways from one national context to another. Within countries, the degree of acceptability of family policy can be seen to vary according to ideological, political and religious convictions. At European level, the Council of Ministers has adopted a cautious and ambivalent approach, in an effort to reconcile seemingly incompatible views about the legitimacy of national and, even more so, supranational intervention in the area of family life.

In this chapter, definitions of family policy and indications of the importance attributed to the family in policy statements are first examined in an attempt to establish whether and how family policy has been conceptualised both at European and national level. The theoretical bases for family policy and the reasons for government intervention in family affairs are then analysed with reference to the concepts of solidarity, redistributive justice and universality. In the final section, the shift from universal towards more targeted family policies is situated in relation to differences in the ways in which social protection has been conceptualised.

## Defining and conceptualising family policy

A number of attempts have been made to find a definition of family policy that can be applied universally (for example Kamerman and Kahn, 1978, p. 3; Schultheis, 1990, p. 74; Dumon, 1994, pp. 325–6; Barbier, 1995, pp. 16–17). The broad definition of social policy formulated by Richard Titmuss (1974, pp. 23–32) in the British context has been widely used as a reference point in policy analysis and can be adapted to family policy for the purposes of making cross-national comparisons. Titmuss described social policy in terms of the principles governing actions directed towards achieving specified ends, through the provision of welfare, minimum standards of income and some measure of progressive redistribution in command over resources, in such a way as to shape the development of society. For a social policy to be described as family policy according to this definition, the family would need to be the deliberate target of specific actions, and the measures initiated should be designed so as to have an impact on family resources and, ultimately, on family structure.

In this section, public policy statements on the family are examined, firstly, at European and, then, at national level to determine to what extent family policy can be identified as an autonomous area of public policy following the above definition. Attention is therefore paid to analysing the process of conception and formulation of actions directed towards family objectives, the ways in which such actions are institutionalised within the public policy framework, and the social recognition of the legitimacy of state intervention.

### Family policy as a European concept

The Treaty establishing the European Economic Community of 1957 was concerned with social provisions only in so far as they affected the mobility of workers and the competitiveness of enterprises (Hantrais, 1995, pp. 1–18). No reference was made to the family. Article 235 gave the Community an opportunity to bring forward proposals in cases where action proved necessary to attain a Community objective and the Treaty did not provide the powers required. The way was therefore open for the Commission to make proposals whenever the protection of the family could be identified as a means of achieving aims such as the raising of the standard of living in member states in support of economic policies (Article 2).

For nearly twenty years after the signing of the EEC Treaty, Community action in the area of family affairs was not called for. By contrast, in its Social Charter of 1961 the Council of Europe, which had the support of a much larger grouping of countries, openly recognised the social importance of the family, stating that: 'The family as a fundamental unit of society has the right to appropriate social, legal and economic protection to ensure its full development.' The duties of the state towards individual family members, whether or not the family unit was legally constituted, were clearly set out: 'Mothers and children, irrespective of marital tatus and family relations, have the right to appropriate social and conomic protection' (part I, paragraphs 16 and 17).

Community documents maintained the silence with regard to the iamily until 1974 when the Council of Ministers' social action programme made two indirect references to the family dimension of policy: in the context of the reconciliation of family responsibilities and job aspirations (discussed in Chapter 7), and oncerning the need for an action programme for migrant workers and members of their families (*Official Journal of the European Communities* C 13, 12.2.74, p. 2). A more focused commitment to a Community responsibility for protecting the family as a social institution was developing in the early 1980s. In 1983, Parliament adopted a Resolution on family policy in the European Community, stating its view that 'family policy should ... become an integral part of all Community policies'. Parliament called on the Commission to draw up an action programme and to introduce a comprehensive family policy and, where appropriate, to harmonise national policies at Community level (*OJEC* C 184, 17.11.83, p. 117).

Resolutions are purely advisory and do not have mandatory authority. No formal action was taken until 1989, when a series of reports (in particular a memorandum from the French Ministry of Social Affairs and Employment, dated 5 October 1987), highlighting disturbing demographic trends, prompted the Commission to draft a Communication on family policies. The document reviewed the changes occurring in society and pointed to the essential role assumed by the family 'in the cohesion and the future of society' (COM(89) 363 final, of 8 August 1989, p. 12).

In addition to the reference to concern about reconciling work and family life and sharing family responsibilities, the other areas of common interest identified in the communication included measures to assist certain categories of families; consideration of the most deprived families; and the impact of Community policies on the family, in particular through the protection of children during childhood. The Commission claimed that Community intervention was justified less on ideological grounds than because the family played an important economic role, serving as a 'touchstone for solidarity between generations' and as a route to equality between men and women (COM(89) 363 final, pp. 3, 15).

A communication is a document issued in the preparatory stages of legislative proposals soliciting views from interested parties or signifying initial thinking. A month after the issue of the Commission's communication, the Council of Ministers responded formally by producing Conclusions, in which they agreed that action should be taken at European level in support of families (*OJEC* C 277/2, 31.10.89). The Council reiterated the points made in the communication about the legitimacy of Community action, stressing the importance of the family as a harmonious environment 'in which its members can flourish, with due regard for freedom of choice as to the number of children'. The action recommended focused on information gathering and the exchange of views, the inclusion of the family dimension in Community social policy, for example in the areas of freedom of movement or equality between men and women, and the monitoring of the impact of social policies on the family. The Conclusions did not propose any policy guidelines, but the Council singled out measures targeting families with special needs, describing them as 'measures tailored to the characteristics or difficulties of some families' (*OJEC* C 277, 31.10.89, p. 2).

A concrete result of the Community's interest in families in the 1980s was the setting up of a network of twelve national experts early in 1989, known as the European Observatory on National Family Policies. The Observatory was given the brief of examining the development of the situation of families and family policies and reporting back annually to the Commission. In the absence of a clearly defined policy area, one of the early reports of the Observatory adopted a broad definition, identifying family policy as 'measures geared at influencing families' (Dumon, 1991, p. 9). However, it excluded unintended outcomes for the family of measures implemented in other policy areas.

By the end of the 1980s, the Community seemed to have legitimised its interest in family affairs, but no legislation had been initiated specifically with the family as its target. Neither the Community Charter of the Fundamental Social Rights of Workers nor the Agreement on Social Policy appended to the 1992 Maastricht Treaty directly addressed family issues. The only mention of the family in the Charter was in the context of measures 'enabling men and women to reconcile occupational and family obligations' (point 16), as an equal treatment measure (see Chapter 7). The Council Recommendation 92/442/EEC on the convergence of social protection objectives and policies, adopted in the period following the signing of the Maastricht Treaty, was more specific with reference to the family: the Council advocated developing targeted benefits for categories of families in need (*OJEC* L 245, 26.8.92, p. 52). Recommendations, like resolutions, are not binding and, in any case, the purpose of this particular recommendation was to encourage member states to reach agreement over policy objectives rather than to impose harmonisation of policy measures.

By the mid-1990s, it could be argued that the Union had still not developed a clearly defined or 'comprehensive' family policy, as requested by the European Parliament in 1983. The family had been placed on the European social policy agenda but not as an autonomous policy area. The general trend towards greater individualisation of rights, promoted under the European equal treatment directives, also cast doubt on the viability of the family unit as a focus for policy (see Chapter 7). In the White Paper on European social policy, the Commission made an unambiguous statement to the effect that social policy affects people not only when they are at work but also in their family life (COM(94) 333, 27 July 1994, p.1). But, again, family policy was not identified as a specific policy area. In the absence of a designated policy programme, concrete proposals for EU legislation on childcare, maternity, parental and paternity leave, and the restructuring of worktime arrangements had been brought forward as equality or health and safety measures (see Chapter 7). References in the White Paper to provision for childcare and parental leave were located within the context of equal opportunities policies. A section on social policy and social protection proposed that social protection systems should be adapted in response to socio-demographic change in such a way as to take account of its impact on, and interrelation with, social and economic policy. In this context, the White Paper stressed that consideration should be given to measures to promote the individualisation of rights and contributions as well as long-term care insurance (COM(94) 333, 27 July 1994, p. 36), two equality measures which would shift the focus away from the family unit.

## From European to national definitions of family policy

If no wholly satisfactory and generally accepted operational definition of family policy has been formulated at European level, the reason may be, in part, that family affairs have remained at the margins of the major social policy concerns of the Union. The reluctance of the Council of Ministers to intervene in family affairs may also be explained by the fact that this is an area where agreement between member states has been particularly difficult to reach because of national ideological and political differences in approaches to family policy. In the Conclusions regarding family policies, echoing the words of the Commission in its communication, the Council noted that any action at Community level would 'have to be pragmatic in order to respect the special features of different national policies already created and the varying socio-economic contexts in which such policies operate' (*OJEC C* 277, 31.10.89, p. 2). The Recommendation on the convergence of social protection objectives and policies was written in the same spirit, implying that social policy was an area where harmonisation and standardisation were no longer considered appropriate or attainable.

Within the European context, family policy affords an interesting example of the application of the principle of subsidiarity, whereby the Council of Ministers intervenes only if member states are unable to take appropriate action at national level (see Chapter 3). In accordance with the subsidiarity principle, when external support is necessary, the preference should be for local rather than national communities to provide assistance, justifying the delegation of action to local authorities, who in turn, if the principle is taken to its logical conclusion, should intervene only if individuals or families are unable to manage their affairs independently. Primary responsibility for their own well-being and that of their immediate relations is thus assumed to reside with families.

Whereas the Council of Ministers and European Commission can be credited with having helped to shape equal opportunities policies, member states have largely continued to develop their own family policy agendas, independently of European legislation. The principle of subsidiarity may have been applied by default, if not by intention.

## National conceptualisations of family policy

The extent to which family policy has been legitimised and institutionalised, has served as the focus of policy programmes and has resulted in measurable outputs in terms of resources and family structures varies substantially from one member state to another. Some countries have a long history of interest in family affairs, which has been translated into constitutional and institutional structures, confirming the social acceptability of state intervention in this policy area. Austria, Belgium, France, Germany, Luxembourg and Portugal have probably gone furthest in lending institutional weight to the recognition of the responsibility of the state as a family policy actor, whereas Ireland, Italy, post-Franco Spain and the United Kingdom have been the strongest advocates of the family as a private domain (see Chapter 2), and they have sought to avoid programmes explicitly targeting the family as a social unit and as the focus of policies. Since the discredit brought on it by the Franco regime, family policy in Spain has been described as lacking 'institutional visibility' (Valiente, 1995, p. 80). In line with the individualisation and equality principles, the Nordic states have also progressively steered away from presenting policies as being intended for the family as an institution. If the criterion is adopted that family policies should have the family as their target population, many of the measures examined in analyses of national family policies do not, strictly speaking, fall within this policy area. The Observatory's loose definition – 'measures geared at influencing families' – implies that many of the provisions it has considered in its reports on national family policies, such as childcare and parental leave, are more properly the domain of the European Commission Network on Childcare and other Measures to Reconcile Employment and Family Responsibilities (1994). Few member states readily admit that policies in these areas are intended to have a direct impact on the family for reasons which are made clearer below in an analysis of policy objectives.

The reluctance of national governments to make policy commitments that might be construed as deliberate intervention in family affairs can be illustrated by comparing approaches to family allowances, the measure most likely to reflect the salience of the family orientation of policy in different national contexts.

Public provision for family allowances was first introduced in Belgium, France, Italy, Spain and the Netherlands in the 1930s, followed by Portugal, Ireland, the United Kingdom, Luxembourg, Finland and Sweden in the 1940s, and Denmark, Germany and Greece in the 1950s. By the mid-1990s, the term used to describe allowances towards the cost of raising children continued to refer to the family only in Austria (*Familienbeihilfen*) and the Latin countries: French-speaking Belgium, France, and Luxembourg used *allocations familiales* and, in the south European countries, the Italians used the terms *assegni familiari*, the Portuguese *abono de familia*, the Spanish *prestaciónes familiares* and the Greeks οικοφενειακο εοιδομα or βοιτιμα. In the other member states, children were identified as the target for benefits: *kinderbijslog* in Flemish-speaking Belgium, *børnepenge* in Denmark, *lapsilisa* in Finland, *Kindergeld* in Germany, *kinderbijslag* in the Netherlands, *barnbidrag* in Sweden and child benefit in Ireland and the United Kingdom. Even though benefits are not paid directly to children, the term used can be taken as an indication that social protection is conceptualised less as a family income supplement than as an individualised right targeted at children.

Analysis of the administrative organisation of family allowances or child benefit also provides an indication of the way in which the family-state or private-public relationship operates in different national contexts. In member states where social security systems are based on the insurance principle, family allowances were sometimes conceived as part of the wage package. Employment-related contributions were consequently the main or sole source of funding. In a few cases, employees do not contribute, as in Belgium, France, Italy and Luxembourg, thereby departing from the shared insurance principle applied in other areas of social protection. In these last three countries, various subsidies have been introduced to relieve the burden on employers, in gradual recognition that the justification for making employers responsible for family affairs has become more tenuous. In Greece, Portugal and Spain, employers and employees share contributions, and the state provides subsidies in Greece and Spain. In Austria, two-thirds of income is from contributions and one-third from taxes (Tálos and Wörister, 1994, p. 222). Funding is solely or mainly from the state in Denmark, Germany, Ireland, the Netherlands, Sweden and the United Kingdom (Melsted, 1988, p. 5; MISSOC, 1995, table II), thus breaking the direct link with employment.

The fact that family allowances or child benefit are considered as an integral part of social security and are funded through social insurance by employers, and in some cases employees, does not, however, demonstrate non-involvement on the part of the state or a lack of commitment to family policy. Often it reflects the origins of family allowances as a supplement to wages, a tradition which was not entirely broken when social security systems were established, as illustrated by the French case (Prost, 1984; Grignon, 1994).

Irrespective of the funding mechanisms and the terminology used, the concept of family allowances as a universal fixed-rate benefit for all families with children has not been evenly applied across the Union. Differential rates have operated for family allowances and child benefit according to the age and rank of children, family size and parental income (see Chapter 3), partially reflecting national definitions of family and public responsibilities. In the mid-1990s, for example, only Portugal and Spain paid the same amount for each child, and in Spain no allowances were paid if parental income was over a set amount. No variations were made according to family income in Belgium, Denmark, France, Ireland, Luxembourg, the Netherlands, Sweden and the United Kingdom. Austria operated a negative tax, providing a supplement for low-income earners who fell outside the tax threshold (Tálos and Wörister, 1994, p. 229). Only in the United Kingdom was the rate higher for the first child than for subsequent children. Only France did not pay family allowances for the first child. Larger families received higher rates of payment in Austria, France, Greece, Ireland, Luxembourg and Sweden. Portugal imposed the lowest age limit for benefits at 15 but with an extension up to 25 for children continuing in education, whereas Denmark, Italy and

Spain did not normally make any concessions after the age of 18, and Sweden after 19 (Melsted, 1988, p. 5; MISSOC, 1995, table X).

Differences in the terms used for family allowances and child benefit, and the ways they are funded and allocated, to some extent reflect the reluctance or otherwise of governments openly to declare an interest in the family. Approaches are, however, far from being consistent over time and space. Policy orientations may differ according to political affiliations, and decisions over family policy are often the subject of acrimonious public and parliamentary debate, as exemplified by the discussions surrounding changes in the laws on abortion, divorce or bioethics (see Chapter 2).

**Family policy objectives**

The aim of the strategy set out in the Council Recommendation on the convergence of social protection objectives and policies was 'to fix common objectives able to guide Member States' policies in order to permit the co-existence of different national systems and to enable them to progress in harmony with one another towards the fundamental objectives of the Community' (*OJEC* L 245, 26.8.92, p. 50). Changing family situations were identified as one of the comparable trends across member states which might lead to common problems, justifying the formulation of common objectives. Concern was, for example, expressed that changes in family structure were affecting the ability of families to provide support for their members (*OJEC* L 245, 26.8.92, p. 49).

The lack of progress in formulating a coherent family policy at European level and the diversity of approaches to policy among EU member states noted above can perhaps best be understood within the context of the lack of consensus among national governments over the possible objectives of family policy. The objectives finally adopted in the recommendation, as compared with those outlined by the Commission in the proposal formulated for a Council recommendation, indicate some of the areas of disagreement. The proposal referred to the need 'to develop family benefits, so as to avoid that [*sic*] a lack of resources will not dissuade anyone from having children' (COM(91) 228 final of 27 June 1991, p. 12). The implication that resources might affect the desire of parents to have children was excised from the final text. In its place, a more neutral form of words was inserted, encouraging member states to develop benefits paid to 'families with the greatest child-related costs, for example because of the number of children, and/or the most disadvantaged families' (*OJEC* L 245, 26.8.92, p. 52).

In this section, consideration is given to the many overlapping and conflicting objectives that have been attributed to family policy at both European and national level. They can be broadly grouped to distinguish between policies designed to redistribute resources horizontally and vertically, and those intended to affect behaviour, including decisions about the timing and number of childbirths, the management of family time and family lifestyles (Barbier, 1995, pp. 20–1). Issues concerning the reconciliation of paid and unpaid work were examined in Chapter 7 and are not developed further here. Instead, the focus is on redistributive objectives and policies aimed at family size and structure.

### Horizontal and vertical redistribution

Most countries have sought to use family policy as a means of redistributing income, either horizontally from individuals or couples without children to those with children in the same income brackets, or vertically from individuals and families on high incomes to those with low incomes, often targeting families most in need. In many cases, both horizontal and vertical redistribution has been pursued, but increasingly emphasis has been placed on helping children at risk in line with the child-centred approach of policy in the 1990s. Whether vertical redistribution is properly a function of family policy is open to debate (see Chapter 10). Efforts to contain costs in an economic context where young people remain dependent on their parents until a later age may also encourage targeting of benefits.

One of the defining characteristics of social policy identified in the previous section was the progressive redistribution in command over resources in such a way as to shape the development of society. Even before family policy was introduced as a branch of social security, in some cases family factors were taken into account in the wage package so as to compensate workers with families for the additional expenditure they incurred, resulting in horizontal redistribution of resources. The principle at the basis of most state organised systems of family allowances as they developed in the interwar and postwar periods was maintained as the dominant objective in systems where benefits are paid for all children at a standard rate, irrespective of income, for so long as young people are considered to be dependent on their parents.

In some countries, the tax system is also used as a horizontal redistributory mechanism. The provision of generous tax relief for high income earners with large families, as through the *quotient familial* system in France, for example, effectively redistributes income from taxes paid by individuals and couples without children to couples with children (see Chapter 3).

Horizontal redistribution through family allowances and child benefit, and tax law can be interpreted in different ways: benefits may be a means of rewarding families for carrying out an important service to the community; they may compensate families for the financial burden of raising offspring; or they may be intended to ensure greater equality between couples with and without children (Brin, 1991, p. 144).

In the early years of social security systems, the policy objective of redistributing income horizontally, for whatever reasons, tended to be taken for granted in most member states. Just as the European Community was forced to recognise that not all population groups were benefiting to the same extent from economic expansion and the general rise in the standard of living during the period of postwar reconstruction, member states were also becoming aware that family responsibilities, particularly in large families, were often associated with poverty and hardship. Income-related or means-tested family allowances and child benefit, ceilings on the level of benefits and supplements for particular types of families have been implemented across the Union. Their aim has been to bring about a vertical redistribution of resources from high to low-income families, whether it be through family policy as in France, through the tax system as in the United Kingdom, or through a minimum income and social solidarity as in the social assistance systems that have developed in all member states, except Greece and Portugal.

Countries that disregard family income when determining the level of family allowances and child benefit may, nevertheless, take account of family factors in calculating social assistance payments, thereby making the family the target of benefits (Millar and Warman, 1996). While individualisation of employment-related entitlements has meant that family income has become less salient in the calculation of rights for women in paid work, family factors may affect entitlements to provisions made for periods spent out of employment, either for family reasons or due to unemployment, reflecting the way in which family obligations and responsibilities are conceptualised (Luckhaus, 1994).

In Belgium, for example, family allowances are not adjusted according to income and might therefore be considered as 'neutral' with regard to the vertical redistribution of resources. However, social assistance and the guaranteed minimum income (*minimex*) may be reclaimed from a partner, parents or direct descendants by the agencies responsible for allocating social assistance (Meulders-Klein and Versailles, 1994, pp. 23–4). In the United Kingdom, the family, as constituted by parents and children, is the unit of assessment for means-tested benefits. Policy could therefore be said to be aimed at the vertical redistribution to low-income families of public funds derived from taxation on higher income earners as a social justice measure.

*Family size and structure*

In several member states, the level of family allowances and child benefit is not the same for each child. In the case, as in the United Kingdom, where a larger sum is allocated for the first child, the inference may be that the economic cost of catering for the needs of the first child are greater than those of subsequent children. In the case, as in France, where the amount paid for the third child and subsequent children is greater, and no allowance is paid for the first child, the economic justification may be that the costs involved in raising larger families are exponentially greater, and that the third child, in particular, may incur higher costs because women are less likely to be able to continue in employment, and it may become necessary for the family to move to another house or flat.

Another reason for supporting larger families is that population growth and renewal are dependent on couples having more children, although it can also be argued that the greatest incentive is needed to produce the first child. Pronatalist objectives may be the justification for state intervention in an attempt to influence family size and stem population decline. There is evidence of pronatalism underpinning family policy in several member states, particularly in its early stages. In Belgium, family allowances were introduced in 1930 in the context of a falling birth-rate and economic recession as a pragmatic response, however, rather than as part of a 'clearly defined social vision' (Meulders-Klein and Versailles, 1994, p. 21). The 1939 *Code de la famille* in France was a reaction to fears about the adverse consequences of population decline and an attempt to create a family-friendly environment in which couples would have an incentive to raise large families (Prost, 1984, pp. 8–10). The origins of family policy in the 1930s in Sweden were also associated with concerns about demographic issues (Pauti, 1992, pp. 963–5). Francoist Spain supported population growth as a source of political power (Valiente, 1995, p. 82). Neither France nor Belgium has been reluctant to make pronatalist objectives explicit. By contrast, post-Franco Spain, the United Kingdom and, until the late 1980s, also the Federal Republic of Germany (FRG) deliberately avoided formulating policies which might be interpreted as encouraging population growth because of its expansionist connotations.

Although pronatalist objectives are directed at families and could therefore be considered as family policy objectives, it has been argued that a distinction should be made between family policy on the one hand and demographic or population policy on the other (Barbier, 1995, pp. 17–18). Whereas the objective of family policy is to redistribute resources so as to eliminate differences in the standards of living for households with and without children, demographic policy is intended to influence the formation and size of families; pronatalist policy aims more specifically to increase family size (Lévy, 1985, p. 3).

While not all population or demographic policies have the family as their main target, for example policies intended to limit migratory flows or to manage population ageing are not family specific, the dividing line between family and demographic policy may sometimes be quite finely drawn. The integration of migrants may involve enabling family members to join a migrant worker. Community care policies for older people may require a major input from close family members, sometimes causing them to lose their own independence as paid workers outside the home. Population ageing may require policies to re-establish the balance between generations by providing incentives to adapt working and reproductive behaviour.

The increasing trend towards targeting and means-testing of benefits has taken place at the same time as family structure has been changing. The growth in the number of unmarried cohabiting couples, lone-parent families and reconstituted families has raised issues about the extent to which governments should be supporting and institutionalising new family forms. Some governments are bound by the national constitution to protect particular family forms – the legitimate married couple in Germany and Ireland or the legitimate child in Greece are cases in point – but most governments avoid formulating policies aimed at overtly and deliberately encouraging new family forms. While not openly promoting alternative family structures, the legitimacy or otherwise of family relationships may apparently be disregarded in policy. The distinction has, for example, progressively been removed between children born to married and unmarried cohabiting couples. The refusal of some governments to take account of unmarried cohabitation is an indication that they are continuing to lend support to the normative family. In Germany, for example, where marriage and the conjugal couple are the centrepiece of the family as an institution, cohabiting couples are not afforded the same rights as married couples (see Chapters 2 and 3).

In countries where the well-being of children is considered paramount, every effort may be made to compensate for any deficiencies that might arise as a result of the breakdown of the normative family, as demonstrated by the support provided for lone-parent families. Policy objectives may, however, be different. In France and the Nordic states, the aim is to provide help so that mothers can participate fully in the workforce and thereby ensure their economic independence, while in Ireland or the United Kingdom the aim has been to make sure that mothers are not prevented from being able to raise children by the need to earn their own income. Reconstituted families have not generally been singled out as a specific target area of policies, except in so far as they may create new pockets of poverty and raise issues about the liability of biological parents to maintain their children.

While the principle of redistribution is readily accepted as a family policy objective, attempts to influence the size or structure of families have met with considerable resistance, as testified in France by the debate over pronatalism (Le Bras, 1991; Lenoir, 1995), in Denmark and Sweden over the participation of fathers in childrearing (Kaul, 1991) or in the United Kingdom over the responsibility of absent fathers to maintain a former spouse and children (Family Policy Studies Centre, 1991).

## Family policies and concepts of welfare

Over the postwar period, governments in EU member states formulated their own family policy objectives in line with their political ideology, their approach to policy making and, in democratic states, as a response to their interpretation of the needs of families in a context of rapid economic and socio-cultural change. In the interwar and postwar periods when social protection systems were developing in the north European countries, agreement may have been relatively easy to reach within countries over the institutionalisation of universal family allowances aimed at protecting and supporting the family as a core unit in society. In the 1940s and 1950s, in a climate of economic expansion and demographic growth, horizontal distribution of resources through family allowances for all couples with children was readily integrated into Nordic and British concepts of welfare based on universal rights and funded by taxation. Universality was less clearly justifiable in countries, such as the original EC member states and Austria, where social protection was derived from the principle that rights should be earned by workers and their family dependants through employment-related insurance contributions. The south European countries that joined the Community in the 1980s largely followed the employment-insurance model, but their welfare systems were less developed than in the founder member states, and financial constraints prevented them from giving priority to families.

Several of the countries where the welfare system was designed with the worker rather than families as the main focus of attention have maintained the strongest and most visible commitment to family policy and have sought to respond to a wide range of needs. Belgium, France, Luxembourg and Germany have been identified as pursuing relatively consistent and coherent family policies (Barbier, 1995). The first three countries have ensured both horizontal and vertical distribution of resources, while Germany has focused more on vertical redistribution. The other EU member states, except for the Nordic countries, have also tended to concentrate on vertical redistribution. As Denmark and Sweden became leaders in terms of the provision of family-friendly and father-sensitive policies, the main focus of attention was not, however, the family unit but rather the needs of children and gender equality.

By the early 1990s, a marked shift was occurring towards individualisation, accompanied by a more diversified and pluralistic approach to welfare across the Union. Family allowances were adjusted according to income in the south European countries and Germany. Ireland and the United Kingdom were progressively shifting away from universalist welfare systems to more targeted benefits and market solutions for all categories of social protection. The new benefits introduced in France from the 1970s were means-tested, resulting in a shift towards vertical rather than horizontal distribution.

Policy measures may be prompted by any number and combination of different objectives, which are likely to vary over time according to factors such as economic circumstances, the political convictions of the government in power or the force of public opinion. In the Europe of the 1980s and 1990s, in a context where the family unit had become less clearly defined and governments were looking for ways of reducing public spending, the objective of prioritising low-income families was more widely accepted, though not without coming into conflict with the advocacy of universal benefits. Agreement over less solidaristic objectives, such as arrangements for parental leave, was proving difficult to achieve both within and between countries, as illustrated by the negotiations at European level.

Irrespective of their other aims, an objective increasingly shared by EU member states was the desire to make policy more accountable, efficient and open to public scrutiny, resulting in tighter regulation and greater control at national level. In the family policy area, the contraction of funds and efficiency drives resulted in a tightening of the focus of family policy objectives, making selectivity and targeting an increasingly common cause across the Union and calling into question the viability of policies, such as family allowances or child benefit, that did not specifically target population groups at risk.

CHAPTER 9

# The family impact of social policies

While the stated and intended outcome of policy measures may not be to influence families, many actions initiated in other policy areas are likely to have an impact on families, as for example through the payment of maintenance awards for young people who continue in education and training after school-leaving age, or the provision of free medical care for children. Even when the family unit is not the explicit and deliberate target of provision, governments are constantly making decisions that require them to take family factors into consideration, as in the case of care for disabled and older people. By deciding that the level of benefits should be adjusted to take account of the income of family members, by issuing more generous payments to large or poor families or to families where the mother stays at home, or by treating unmarried cohabiting couples differently from married couples, governments may be making statements about the normative family that society should be supporting (Land and Parker, 1978; Schultheis, 1991; Taylor-Gooby, 1991a, pp. 149–50).

Not all EU member states have gone to the same lengths to institutionalise family policy. Nor do they all appear to afford the same importance in the policy-making process to family affairs. In this chapter, an attempt is made to determine the extent to which policies formulated with the family as the stated target for intervention, as well as those where the outcome for the family is less direct, may have an impact on the resources and/or behaviour of families. The effects of policy are not easy to measure. Econometric studies give the impression that an increase in tax relief or in the level of benefits, by translating directly into greater resources, does have a measurable effect on decisions about whether or not women continue in employment outside the home and whether or not couples have more children (Becker, 1986; Ekert-Jaffé, 1986; Joshi, 1990). Sociologists are more cautious and seek rather to explain behaviour as the possible outcome of a combination of factors, including the wider socio-economic and political climate (Gittins, 1993; Hoem, 1993; Pitrou, 1994).

From an international comparative perspective, the situation is even more complex. The same policy measures may or may not be intended to meet the same objectives. Policies may have unintended

153

effects that vary from one national context to another, as for example in the case of family allowances or child benefit, paid parental leave and lone-parent benefit, which are conceptualised quite differently across the Union (see Chapters 7 and 8).

In the first section of this chapter, consideration is given to the findings from studies which have attempted to assess the impact on resources and behaviour of policies deliberately targeting families. The possible effects, intended or otherwise, on the family of policies pursued in areas such as health, education and caring are then examined. In conclusion, the combined impact on the family of a whole range of policy measures is explored in an effort to evaluate the effectiveness of policy in bringing about a redistribution of resources towards families and in changing behaviour by creating a family-friendly environment.

## The impact of family policies on families

When family policy is defined in terms of objectives and measures deliberately targeting the family unit with the intention of having an impact on resources and behaviour, not all countries are found to display the same level of commitment to family affairs as a legitimate area of policy (see Chapter 10). Family allowances represent the measure most extensively understood as properly belonging to family policy, although here too a paradigmatic shift has occurred in many EU member states, signalled by the change of title from family allowances to child benefit in a number of countries (see Chapter 8). Support for families in the Nordic states, in particular, has to be located within the wider context of equal opportunities and individualised welfare. Although childcare, maternity, paternity and parental leave and other measures to help parents reconcile employment and family life have not been identified in all member states as family policy measures, they can be considered as a proxy for family policies in cases where they are intended to encourage redistribution both between and within households. Their possible impact on the resources and behaviour of families is therefore also examined in this section.

### The impact of family policies on resources

Many attempts have been made to measure the effect of family policies on the resources of families across the Union. In addition to the regular monitoring by Eurostat, the European Observatory on National Family Policies and the European Commission Network on Childcare and other Measures to Reconcile Employment and Family Responsibilities, and despite their methodological limitations, two European-wide studies, in particular, have provided useful data on the redistributive effect of policies in member states. In a project commissioned by the German Bundesministerium für Familie und Senioren of family policy in the twelve EC member states in the early 1990s, Erika Neubauer *et al.* (1993) attempted to assess the financial value of a narrowly defined range of family support measures. In a study commissioned by the British Department of Social Security, Jonathan Bradshaw *et al.* (1993) sought to identify and quantify the composition of what the authors described as the 'child benefit package' for different model families, or family types, in the twelve EC member states, and also Australia, Japan, Norway and the United States (Swedish data were added later). The package included not only cash benefits and tax relief but also services in kind which provide support for families with children. The study presents a snapshot of particular family types at a specific point in time rather than an analysis of the dynamics of family relationships.

These and other international comparisons suggest that the family impact of financial incentives may vary substantially from one country to another. Different measurements produce broadly similar rankings, but with some notable deviations. When expenditure on family/maternity is measured as a percentage of total social protection spending, Denmark, Ireland, Luxembourg and the United Kingdom, three of which have not given a high profile to family affairs, are found to devote the largest proportion to families, with Greece and Spain at the other end of the scale showing an almost negligible amount (Eurostat, 1994b, table 5). Denmark, Ireland and Luxembourg were the only countries, according to Eurostat data, where the proportion had increased during the 1980s. In Denmark and Luxembourg, in particular, and also in France, Germany and the Netherlands, the amount received *per capita* in benefits was well above the European average; in Belgium, Ireland and the United Kingdom, it was close to the average; and in Greece, Italy, Portugal and Spain far below the average.

Adopting a different approach, in their study Bradshaw *et al.* (1993, pp. 36–7) looked at the value of universal and income-related family benefits for different family types and found that, in EU countries, low-income families with one three-year-old child and lone-parent families with one young child received the most generous allowances in the United Kingdom and France (in that order). For higher income earners, France and Denmark were most generous to lone-parent families. Belgium and Luxembourg were more supportive of larger couple families. Greece, Portugal, Ireland and Spain consistently showed the lowest levels.

When tax relief for children and spouses is added to benefits and differential payments, the pattern changes (Neubauer, 1993, pp. 300–2). In the early 1990s, the arrival of the first child produced the largest increase to family income from benefits and tax relief in Denmark, followed by Belgium. Italy showed the smallest increase. For families with two children, France headed the list, again followed by Belgium. Denmark was in third place well ahead of the other member states. The United Kingdom was further down the list, and Ireland made the smallest addition to income for this family size. The rank order was similar with three children, but the difference between the most and the least generous contributions was even more marked: France was by far the most generous state, once more followed by Belgium; Luxembourg and Denmark provided a much lower level of support; Germany, Greece, Italy and the Netherlands held an intermediate position; Portugal and Ireland were again the least generous states, and the United Kingdom had moved further down the list. Comparable data were not available for Spain but, in the absence of universal family allowances and given the low level of tax relief, it seems likely that Spain would rank even lower than Ireland.

Using the model family approach, Bradshaw *et al.* (1993, pp. 43–4) also found that, as family size increased, tax concessions became progressively much more advantageous for couples with children in Belgium, France and Luxembourg, whereas in Spain, particularly, and also in Greece and Ireland, their mitigating effect was relatively small.

The findings from these studies suggest that families on average incomes with more than one child are likely to receive more financial support from the combined effect of family benefit and tax relief in Belgium, France, Luxembourg and Denmark. Families in Greece, Ireland, Italy, Portugal and Spain receive the least support. The seemingly advantageous position of the United Kingdom in terms of the proportion of social protection spending devoted to families is counteracted by a relatively low level of allowances and tax relief.

### The impact of family policies on behaviour

Family policy evaluation has often examined the possible effects on behaviour of measures designed to redistribute resources to families in Europe (for example Tabah and Maugué, 1989). An explicit or implicit objective of policy may be to influence decisions by couples about whether and when to have children and how many (see Chapter 8). In countries that have actively pursued pronatalist policies, attempts have been made to assess the possible impact of policy on fertility rates and family size (Messu, 1994).

Measures encouraging women to enter and/or remain in employment, or discouraging them from doing so, may also be intended to have an effect on birth-rates by making it possible for women to engage in paid work outside the home without forgoing motherhood (Calot, 1980).

While some commentators believe that policy can influence decisions about reproduction (Ekert-Jaffé, 1986), many observers and policy makers reject the idea that family policy can have an effect on demographic trends, arguing that fluctuations in the birth-rate are more likely to be attributable to economic factors and broad cultural and social forces (Hoem, 1993). In this section, an attempt is made to explore some of the evidence in support of the theory that behaviour might be explained as a possible outcome of policy by examining the relationship between the level of state intervention, economic activity rates and fertility rates across the Union, using national-level data.

From the material presented in previous chapters, several patterns can be identified in the policy–employment–family relationship for the EU member states. In one grouping of countries, high female activity rates are matched by relatively high fertility rates and generous support for families, either as an equality measure, for example in Denmark, Finland and Sweden, or with emphasis on the family as a fundamental reproductive unit, as in Belgium and France. Lower female economic activity rates and lower fertility rates may be found in conjunction with generous policy provision for women who revert to the homemaker role, as in Austria, Germany and Luxembourg, and to a lesser extent in the Netherlands. The United Kingdom combines relatively high birth-rates and female activity rates with a low level of provision for women as working mothers. Ireland records high fertility rates but low female activity rates, without measures intended to encourage family building or women's employment. Greece, Italy, Portugal and Spain all display low fertility rates. Portugal is distinguished by its relatively high female activity rates. Italy has an uneven pattern of provision for families and presents a case where support for women as working mothers is associated with low female economic activity rates. Greece and Spain rank low for their fertility and female economic activity rates, and their formal provision for women as working mothers is also under-developed, even though the younger generation of Spanish women are adopting more continuous patterns of employment (see Chapter 7).

In the first grouping, where high female activity rates are matched by relatively high fertility rates and generous support for families, France affords an interesting example of a country that has implemented deliberate pronatalist policies. It has been argued, for example, that French family policy was relatively successful in raising the birth-rate and maintaining it at a higher level than in neighbouring countries (Brin, 1991, p. 145). Following the same logic, the decline in fertility rates from the mid-1960s could be explained by changes in legislation on birth control, marriage and gender relations, combined with an erosion of the level of family allowances (Messu, 1994, p. 583).

The higher fertility rates observed at certain periods in Sweden have also been explained as the consequence of family policy measures (Pauti, 1992). Like the French, the Swedes were concerned about population decline in the 1930s. Policy makers in Sweden stressed the importance of raising the standard of living of couples with children to the same level as those without offspring through a fixed-rate benefit for all children. When the social security system was instituted in 1945 in France, family allowances were paid at higher rates for the third and subsequent children, with no allowance for the first child. By 1960, fertility rates in France and Sweden were at almost the same level but behind Ireland, the Netherlands, Portugal and Spain (see Figure 1.2). By the mid-1970s, Sweden had introduced paid parental leave to replace maternity leave and was extending public provision of childcare, as measures recognising the importance of women's economic activity. Despite its supportive policies, in the 1970s Sweden was among the countries with the lowest fertility rates in Western Europe. While France was also responding to the demand for measures to help women combine employment and family life, the fertility rate had remained above the level in Sweden but was still well below the five member states with the highest levels, even though they were not pursuing similar family policies (see Figure 1.2, and Chapters 7 and 8). Then, in 1982, Sweden introduced differential child benefit rates from the third child and raised the level of allowances, whereas other countries had not uprated their child benefit. By the 1990s, Sweden had a higher fertility rate than all the EU member states, not it is argued, however, because of its pronatalist measures but because it had sought to make employment and family life compatible so that couples did not need to choose between women's paid work and childraising (Pauti, 1992, p. 983). Employment, according to the Swedish interpretation, serves as the means of self-fulfilment. Any increase in the fertility rate might, therefore, be seen as a side-effect of measures designed to help couples combine work and childraising, thereby creating a family- and women-friendly environment (Hoem, 1993, pp. 116–18).

In the past, the same arguments could have been applied broadly to France, but with two differences. Firstly, French governments began concentrating resources much earlier on large families in a deliberate attempt to influence family size (legislation to encourage large families dates back to the 1920s). Secondly, in the 1970s women in Sweden were entering employment as part-time workers, whereas in France they were more often employed on a full-time basis.

Comparisons with Denmark and Finland do not lend strong support to claims about the influence of family-friendly policies on fertility rates. Both countries have good records for the provision of leave and childcare and relatively high levels of female part-time work, as in Sweden. However, while fertility rates began to increase in Sweden from the early 1980s, the upturn came much later in Denmark and Finland, and a particularly large proportion of Finnish women were remaining childless (Prioux, 1989, table 5; Eurostat, 1995a, table E-6; Eurostat, 1995e, table 2), indicating that a similar policy environment may not have been achieving the same effect. Moreover, Denmark was reluctant to take measures that might result in women being segregated if special treatment was accorded to them (Carlsen and Larsen, 1993, p. 10).

Ireland and the United Kingdom both had a higher fertility rate than France in the mid-1990s. In 1994, after recording the highest fertility rate in Europe for many years, Ireland was still second only to Sweden (see Figure 1.2). Yet, neither Ireland nor the United Kingdom had sought to encourage large families or put in place leave and childcare arrangements designed to make it easier for women to remain in employment. In Ireland, female economic activity rates have grown more slowly than in most other EU member states. The United Kingdom shows similar overall levels to France, but with women more often employed on a part-time basis. The Anglo-French comparison would suggest that the attention devoted to family measures in France may have contributed to the ability of women to remain in full-time continuous employment when they have young children and may therefore have prevented the fertility rate from falling to a lower level than it might otherwise have done (Hantrais, 1992).

In the grouping of countries which combine relatively low fertility rates and low female economic activity rates with seemingly supportive family policies, Germany displays a particularly low fertility rate despite generous provision for women as mothers when they stay at home to look after young children. The proportion of women who remain childless is also particularly high. The impact of family policy in this case may be that women are rejecting the enforced choice between motherhood and employment (Ostner, 1993).

The south European member states also display contrasting patterns. In Portugal, high female economic activity rates are recorded for women with young children, but fertility rates have fallen to low levels in a context where public provision for families is poor. Italy has low female economic activity rates, combined with the lowest fertility rates in the Union and very uneven provision of measures for families and for women as mothers from one region to another. In the north where policy is most supportive, fertility rates have fallen to a particularly low level. Greece and Spain saw their fertility rates decline at the same time as women were increasing their labour market participation, and when equality measures were being developed in the absence of any substantial financial support for families.

These examples suggest that no direct and irrefutable link can be established between policy outcomes and policy measures either for families or for women as mothers. Rather, policies targeting families may be one of any number of factors combining at a particular point in time in different configurations to produce outcomes which may or may not be intended.

## The impact of social policies on families

It is not difficult to demonstrate that most social policies may have an impact on families in one way or another. It is much more difficult to measure the effect of a particular policy and to track the linkages between its intended and actual outcomes for families, the more so when the effect is not directly quantifiable in monetary terms but may be translated into behaviour. In this section, different attempts to identify policies with a family dimension are considered, before drawing together the findings of studies aimed at evaluating the possible impact on families of a range of social policies.

### Social policies with a family impact

The Council of Ministers' Conclusions on family policies in 1989 recommended that the impact of social policies on the family should be monitored (*Official Journal of the European Communities* C 277/2, 31.10.89). The brief of the European Observatory on National Family Policies was to carry out this task and report back regularly to the European Commission. In its reports, the Observatory excludes policies which have an impact on the family if their agreed goal is not family well-being, but it aims to cover measures concerned with the protection of women's health at the workplace if they are designed to support women as mothers. If their aim is to protect women as individual citizens and workers, they belong to health policy and are discounted.

Among the deliberate measures or instruments indicating the presence of family policies, Sheila Kamerman and Alfred Kahn

(1978) included childcare, child allowances, tax benefits, income maintenance and some housing policies, specifically aimed at the family, as well as policies which have an impact on the family even if their agreed goal is not family well-being. The German study by Neubauer *et.al.* (1993) examined all these areas and also looked at education and training, caring for older people and measures to combat poverty. The international comparison of child support measures by Bradshaw *et al.* (1993) included tax allowances in respect of childcare, housing, health care and services reducing the costs of schooling and pre-school care.

In an analysis of family policy in Europe, Jean-Claude Barbier (1994, pp. 52–3) identified three areas of public intervention which are not generally included in family policy but may have an impact on the family: education, which may be organised in conjunction with childcare provision; support for carers whether in cash or kind; proactive (job creation) and passive (unemployment benefits) employment policies. He also presented six categories of transfer payments which have an impact on families: social benefits directed at families, including family allowances or child, housing and maternity benefit; transfer payments, such as income support, not directly aimed at families but which may affect family resources; tax relief; benefits in kind through the public provision of services for families, covering childcare and facilities for mothers; derived benefits through health care or pensions; and reductions for families in the purchase of goods and services. He added a further category concerned with the provision of time through measures such as flexible working hours, parental leave, opening hours for services.

In the analysis below, the family impact of some of the social policy measures most frequently examined in comparative studies are briefly presented as a further dimension to the overall picture of the family as a beneficiary of public policy.

## *The family impact of housing subsidies*

Although in several countries the state provides support towards housing costs, only in France is an explicit link made between the family and housing by treating housing benefit and social housing as an integral part of family policy within social security, in a scheme administered by the Caisses d'Allocations Familiales (CAF). Only Denmark, France, Germany and the United Kingdom make direct provision to meet the housing costs of recipients of social assistance and individuals on very low incomes (MISSOC, 1995, table XII).

As Bradshaw *et al.* (1993, p. 45) have argued, housing costs and subsidies are extremely difficult to deal with in comparative studies, in particular due to national differences in tenure arrangements and regional variations within countries. Some member states, namely Luxembourg, Portugal and Spain, had no direct subsidy schemes in the early 1990s. In Ireland and Italy, subsidies were available only to unemployed families. The scheme in France was found to produce the biggest percentage reductions in rent and local taxes for families with low earnings. The German, Greek and British schemes were most supportive to unemployed families (Bradshaw *et al.* 1993, p. 47).

When housing costs are excluded from the average child benefit package, Sweden (subsequently added to the study, as reported in Bradshaw *et al.*, 1994, p. 22), Luxembourg, France and Belgium (in that order) were by far the most generous countries. When housing costs were included, France moved into first position, followed by Luxembourg, Belgium and Sweden. Denmark, Germany, the United Kingdom and the Netherlands formed an intermediate grouping both before and after housing costs. When housing costs were included, the positions of the United Kingdom and Germany were reversed. Portugal, Italy, Ireland, Spain and Greece, respectively, were ranked at the bottom of the list. Greece remained in the last position, whatever the measures used, whereas Italy and Portugal, and Ireland and Spain changed places.

## *The family impact of educational provision*

Free education can be seen as a significant state benefit for parents, and grants for further and higher education provide support for children who continue in education after compulsory schooling. In their study of twelve EC member states, Neubauer *et al.* (1993) found that education as an instrument of family policy becomes increasingly important as children grow older. The length of time spent in education differs, however, from one member state to another: full-time compulsory schooling ranges from eight years in Italy to eleven in the Netherlands and the United Kingdom, but children may subsequently spend longer in full-time further or higher education in one country than another.

The availability of schooling affects families in two ways. When children enter publicly provided nursery or infant schooling, parents are partially relieved of their caring duties. Children who remain in education or training after completing compulsory schooling may incur higher costs for their parents, both because they continue to be dependent on them for a longer period than might otherwise have been the case and because further and higher education may not be provided free of charge.

The responsibility of parents for older children due to later labour market entry and disproportionately high levels of unemployment among young people, in the absence of appropriate unemployment benefit, also increases the financial burden on parents. Some countries – Belgium, Germany, Greece, Luxembourg and Portugal – take account of these costs by extending the age limit on family allowances and child benefit. The age limit for tax relief is raised in these countries and also in France, Italy and Spain. In Belgium, France, Germany and Luxembourg, the financial assistance given to parents towards the costs of education is particularly generous and is estimated, in the most favourable case, to cover as much as half the maintenance costs of schoolchildren and students. In most countries, public support is provided for children in further or higher education through grants towards the cost of education or low-interest loans (Neubauer *et al.*, 1993, p. 604). Although much larger proportions of men and women aged 22 to 25 are classified as students in Denmark, Finland, France, Germany and Spain, than in Ireland, Portugal or the United Kingdom (OECD, 1993, table S15), no direct link has been found between the kind of support provided and the level and length of participation in education or the success rates of children (Neubauer *et al.*, 1993, pp. 604–5).

In their study of child support packages in different countries, Bradshaw *et al.* (1993, pp. 49–52) took account of school costs and benefits, including pre-school provision, transport, uniforms, meals and books. They found that childcare costs exceeded the total level of child benefits in nine EC member states – Belgium, France and Luxembourg were exceptions – for all types of families. They therefore concluded that the cost of paying for full-time pre-school care could more than cancel out the value of cash benefits paid to families in respect of children. By comparison with pre-school costs, the other spending associated with schooling was trivial, except in the Benelux countries where parents were expected to contribute to books and outings, and in Greece where private tuition was widespread.

## The family impact of public provision for health and caring

Health care is an important benefit for families. Within the Union, almost the entire population is protected either on the basis of residence, as in Denmark, Finland, Ireland, Italy, Portugal, Sweden and the United Kingdom, or through earnings-related insurance contributions which also cover dependants. Under insurance schemes, pensioners, unemployed and disabled people, as well as the recipients of social assistance, are normally entitled to treatment, even though they are not paying insurance contributions. The cost of health care, nevertheless, varies from one country to another both because of the way that provision is structured and because patients may be required to make a contribution towards doctors' fees, hospital charges and medicines. In their study of the child support package, Bradshaw *et al.* (1993, pp. 53–4) took account of the costs to families of health care. Denmark, Germany, the Netherlands and the United Kingdom made no charges for services provided to children, and in the United Kingdom parents were also exempted from charges in low-income families. In France and Ireland, families were found to incur relatively high health costs, except if the parents were unemployed.

Significant variations in the family support measures available to parents across the Union have also been reported by the European Commission Network on Childcare, which began monitoring arrangements in member states in 1986 before the European Observatory on National Family Policies was established. In the late 1980s, for example, far larger proportions of pre-school children were catered for by publicly provided services in Belgium, Denmark and France than in other member states; provision in Ireland, Luxembourg, the Netherlands, Portugal and the United Kingdom was poor (Moss, 1990, table 3). By the early 1990s, parents in Belgium, Germany, Portugal, Spain and Sweden could take paid leave to care for sick children (European Commission Network on Childcare and other Measures to Reconcile Employment and Family Responsibilities, 1994, pp. 58–9).

The availability of carers to look after not only young children but also disabled and older people has become increasingly problematic due to population ageing and the growing commitment of women to the labour force (see Chapters 5 and 6). From the 1980s, most member states were moving towards a policy of community care and de-institutionalisation, ostensibly in response to the demand for older people to remain in the community but more probably as a means of reducing costs (Jani-Le Bris, 1993; Lesemann and Martin, 1993; Attias-Donfut, 1995). In the early 1990s while state provision of childcare facilities was being extended, family members were coming under increasing pressure to exercise responsibility for older people, albeit with marked differences across the Union. The Nordic countries continued to accept that the state had a responsibility for both child and elder care, and it formally recognised the contribution made by informal carers. In Italy and Spain, formal service provision was made only in cases where no relatives were available to meet these obligations. State support was seen as a substitute for family care (Millar and Warman, 1996). The impact on families in countries, such as France, Germany and Italy, where relatives have been obliged by law to contribute to domiciliary and residential services on a means-tested basis is that care for older people may be seen as a financial, moral and physical burden. The institution of care insurance for older and disabled people, as in Germany and the Netherlands, can bc regarded as an attempt to relieve both the state and families of the financial burden. In countries where family care-givers perform a duty expected of them by society, the effect on family income and on the ability of women to engage in paid work outside the home may not be negligible.

Carers in all member states have access to home-care services, financial allowances in the form of social security payments and/or employment-related safeguards, but different choices have been made about how to organise and fund care, and levels of public provision differ widely from one country to another and from one region to another within countries (Glendinning and McLaughlin, 1993; Lesemann and Martin, 1993; Attias-Donfut, 1995). France, Germany and the Netherlands have developed a welfare mix, involving the concept of care insurance. Some national governments have offered financial support both to informal carers and to disabled and older people (Finland, France, Sweden and the United Kingdom), while others have only provided financial support to the care-receiver (Austria, Germany, the Netherlands and Portugal). Payments are made only to the care-giver in Belgium, Denmark, Ireland and Italy (Millar and Warman, 1996).

The impact on families of the public provision of support for caring, whether it be for disabled and older people or children, is likely to be important in terms not only of resources but also of the willingness and ability of family members to assume responsibility for relatives. In the Nordic states, generous public provision has enabled the vast majority of children to be cared for outside the home, while most older people continue to live in their own homes, often supported by informal carers, sometimes paid for by local authorities. Since 1989, informal carers in Sweden can take paid leave covered by health insurance for up to 30 days to look after a terminally ill relative (Johansson and Thorslund, 1993). By the mid-1990s, Germany had gone furthest in developing a care insurance solution for older and disabled people, thereby potentially relieving families and the state of direct responsibility, but childcare continued to be conceptualised essentially as thc prerogative of the child's mother in the home. The south European member states still relied heavily on family networks both for childcare and elder care, supported by services that varied in number and quality from one locality to another. The impact on families of state intervention in the provision of caring thus highlights important differences in the way the public–private relationship is understood and implemented in EU member states.

## The family impact of policies to combat poverty and social exclusion

Whereas in the 1970s poverty was essentially the lot of older people, by the 1990s large numbers of people of working age were socially excluded, often as a result of long-term unemployment. This 'new poverty' was particularly prevalent among families with children, and especially lone-parent families. European studies in the early 1980s suggested that larger families were more prone to suffer from poverty not only due to the additional expenditure incurred but also because of the opportunity costs, since household income fell if women were obliged to leave the labour market to care for children (Room, 1991).

Most EU member states have progressively introduced either means-testing or income ceilings on benefits in order to direct resources towards families with the greatest need. Where family allowances are paid only to families with low incomes, as in Italy and Spain, resources are effectively redistributed to poorer families. The family supplement (*complément familial*), introduced by legislation in France in 1977, was a means-tested differential payment aimed at low-income families with young children aged under three or with three or more children over the age of three. Policies providing generous tax relief for large families, by contrast, do nothing to relieve poverty; rather they are likely to have the opposite effect. Since they apply only to wealthier families, they result in horizontal rather than vertical redistribution, as in France and Luxembourg (see Chapters 3 and 8).

In a few countries, policies designed to guarantee resources through social assistance or a minimum income may target lone-parent families for special support. France, Ireland and the United Kingdom provide a means-tested benefit for lone parents. The *allocation de parent isolé* (API) was instituted in 1976 in France and represented an important departure from traditional universal family allowances. Its impact has been compared with that of the *revenu minimum d'insertion* (RMI), based on the principle of national solidarity (Messu, 1994, p. 586) and, significantly, both benefits are administered by the Caisse Nationale des Allocations Familiales.

The impact on families of benefits intended to assist underprivileged groups is difficult to measure since few countries monitor take-up rates. Moreover, the social acceptability of welfare benefits produces variations between countries. Some member states have a long tradition of providing means-tested benefits. Elsewhere, entitlements may not be taken up because means-tested benefits require some investigation of personal circumstances and are therefore considered as stigmatising on beneficiaries. Take-up of family credit in the United Kingdom, for example, may, at the most, be 67 per cent (Marsh and McKay, 1993, pp. 182–3). In addition, the available data are unreliable and difficult to interpret because schemes are generally administered locally, with regional disparities contributing to very different levels of provision. Neither Greece nor Portugal has a general social assistance scheme. It seems likely that only a small proportion of families living in poverty in the south European countries actually receive any support from local services not only because resources are limited but also because potential beneficiaries are ill informed about their rights.

## The family impact of time policies

Flexible working hours are sometimes presented as a panacea for dual-earner couples seeking to combine paid employment with raising children (Haut Conseil de la Population et de la Famille, 1987, pp. 35–6). The provision for paid maternity, parental and paternity leave may affect the ability of women to continue in employment, as in the Nordic states and France, or it may act as a pressure on women to leave the workforce when they have children, as in Germany. Part-time working arrangements may provide flexibility without sacrificing employment security as in the Netherlands and the Nordic states, or in France where working hours can be reduced to four-fifths time to free mothers to look after young children on the weekday when there is no schooling. The 'flexibility' afforded by part-time work when imposed by employers may, however, have a negative impact on families if it results in the loss of security or unsocial working hours (see Chapter 7), and even when conditions are not directly discriminatory, part-time workers may be sidelined because their commitment to the job is held to be less than that of full-time workers.

Despite the fact that different forms of leave and worktime arrangements are, in theory, available to both men and women, in practice it is women who most often interrupt their employment or reduce their working hours to look after young children (see Chapter 5). The impact of policies affecting time organisation may therefore be to segregate women into jobs where shorter working hours or flexitime are available. Since public sector employment has often been at the forefront in instituting family-friendly measures while protecting jobs, in most EU member states, women are concentrated in the lower and medium ranks of public sector employment (Rubery and Fagan, 1993, pp. 78–81). By contrast, the long working hours often required of middle and senior management in the private sector, rewarded by high pay, tend to exclude women (Hantrais, 1993).

Rather than reducing gender inequality and encouraging a redistribution of household labour, the unintended impact of public policies creating more flexible worktime arrangements may have been to reinforce the gendered division of roles and to militate against family togetherness. While women are more often than men employed in part-time casual jobs and interrupt their employment to look after young children, men work longer hours and are more frequently in full-time continuous employment. The male breadwinner role is thus perpetuated, and men are dissuaded from making a greater contribution to domestic work, even in the Nordic states where women have come to play a much more important role in the labour force and where the emphasis is firmly on gender equality (Nousiainen, 1995).

## The effectiveness of family impact policies

Whatever the differences and fluctuations in the objectives of family policy in member states, many of the instruments used are the same, even though they may be adapted to suit the specific conditions pertaining from one country to another and are found to be achieving different objectives. Policy instruments may be used without reliable evidence as to their effectiveness, as indicated above in the discussion about pronatalist policies. A broad objective underlying statements on family policy and references to the family impact of social policy is to create what might be described as a family-sensitive or family-friendly environment. In this concluding section, the possible impact of family policies is re-examined in an attempt to assess their effectiveness in achieving this and other objectives.

One of the aims of the 1939 *Code de la famille* in France was to create an environment in which parents would want to give birth to children and to devote themselves to childrearing. The references to the family in national constitutions, particularly in the case of Portugal, also stressed the importance the state attached to protecting and supporting families as a valued social institution. The postwar baby boom throughout Europe might be interpreted as an indication that family building was a socially accepted goal and that the socio-economic climate of the time was conducive and supportive. The extent to which specific family policies can be credited with being responsible for the demographic upturn is less obvious. While family affairs have consistently been on national policy agendas in Belgium, France and Luxembourg, other states have been reluctant to interfere directly in family matters (see Chapter 7). After many years of apparent neglect, by the early 1990s the family had, however, become a focus for political debate and an election issue among parties from different sides of the political spectrum in a context where population ageing and family breakdown were seen as common social problems. In Greece, Ireland, Italy, Luxembourg and the United Kingdom, politicians were looking to the family as a topic that would unite the electorate, but in Spain it was not seen as an issue for public debate.

Although political rhetoric may help to create a favourable climate of opinion, it needs to be accompanied by concrete measures if politicians are to convince voters that they mean what they say. Even then, policies may not produce the outcomes intended. Christiane Dienel (1995) has argued that institutionalisation of family policy is not necessarily a precondition for effectiveness: Belgium and Denmark are countries with a family policy which can be described as effective in creating a positive environment for families, without being highly institutionalised. Nor is centralisation always synonymous with effectiveness or *vice versa*: France is cited as a case where central policy decision making and institutionalisation appear to be effective, while in Germany or Italy decentralisation is associated with inefficiency.

When effectiveness is measured in terms of the extent to which resources are redistributed to families (horizontal redistribution), thus mitigating the costs of raising children, no EU member state can be said to compensate families fully for the additional expenditure incurred from having a family. In general, the estimated costs of raising offspring are found to increase as children grow older; the costs incurred by the first child may be greater than for subsequent children; and the overall burden on households also increases with the number of children (Grignon and Villac, 1993). Although some account is taken of these factors, in the vast majority of cases family benefits and tax relief fall far short of family expenditure on children. In this respect, Belgium and France are often cited as the EU member states that have been most effective in compensating for the additional costs families incur by having children (Neubauer *et al.*, 1993, p. 610).

Both countries are much less effective in redistributing resources vertically. In terms of direct cash benefits to families, Italy and Spain are probably more effective in ensuring vertical redistribution since family allowances are concentrated on lower income families. Despite the United Kingdom's reputation for not intervening in family affairs, and the focus in Denmark on individuals rather than families, in the early 1990s, with Luxembourg, they were ahead of France for average spending per child aged under fifteen derived from child, maternity and housing benefits (Boissières, 1994, p. 1 – 176). The United Kingdom was also one of the countries which had gone furthest in applying means-testing in order to direct resources to those most in need.

When cash benefits are combined with services in kind, four countries – France, Luxembourg, Belgium and Denmark (to which Sweden could be added) – are found to provide the most generous child support packages. Families in Italy, Portugal, Spain, Ireland and Greece, in that order, receive the least generous packages (Bradshaw *et al.*, 1993, p. 74). In an assessment of the effectiveness of the package in improving the access of families to resources and in influencing behaviour, the authors of the child support study looked at the socio-economic characteristics of each country. They had hypothesised that member states with a high proportion of children in the population might be unable to sustain a high level of benefits. This was not substantiated by the evidence, although they did find that lower levels of gross domestic product (GDP) *per capita* were associated with poorer child support packages. France was shown to have a more generous child support package than might have been anticipated from its GDP *per capita*. No strong linear relationship was noted between fertility rates and the level or form of family benefits. Only Denmark showed evidence of a link between the generosity of the child support package paid to lone parents and their proportion in the population, and this could be interpreted as either cause or effect. No strong relationship could be detected between female participation rates and child benefits: low activity rates in Belgium and Luxembourg were accompanied by generous child benefits, whereas high activity rates for Danish women were associated with lower child benefits. Religious convictions, ideological persuasions and the presence or otherwise of women in the decision-making process did not seem to have a discernible affect on the level of child support (Bradshaw *et al.*, 1993, pp. 74–84).

In an assessment of the commitment of countries to promoting families, Neubauer *et al.* (1993, p. 611) categorised Belgium, Denmark, Germany, France and Luxembourg as the most supportive member states (Austria, Finland and Sweden would probably also have been placed in this group had they been members of the Community); Ireland, the Netherlands and the United Kingdom were characterised by their selective support for families; and Greece, Italy, Portugal and Spain were identified as countries concentrating their efforts on families with special needs.

The member states in the first category have in common their high *per capita* gross national product (GNP), and therefore their ability to provide a high level of support for families, but several subcategories can usefully be identified to distinguish between family policies in terms of their effectiveness in creating a family-friendly environment.

The Nordic states have pursued social policies ensuring a high level of support for all families with the objective of encouraging the sharing of childcare and household tasks in a context where individual rights, including those of children, have been actively promoted. They are generally recognised as having enabled parents to raise children in a supportive environment sensitive to the needs not only of children as individuals but also of parents wanting to engage in paid employment (Pauti, 1992; Hoem, 1993), although reservations are expressed about the effectiveness of policies in promoting gender equality (Kaul, 1991; Skrede, 1995).

Austria, Belgium, France, Germany and Luxembourg have also directed resources towards the family and sought to create an environment favourable to family building, but where the emphasis has been more strongly on the family unit, as in Belgium, France and Luxembourg, or on the married couple and the legitimate family, as in Austria and Germany. The success of these two countries in achieving the objective of family-friendliness is less convincing in that they have some of the lowest fertility rates in the Union as well as a relatively high proportion of childless couples.

Although Ireland, the Netherlands and the United Kingdom have been grouped together for their selective policies towards children, they represent rather different cases in terms of policy priorities and outcomes. Until the early 1990s, Ireland was displaying a much higher fertility rate than its European partners, despite the lack of direct and explicit public support for families. The United Kingdom was characterised by its apparent non-commitment to universal provision of facilities and its focus on means-tested benefits for low-income families. The Netherlands had not promoted policies to support lone mothers or to help women combine employment and family life, as in Germany. Although the working environment was supportive towards women as mothers and part-time workers, the Netherlands registered one of the highest rates in Europe for childless women (Prioux, 1989, table 5).

If the south European countries can be described as family-friendly, it is due to the support traditionally provided by family networks rather than to public policy. Although low cohabitation and divorce rates in the mid-1990s suggested that the institutional family was still socially accepted, the low fertility rates indicated that couples were deciding against family building or postponing it in the absence of convincing arguments to persuade them otherwise.

These examples show that family policy is a relative concept and that political rhetoric and the visibility of family impact policies do not necessarily provide an accurate reflection of the extent to which a society can be considered to offer a supportive environment for family formation and childrearing.

# CHAPTER 10

# Integrating European families and family policies

When the European Economic Community was established in 1957 with the signing of the Treaty of Rome, the founding member states were in agreement about the need to improve living and working conditions. The functioning of the common market was expected to achieve this objective by favouring 'the harmonisation of social systems' through 'the approximation of provisions laid down by law, regulation or administrative action' (Article 117). The section in the Treaty covering social policy (Articles 117–28) focused, however, on working conditions and made no reference to the standard of living of families.

Despite the fact that important changes were being identified in family structure in the northern and central regions of Europe as early as the 1960s, the family did not move onto the Community's policy agenda until the mid-1980s. Policies aimed at promoting the well-being of families became an area of common interest among member states, primarily as a result of concern over the demographic situation. By then, harmonisation of national social protection systems was no longer a keyword in European negotiations. Rather, convergence of social protection objectives and policies was being sought on the grounds that comparable trends – population ageing, changing family situations, high levels of unemployment and the spread of poverty – were leading to common problems that policy makers in all member states needed to address. By the early 1990s, when the Maastricht Treaty on European Union was signed, the Council of Ministers was recommending a convergence strategy that involved fixing common objectives to guide policies and enable national systems to co-exist and progress in harmony (*Official Journal of the European Communities* L 245, 26.8.92, p. 50). The Council recognised national diversity and the importance of the idiosyncratic socio-cultural factors which had shaped each system, but the expectation was that, by monitoring and analysing the impact of national family policies, some convergence might take place between member states, possibly as they sought to emulate one another or learnt from each other's experience.

In this concluding chapter, firstly, the 'common' trends recorded by socio-demographic indicators for the EU member states are analysed to determine whether a model, or models can be identified, towards which European families may be converging. Secondly, these trends and models are located with reference to national policy contexts and in relation to European legislation, leading to an assessment, in the final section, of the extent to which the family policies of EU member states are apparently becoming more integrated.

## Towards European family models

Throughout this book, families and family policies in Europe have been examined in isolation from the rest of the world as if they had an autonomous and coherent existence. The Union does, however, share a number of demographic features with the rest of the developed world which distinguish it from developing countries. At the approach of the twenty-first century, the Union has in common with most developed countries low population growth rates, which could be attributed essentially to couples exercising their freedom of choice to determine and control the timing and number of births. As a result, in the mid-1990s the proportion of young people in developed countries was in the order of 20 per cent, compared with 40 per cent or more in the developing world. Greater life expectancy in combination with low birth-rates was leading to demographic ageing, with increasingly higher proportions of the population over the age of 65, reaching 12 to 15 per cent in the developed countries, compared with 4 per cent or less in the developing world. Predictions for the year 2025 suggested, however, that the demographic transition that was underway in developing countries would result in even larger proportions of older people, in a socio-economic context where the burden of ageing could present intractable problems (European Commission, 1995, pp. 11–12). By comparison, the demographic difficulties of the developed countries would be more manageable.

In this section, trends across the Union are examined in relation to other developed countries. The patterning of demographic indicators, and particularly of family structures, is then considered across the countries of the Union in order to test theories about the diffusion and convergence of European family models.

### Families in the developing world

The EU member states are distinguished from the rest of the developed world by their moderate demographic growth and their high population density. In addition to internal similarity between member states with regard to migration models and mortality patterns, they are also distinguished from Central and Eastern Europe by their patterns of family building (European Commission, 1995, pp. 14–16). Women in the Union tend to marry and have their first child at a later age, over 24, compared with under 22.5 in Central and Eastern Europe. Whereas fertility trends have followed erratic patterns in the East during the twentieth century, within the Union similar fluctuations could be observed across member states: between 1920 and the mid-1930s fertility rates fell; they rose in the late 1930s and then dropped again after the Second World War, before climbing steeply during the 1950s and into the early 1960s, when a prolonged decline began, but with some indications of an upturn from the mid-1980s in the Nordic states. The same overall fluctuations occurred in Australia and the United States, but several years earlier. In Japan, the demographic decline began sooner and, by the 1990s, population ageing had progressed much further than in Europe (European Commission, 1995, p. 13).

In the EU member states, the slowing down of population growth and demographic ageing were associated with greater life expectancy, the postponement of marriage, an increasing number of consensual unions, a growing number of divorces, longer periods of cohabitation of children with their parents and changing gender relations as more women entered the labour market. Eurostat averages over the period 1965–94 confirm these overall trends. They show a prolonged fall in total fertility rates, a fairly consistent decline in gross marriage rates, rising numbers of live births outside marriage and a rise in divorce rates up to 1985, followed, however, by a decline in the early 1990s, and rising levels of female economic activity among women with young children (see Chapters 1 and 5). By the late 1980s, the relatively high levels of unmarried cohabitation, extramarital births and divorces, and the importance attributed to equal opportunities in many member states, particularly the Nordic countries, had brought them closer to patterns in North America than to their south European partners (Barrère-Maurisson and Marchand, 1990).

The findings from a Eurobarometer survey in 1993, based on a representative sample for the twelve member states in the early 1990s, provide a picture of a less destabilised European family. According to Eurobarometer data, most Europeans (60.4 per cent) were living in a couple; 53.5 per cent of respondents were married, 2.3 per cent remarried and 4.5 per cent divorced or separated; 7.8 per cent had lived in a consensual union before marrying; men were more likely than women to have cohabited, particularly in the 25–39 age group; men aged over 40 were more likely than women to have remarried. Most couples (over 80 per cent) would have children at some point in their lives. At the time of the survey, 41.5 per cent of all respondents aged fifteen or over had children living with them. More than 70 per cent of parents with two or more children were married (Malpas and Lambert, 1993, tables 1.4a, 1.8). Comparisons with surveys conducted more than a decade earlier indicated a slight rise in the proportion of respondents who were not parents; the proportion of families with two children had remained almost constant, and families with three or more children had declined by 2.5 per cent (Malpas and Lambert, 1993, p. 23).

In the 1993 survey, the main factors contributing to a successful union were mutual respect and love. Faithfulness was the hallmark of marriage. The family was the central value for the majority of Europeans, and they were convinced of the importance of children. Most respondents remained opposed to lone parenthood and to divorce where young children are involved. They were non-committal about consensual unions. More than three-quarters of respondents expressed the view that mothers should stay at home to look after their children; even the least supportive group – women aged between 15 and 24 – were strongly (two-thirds) in favour of mothers staying at home, although they were also aware that having children was an obstacle to women working. Respondents thought that mothers should perform caring tasks, while fathers were expected to be involved in playing with children or punishing them (Malpas and Lambert, 1993, graph 2.2, tables 2.1, 2.4–5, 2.16, 3.10, 3.14, 4.3 4.7, 4.10, 4.17).

When contrasted with the more coherent model of the 1960s, firmly based on the child-centred married couple, the demographic trends observed in the Union in the last quarter of the twentieth century have been interpreted as heralding a new European family model, characterised by growing fragmentation and instability (Tabah and Maugué, 1989, pp. 50–1). This claim found some support in the 1990s: couples were more often living together before marriage, the opprobrium associated with divorce and lone parenthood was lessening, and more children were experiencing life in reconstituted households. Aggregate-level data suggest, however, that the vast majority of families in the late twentieth century across the Union were still composed of married parents living together with a small number of children, whom they were strongly committed to raising themselves.

## *Intra-European family patterns*

The picture of the average family as portrayed by Eurostat and Eurobarometer data conceals marked national differences. Scrutiny of fertility and childrearing patterns, of marriage and female economic activity rates in individual member states, and of attitudes towards them might seem to suggest that, since the 1960s, the Nordic countries, like North America, have been setting trends which are subsequently followed by the member states in the centre of the Union and then by the south European countries. Time series data for the number of divorces, consensual unions, extramarital births, lone parenthood and reconstituted families between the 1960s and 1990s point to an apparent diffusion from the north towards the south, albeit with disparities in pace, timing and degree (see Chapters 1 and 5). One hypothesis that has been formulated on the basis of these data is that greater demographic similarity might, ultimately, be the outcome, particularly since one of the main driving forces behind the changes is the aspiration of women for greater autonomy and freedom of choice, which has been spreading across the Union since the 1960s (European Commission, 1995, pp. 18–19).

The convergence thesis with reference to the family seems to be premised on the assumption that all couples, or more especially all women, whatever their socio-cultural environment, are aspiring to greater freedom of choice as far as family size and structure are concerned and that they are all intent on gaining autonomy by being economically independent and exploiting their skills and qualifications to the full. Freedom of choice is taken to mean that most women would want to reproduce within a relatively stable heterosexual relationship, and that they aspire to having two children, while also pursuing a career path offering opportunities equal to those of their male counterparts, but without sacrificing the flexibility to organise employment and family life in the most harmonious way possible. The data from national studies, considered below, tend to refute the case for a single family model based on these criteria.

*Towards a dominant family model . . .*

According to the diffusion thesis, as more women are able to achieve their aspirations, they might be expected to adopt the corresponding family model, which by the 1990s was most clearly articulated in the north of the Union. Analysis of family arrangements in the Nordic states suggests, however, that they may not share a single family model and that socio-cultural factors make it unlikely that other countries in the Union will follow the same development.

On the basis of the demographic data assembled in previous chapters, the so-called Nordic family model encapsulates a variety of family forms: most couples delay, or postpone marriage and childbearing, sometimes indefinitely; they live in consensual unions and have a small number of children who continue to reside with their parents and remain dependent on them until they are well into their twenties; separation or divorce are the outcome of most unions; new family relationships are formed, intercalated with periods when women live alone with their children; large numbers of households are composed of a single person; child and elder care is shared between women and the state; women are engaging in economic activity even when they have young children; they are often employed on a part-time basis and are more likely to be unemployed than their male counterparts; the contribution made by women to family resources from paid work is accompanied by a more equal – but still unequal – sharing of household labour. Although women who engage in paid work outside the home when they have young children are generally supported by public opinion, they are very much aware of the adverse effects that children can have on employment opportunities (Kaul, 1991; Carlsen and Larsen, 1993; Hoem, 1993; Malpas and Lambert, 1993).

Even though, at the superficial level, the demographic trends observed in the Nordic states might appear to be followed, firstly, by the countries in the central area of the Union and, then, by those in the south, the conclusion cannot be drawn that EU member states will ultimately converge towards a single family model or that the division between north and south can simply be attributed to a time lag. The fallacy in the diffusion and, more especially, convergence theses is their failure to consider the family as a dynamic organism and to take account of the fact that similar aspirations may be associated with quite different configurations from one national context to another, since they are the outcome of complex processes of negotiation and historical compromise.

The extent to which, by the middle of the last decade of the twentieth century, the fifteen EU member states were moving towards the model sketched out above is refuted by the available data. Even as fertility rates were falling to record lows in the south European countries and Germany, the Nordic states had reversed the trend, without ever reaching the same low point. Marriage rates were fluctuating in such a way that no clear pattern emerged for the north or the south: after reaching a particularly high level in the 1970s, Portugal was, with Denmark, well above the other member states. Despite high levels of unmarried cohabitation, Denmark and the United Kingdom were displaying relatively high marriage and divorce rates, while marriage had sunk to low levels in Sweden, France, Ireland and Finland, in that order. In Ireland, divorce was still illegal; Greece, Italy and Spain recorded very low levels, despite the fact that no-fault divorce had been legalised for more than a decade. Compared with the 1960s, the divide had widened between the north and the south with regard to trends in extramarital birth-rates, consensual unions and lone parenthood, with no clear indication that all the member states in the centre of the Union were moving towards the high rates recorded in the north.

Nor did patterns of female economic activity appear to be converging towards a single model. Labour market participation had increased everywhere for women since the 1970s, reaching levels close to those of men in the Nordic states. Gender disparities continued to be especially marked in the south European member states, except Portugal, and also in Ireland and Luxembourg. Activity patterns had become more continuous for women with young children, particularly in the north, and more women were returning to employment after raising young children in Luxembourg, the Netherlands and the United Kingdom (see Chapter 5). In Ireland, female economic activity was essentially confined to young single women without children. In some cases, relatively high activity rates corresponded to high levels of part-time work, as in the Nordic states and the United Kingdom. Part-time working arrangements were also characteristic of women's employment in the Netherlands where overall activity rates were not so high. In the EU member states where women had apparently made the greatest gains, bringing them close to male working patterns, gender segregation had not disappeared, and the gap in wage differentials had not necessarily been closed to a greater extent than in cases where women had less of a stronghold in the labour market and did not leave employment when they had young children (Rubery and Fagan, 1993, 1994).

### ... or a plurality of family models?

Analysis of the available trend data suggests that the diffusion and convergence theses cannot be applied systematically with reference to a single model, such as that provided by the Nordic states in the late twentieth century. Rather, as argued here, it may be more meaningful to attempt to interpret socio-demographic indicators in terms of a plurality of family forms or arrangements of private life, some of which are more tightly focused on the concept of the family than others. These family arrangements can be depicted using overlapping clusters of countries sharing similar characteristics. The same countries would not, however, necessarily belong to a particular cluster for all variables or at all times. EU member states can be roughly allocated to three main or broad groupings, representing a continuum between north and south, but with different configurations according to the variables concerned.

The Nordic states are generally presented as the exponents of a de-institutionalised family model based on gender equality and the reconciliation of employment and family life. Sweden probably comes closest to the 'ideal type' as gauged by the combination of high levels of fertility, unmarried cohabitation, extramarital births, divorce and female economic activity. Finland is lower on the scale than the other two Nordic states for consensual unions and extramarital births. Denmark shows a lower fertility rate than the other countries, a high level of lone parenthood and a higher marriage rate, which brings it closer to the next cluster of member states. Data from the 1993 Eurobarometer survey confirm that attitudes towards cohabitation, divorce and lone parenthood are less negative in Denmark than in most other EU member states (Finland and Sweden were not covered by the survey), and that mothers are less often expected to stay at home to look after children, but the proportion of respondents who recognised that children can be an obstacle to women's employment was close to the European average (Malpas and Lambert, 1993, tables 3.10, 3.14, 4.13).

Belgium, France and the United Kingdom overlap, in some respects, with the Nordic cluster of countries, although Belgium is closer to the next cluster for most of the indicators considered here. Female economic activity rates in Belgium and France are closer to those of the Nordic countries for women in the 25 to 29 age group, and the mother at home model finds relatively little support in Belgium. Fertility rates, and proportions of consensual unions and extramarital births are relatively high in both France and the United Kingdom, compared with other member states in the geographic centre of the Union, while the marriage rate is low for France. The United Kingdom records relatively high marriage and lone parenthood levels and the highest divorce rate in the Union.

Austria, Belgium, Germany, Luxembourg and the Netherlands form a second cluster of countries, although Germany displays patterns of employment among women that take the same continuous form as in the Nordic states, but at a lower level. Germany is also distinguished from the other countries in this cluster by its low fertility rate, one of the lowest in the Union. Attitudinal data place Germany very high among the countries supporting mothers who stay at home, while attributing low importance to children and recognising their negative impact on women's employment.

In all the countries in this cluster, marriage rates have remained moderate to high, and divorce has not risen to the same level as in the United Kingdom. Fertility rates (with the exception of Luxembourg) and extramarital births are relatively low. Levels of lone parenthood are fairly high, despite mainly negative attitudes. The number of consensual unions is about average, and childbearing takes place essentially within the context of marriage, despite the fact that cohabitation more often meets with approval in these member states than elsewhere in the Union. Luxembourg and the Netherlands have in common that women tend to leave the workforce when they have children and do not regain their previous levels of employment, a pattern consistent with public opinion. Nor are children seen there as an obstacle to women's employment. In some respects, attitudes in the Netherlands are closer to those in the United Kingdom than for their continental neighbours: the British and Dutch attribute a similarly low level of importance to children, and they are more tolerant of divorce and lone parenthood. They also have in common their conception of the private lives of individuals. They diverge, however, over attitudes towards mothers staying at home to look after their children: the Netherlands are supportive; the United Kingdom less so. In this cluster of countries, Luxembourg could be regarded as being closest to an 'ideal type' where family values, the institution of marriage and the male breadwinner model receive strong support.

The cluster formed by the south European member states, including Italy, also overlaps with other groupings. Marriage rates are relatively low, but not so low as in Sweden, and Portugal stands out as having the second highest marriage rate in the Union. Divorce rates are low in Greece, Italy and Spain. Divorce, remarriage and cohabitation are viewed less negatively in Spain than in the other three countries. Fertility rates are among the lowest in the Union, particularly in northern Italy and Spain. Somewhat paradoxically, children are said to be of greater importance in the south European countries, according to survey respondents, than elsewhere in the Union. Extramarital births are particularly low in Greece, Italy and Spain but higher in Portugal than in some of the central EU member states. Lone parenthood is less widespread than elsewhere in the Union and is viewed negatively, especially in Greece. Female economic activity rates in Greece, Italy and Spain are consistently below the levels reached in the other member states, whereas Portugal registers some of the highest initial rates and maintains them for women with young children. Views about women staying at home to look after children are most supportive in Portugal, although, as in the other three countries, children are not seen as an obstacle to women's employment. Greece might be taken to represent the Mediterranean 'ideal type', where the male breadwinner model is dominant, and where traditional family values remain strong and centred on children produced within marriage and raised by a married couple.

Ireland does not fit in easily with the other member states in the central area of the Union, nor with the United Kingdom, nor with the south European countries. High fertility rates combine with low marriage rates, the absence of divorce, relatively low extramarital birth-rates and low levels of lone parenthood. Attitudes towards remarriage and cohabitation are negative, while divorce and lone parenthood are more acceptable, and very low importance is attributed to children. Female economic activity rates are among the lowest in the Union for women with children. There is little support for mothers staying at home to look after children, and the rating for children as an obstacle to women's employment is close to the European average.

Whereas similar fluctuations may have been recorded in respect of several demographic indicators over the postwar period, and trends can generally be said to be moving in the same overall direction, conferring a distinctive profile on the Union in comparison with other developed countries, intra-European differences make it difficult to identify a single family model characterising the Union as a whole or towards which all member states are converging. In addition, as at the international level, the particular family model that is dominant in any country at a given point in time conceals important internal variations associated with factors such as age, socio-occupational status, ethnicity and geographical origins, which it has not been possible to examine here but which should not be forgotten. The overlapping clusters arrangement may offer a more meaningful representation of European families from a socio-demographic perspective, while also highlighting internal differentiation between member states which would seem to provide grounds for refuting, or at least modifying, both the diffusion and convergence theses.

## Diverging national family policy-making contexts

Much attention has been paid throughout this book to exploring the socio-cultural factors shaping institutional processes. The attempts of policy makers to influence demographic trends and family structures have been examined in some detail, and reference has been made to the broader social policy context and to the family impact of policies implemented in other areas. While the Council of Ministers considered that action at European level was justified in so far as EU member states were said to be facing the same problems and might therefore be able to identify shared objectives, the analysis in the previous section would seem to suggest that the problems being tackled at national level are not so similar as might have been supposed and that the issues national governments are facing may not be responsive to the same policy solutions. The 1992 Council Recommendation on the convergence of social protection objectives and policies mentioned only three aims with respect to families where agreement had been reached over the need for action by member states: the development of benefits for families with the greatest child-related costs or the most disadvantaged families; the integration of persons wanting to enter the labour market after raising children; and the removal of obstacles to employment for parents through measures to reconcile family and professional responsibilities (92/442/EEC, *OJEC* L 245, 26.8.92, p. 52). The 1989 Communication from the Commission on family policies (COM(89) 363 final of 8 August 1989) was more specific in defining the categories of families who might need support as single-parent and large families. Reference was also made to the impact of other Community policies on the family, and particularly on child protection. Recognising that diversity is rooted in national cultures, the Council recommended, however, that members states should be left to determine how their social protection schemes are funded and organised, in the expectation that, by setting common objectives, national systems will ultimately converge.

Analysis of administrative structures, objectives, instruments and outputs across member states in preceding chapters has highlighted a plurality of approaches to family policy making. Even when demographic trends may appear to be resulting in similar patterns of family and household change (smaller family and household size, non-institutionalised family forms, rising levels of lone parenthood and larger proportions of reconstituted families), the extent to which these family forms are perceived by both the population at large and by policy makers as problematic, and the degree to which state intervention is considered necessary or legitimate vary from one member state to another. Rather than providing enduring solutions to a common set of problems, approaches to family policy across the Union generally represent a compromise worked out in each national context in the face of competing, and often conflicting, demands.

A number of different parameters have been used in this book to identify patterns of family policy making within the European Union: administrative frameworks, the visibility of government policy, the instruments used for implementing policy, outcomes in terms of resources and behaviour, and the family impact of social policies.

The analysis carried out in the course of this book has pointed to a range of issues that are central to family policy, or what have been described as policies with a family impact: the extent to which state intervention in family affairs is considered legitimate; whether family policy is perceived as a discrete and autonomous area of social policy; the consistency or otherwise of the aims and objectives of family policy at national level and whether they command a consensus; the extent to which the state exercises control over families.

An attempt is made in this section to answer these questions by drawing together the material on the national patterns examined in previous chapters. The diffusion and convergence theses are tested further by examining different policy-making contexts and national responses. Again, overlapping clusters of countries can be identified according to criteria such as the relative acceptability and coherence of family policy as a concept and the extent to which family responsibilities have been socialised.

## The legitimacy of family policy

State intervention in family life has been accepted to a different extent from one country to another. It is seen in the Nordic countries as an everyday occurrence, though it is not necessarily identified with family policy. France is frequently quoted as a country where family policy has acquired a particularly high degree of legitimacy (Tabah and Maugué, 1989, p. 57; Schultheis, 1991, p. 17; Commaille, 1994a, pp. 126–36). The principle of state intervention in family affairs has also been widely accepted in Belgium, Germany and Luxembourg.

At the other extreme, in some parts of the Union, the family is seen as a private domain with which the state should not interfere. The United Kingdom is often cited as one of the countries where the state has been most reluctant to intervene, unless family members are at risk (Tabah and Maugué, 1989, p. 58; Department of Health, 1989). In Greece, Ireland, Italy, Portugal and Spain, the state is committed in the national constitution to protecting the family. In Ireland, this commitment has been interpreted as meaning that the family should be protected against outside intrusion (Kiely and Richardson, 1994), and in Italy and Spain, where state intervention was discredited by Fascist regimes, central government action is only considered justified if other 'private' solutions are unsuccessful (Sgritta and Zanatta, 1994; Valiente, 1995).

The concept of legitimacy can be examined from another angle: the state may also intervene to establish the legitimacy of a family unit, for example by setting the legal age for marriage and the conditions under which divorce and abortion can take place. In Belgium, Germany, Luxembourg and the Netherlands, and also in the south European countries, the state has recognised the married couple and children born within marriage as the legitimate family unit but has been slow to acknowledge non-marital family forms.

In the Nordic states, in France and the United Kingdom, the legal framework governing the family has been liberalised to legitimate new family forms, including consensual unions and children born out of wedlock. The rights of children and of women, and also of fathers (custody after divorce), have progressively been written into legal codes, as well as the responsibilities of parents towards their offspring (paternity and maintenance). While endorsing the loosening of the family ties institutionalised by marriage, the state has, however, intervened to determine the rights and obligations of biologically related family members.

## *The coherence of family policy*

In countries where state intervention in family life has a high degree of legitimacy, family policy has often developed as a discrete area of social policy, with its own designated administrative structures and sources of funding (see Chapter 3). Again, France can be identified as one of the member states which has probably gone furthest towards creating an autonomous area of policy, in so far as any policy domain can operate in isolation. Germany and Luxembourg have also given a high profile to family affairs at governmental level and, like France, have a strong tradition of family associations. In recognition of the importance of the family impact of policies implemented in other areas, several countries have established interministerial committees to monitor the effects of a range of social policies on families. While Ireland, the Netherlands and the United Kingdom have consistently avoided promoting family policy as such, Italy and Spain, in particular, have moved from a high to a low profile position.

The method of funding family policy in terms of cash benefits reflects the nature of each country's social protection system rather than the institutional importance attributed to family matters. Benefits may be funded from taxation, as in the Nordic states, Ireland and the United Kingdom. In insurance-based social security systems, they may be funded entirely from contributions, as in Belgium, Greece, Italy, Portugal and Spain, or they may be tax financed or funded from public means as in Germany and the Netherlands. Austria and Luxembourg have a mixed funding arrangement, and France has moved from funding solely by employers' contributions to a mixed system, largely in recognition of the fact that employers could no longer be expected to have sole responsibility for this area of welfare. Although the link with earnings is generally clear in the case of maternity benefits, it is less so for family allowances/child benefit, which may only be earnings related in the sense that, in some countries, they are paid solely to low-income families.

The family dimension of taxation is not confined to the funding of child benefit (see Chapter 3). Tax law may also impact on families in other ways. Its effect is most visible in countries where account is taken of family members, as with the *quotient familial* in France and Luxembourg, and to some extent in Belgium where the household is the unit of assessment. Childcare costs are taken into account in Belgium, France, Greece and Spain, whereas Denmark, Ireland, the Netherlands and the United Kingdom do not grant tax relief for children and, increasingly, the family link has been broken with the shift towards individual taxation.

National benefits systems have also been developing in line with the individualisation of rights, as women have gained their own entitlements through employment or recognition of time spent raising children or caring for older people. Paradoxically, the shift towards greater targeting of benefits on low-income groups has, at the same time, led to more attention being devoted to the family unit, since additional payments may be made according to family size, and the income of other family members may affect eligibility to social assistance (Luckhaus, 1994)

Another trend in the state–family relationship is that most countries have been devolving responsibility for family affairs from central to local or regional government, resulting in regional variations and confusion between family measures and means-tested schemes. In the Nordic countries, local government has almost complete discretion, and in Austria and Germany the *Länder* have extensive powers in the organisation of services. Where, as in the south European countries, measures target low-income families, at the local level family policy may merge with social assistance, and its coherence may thereby be undermined.

## The socialisation of families

In most EU member states, the objectives of family policy and of policies that have an impact on families are decided at national level. Historically, family policy was primarily concerned with achieving greater social justice by redistributing resources horizontally from people without to those with children. In principle, countries which operate social protection systems providing universal flat-rate benefits, as in the Nordic states, or which make generous tax concessions to families, as in Belgium, France and Luxembourg, are likely to be more successful in redistributing resources horizontally (see Chapter 9).

For some commentators (for example Brin, 1991, p. 144), the term 'family policy' should be reserved for measures that redistribute resources horizontally. Vertical redistribution, by transferring resources from wealthier to poorer families, should more properly be described as policy to combat social exclusion. In this sense, it can be said that Ireland, Spain and the United

Kingdom, which concentrate on low-income or problem families, are not pursuing family policies. Analysis suggests that France, Belgium and Luxembourg may be redistributing more resources both horizontally and vertically than other member states, whereas the United Kingdom, by concentrating on less privileged groups, may be more effective in achieving vertical redistribution (Bradshaw *et al.*, 1993; Neubauer *et al.*, 1993).

Family policies may also be expected, and intended, to affect behaviour. Many analysts have attempted to assess the effect of policies on family size and on women's working patterns. The findings are inconclusive (see Chapter 9). The effect on family size of increasing the level of benefits (unless they are brought up to a very high level), if discernible, is almost negligible (Ekert-Jaffé, 1986; Grignon and Villac, 1993), calling into question the efforts made in France, in particular, to link family policy with population policy. The arguments in support of the claims that the provision of childcare encourages more women to go out to work and that women working outside the home have fewer children are more persuasive but would seem to be refuted by the Swedish example (Hoem, 1993). The disincentive effect of benefits on work has been extensively studied, particularly in the case of single mothers (Marsh and McKay, 1993; Messu, 1994). Comparative analysis of France and the United Kingdom suggests that by treating lone parenthood simply as another category of families within family policy requiring additional support, single mothers in France have not been stigmatised or discouraged from working to the same extent as in the United Kingdom where they are classified as a social assistance benefit category. By the early 1990s, the situation of many lone mothers in France was deteriorating, however, and they were being forced to resort to the *revenu minimum d'insertion* as they were unable to find employment and were no longer entitled to lone-parent benefit (Martin, 1995, p. 59).

In judging the impact of family policies, a useful criterion is whether policy contributes to creating a family-friendly environment in which couples want to raise children. The 1993 Eurobarometer survey found the factors that were most influential in determining the number of children couples wanted were housing, the economic situation and unemployment, the cost of bringing up children, worktime flexibility, the availability of good quality childcare and parental leave, in that order (Malpas and Lambert, 1993, table 6.5). Neither family benefits nor tax relief had much importance, suggesting that it may not be the direct and visible family-labelled policies which are most effective in persuading couples to have children, but rather the wider social and economic environment, as evidenced by the situation in Sweden (Hoem, 1993).

To some extent, perceptions of the factors affecting family size relate to the prevalence of specific conditions in the countries concerned. In the same survey, family stability was considered particularly important in Denmark, France and the United Kingdom, where extramarital births and consensual unions are most prevalent. High scores were recorded for this factor in Ireland and Italy, where family structures are also being called into question, as indicated by the debate over abortion and divorce in Ireland and by the steep fall in fertility rates in Italy. Housing was a particular concern in Denmark, Germany, Spain and the United Kingdom, which represent quite different housing situations (Bradshaw *et al.*, 1993). Respondents in Spain, Greece, Italy and France were most concerned about the economic situation and unemployment, understandably so since they were the countries with relatively high levels of unemployment in the mid-1990s; Spain was well above the European average (see Figure 5.5).

The impact of state intervention has also been assessed in terms of the extent to which families have been relieved of certain responsibilities. In the 1970s, the concept of 'familism' was used to indicate the degree of commitment to the idea of the family, the centrality or otherwise of the family in the lives of social actors, the ideal structure, scope and forms of the family held by members of a society (for example Morgan, 1975, p. 8). Reference was made in the 1990s to the concept of 'de-familisation' to portray the socialisation of what were previously considered as family responsibilities. According to Eithne McLaughlin and Caroline Glendinning (1994, p. 65), 'de-familisation is about the terms and conditions under which people engage in families, and the extent to which they can uphold an acceptable standard of living independently of (patriarchal) "family" participation'. It has been argued that de-familisation may have been taken further in social democratic states than in conservative corporatist or liberal regimes (Taylor-Gooby, 1991b, p. 97). The examples quoted in this and previous chapters would seem to lend some support to these arguments: the Nordic countries are distinguished from most other member states by the extent to which family care tasks have been taken over by the state, but countries that support state intervention in family matters are also characterised by the 'de-privatisation' or de-familisation of families, as in France or Luxembourg.

## Towards European integration of families and family policies?

The limitations of the diffusion and convergence theses would seem to apply to both family patterns and family policy models, at least in the last decade of the twentieth century. Even if, at the objective level, EU member states appear to be facing many of the same problems in the area of family affairs, issues are not conceptualised in the same way. The single mother would be seen as a social outcast in Greece, whereas the frail parent would be supported by the family and the wider social network. In Sweden, the state would automatically provide support in both cases. The child with a working mother in Portugal would be cared for by the local community, whereas the state would make available public childcare facilities in France, and families would be left to make their own arrangements in the United Kingdom, unless children were considered to be at risk. Parental leave would remove the mother from the workforce in Germany, whereas in France it would serve as a temporary break from employment, or an extended maternity leave, and in Sweden it would be shared with the father as part of the equality strategy. Part-time work would be seen by most women as a convenient means of combining employment and family life in Denmark, the Netherlands and the United Kingdom, but as an option to be avoided by many women in France because of its negative impact on career prospects.

European legislation introducing measures such as parental leave and the provision of childcare, or regulating working conditions, would seem to be based on the assumption that the same instrument can be applied to produce the same effect in what may be very different policy environments. It is significant that many of the measures that are most commonly considered as belonging to family policy in the strict sense, particularly family allowances, or child benefit, are not found to be very effective in compensating families for the additional load incurred, especially when universal and paid at a fixed rate; nor are they cited as the most important factors taken into account by couples in decisions about family building.

The evidence from EU member states would seem to suggest that the postwar baby boom across Europe may be explained by economic growth and the climate of optimism associated with full employment, rising standards of living, social security and peace, rather than by family policies, and more especially the pronatalist ideology. The decline in family size made possible by the availability of effective contraception took place at a time when the mood of optimism was fading, women were increasingly entering employment both because of female emancipation and for economic reasons, unemployment was growing in the wake of the oil crises, and governments were looking for ways of reducing public spending.

Over the postwar period, family policy, as practised in most member states, would not appear to have been a major factor either in redistributing resources more equitably or in bringing about significant changes in behaviour. Nor can it be identified as an important force encouraging convergence of family building patterns and family structures across the Union. The information analysed in this book suggests rather that a variety of models and trends can be distinguished and that they are determined largely by the complex mix of socio-economic, political and cultural traditions peculiar to each member state. This does not mean that countries cannot learn from one another's experience, but any attempt at policy transfer needs to take account of the particular environments within which policies originate and the conditions under which they are to be implemented. Rather than looking for evidence of convergence or divergence, comparative analysis is likely to make a greater contribution to the understanding of national systems if it concentrates on trying to unravel the cultural embeddedness of different family forms and of the institutions involved in the policy-making process.

# Bibliography

Alberdi, I. (1979) *Historia y sociología del divorcio en España* (Madrid: Centro de Investigaciones Sociológicas).

Alberdi, I. (ed.) (1994) 'Informe sobre la situación de la familia en España'. Unpublished report to the Ministerio de Asuntos Sociales, Madrid.

Amaro, F. (1994a) 'Family Policy Based on a Network of Family and Infrastructures', in M. Teirlinck (co-ordinator), 'The European Union and the Family', *Social Europe*, 1/94, pp. 87–9.

Amaro, F. (1994b) 'Portugal: Improvement of the Quality of Family Life', in W. Dumon (ed.), *Changing Family Policies in the Member States of the European Union* (Brussels: Commission of the European Communities, DG V/European Observatory on National Family Policies), pp. 255–70.

Anderson, M. (ed.) (1971) *Sociology of the Family. Selected Readings* (Harmondsworth, Penguin).

Ariès, P. (1948) *Histoire des populations françaises et de leurs attitudes devant la vie depuis le XVIIIᵉ siècle*, 1st edn (Paris: Le Seuil).

Assier-Andrieu, L. and Commaille, J. (eds) (1995) *Politique des lois en Europe: la filiation comme modèle de comparaison* (Paris: LGDJ, Collection Droit et Société).

Attias-Donfut, C. (ed.) (1995) *Les solidarités entre générations: vieillesse, familles, État* (Paris: Nathan).

Bak, M. (1989) 'Introduction', in K. Boh, M. Bak, C. Clason, M. Pankratova, J. Qvortrup, G.B. Sgritta and K. Waerness (eds), *Changing Patterns of European Family Life: a Comparative Analysis of 14 European Countries* (London and New York: Routledge), pp. 1–13.

Baldwin, S. (1991) 'Statistiques communautaires sur la population et les ménages: harmonisation et standardisation', in 'Actes du colloque: "Beyond National Statistics: Household and Family Patterns in Comparative Perspective"', *INSÉÉ Méthodes*, no. 8, February, pp. 111–16.

Barbier, J-C. (1994) 'Administrative Categories and Social Protection for Families in Europe', *Cross-National Research Papers*, vol. 4, no. 1, pp. 48–57.

Barbier, J-C. (1995) 'Public Policies with a Family Dimension in the European Union: An Analytical Framework for Comparison and Evaluation', *Cross-National Research Papers*, vol. 4, no. 3, pp. 15–32.

Barker, D.L. and Allen, S. (eds) (1976) *Dependence and Exploitation in Work and Marriage* (London/New York: Longman).

Barrère-Maurisson, M-A. (1992) *La division familiale du travail: la vie en double* (Paris: PUF).

Barrère-Maurisson, M-A., Daune-Richard, A-M. and Letablier, M-T. (1989) 'Le travail à temps partiel plus développé au Royaume-Uni qu'en France', *Économie et statistique*, no. 220, pp. 47–56.

Barrère-Maurisson, M-A. and Marchand, O. (1990) 'Structures familiales et marchés du travail dans les pays développés. Une nette opposition entre le Nord et le Sud', *Économie et statistique*, no. 235, pp. 19–30.

Becker, G. (1986) 'The Economic Approach to Human Behaviour', in J. Elster (ed.), *Rational Choice* (Oxford: Blackwell), pp. 108–22.

Beechey, V. (1979) 'On Patriarchy', *Feminist Review*, no. 3, pp. 66–82.

Beechey, V. and Perkins, T. (1987) *A Matter of Hours: Women, Part-Time Work and the Labour Market* (Cambridge: Polity Press).

Bengtson, B. (1988) 'New Legislation in Swedish Family Law. Modern Legislation for Modern People', *Current Sweden*, no. 366.

Berthod-Wurmser, M. (ed.) (1994) *La santé en Europe* (Paris: La Documentation Française).

Besson, J-L. and Comte, M. (1994) 'La notion de chômage en Europe: une étude méthodologique', *Revue d'économie politique*, vol. 104, no. 4, pp. 540–70.

Bimbi, F. (1993) 'Gender, "Gift Relationship" and Welfare State Cultures in Italy', in J. Lewis (ed.), *Women and Social Policies: Work, Family and the State* (Aldershot/Vermont: Edward Elgar), pp. 138–69.

Björnberg, U. (ed.) (1992) *European Parents in the 1990s: Contradictions and Comparisons* (New Brunswick/London: Transaction Publishers).

Björnberg, U. (1994) 'Reconciling Family and Employment in Sweden', *Cross-National Research Papers*, vol. 4, no. 2, pp. 59–67.

Blossfeld, H-P. (1994) *Family Cycle and Growth in Women's Part-time Employment in Western European Countries* (Brussels: European Commission, Directorate General V), V/699/94.

Boissières, C. (1993a) 'Les familles et le système d'imposition français', *Recherches et prévisions*, no. 34, pp. 31–7.

Boissières, C. (1993b) 'Les prestations fiscales européennes: des principes différents', *Recherches et prévisions*, no. 34, pp. 39–45.

Boissières, C. (1994) 'La protection sociale européenne. Approche macro-économique', *CAF statistiques: prestations familiales – année 93* (Paris: CNAF), pp. 1 – 169–82.

Bonke, J. (1993) 'The Distribution of Time and Money in the Family', in S. Carlsen and J.E. Larsen (eds), *The Equality Dilemma: Reconciling Working Life and Family Life, Viewed in an*

*Equality Perspective. The Danish Example* (Copenhagen: Danish Equal Status Council), pp. 131–42.

Borchorst, A. (1993) 'Working Lives and Family Lives in Western Europe', in S. Carlsen and J.E. Larsen (eds), *The Equality Dilemma: Reconciling Working Life and Family Life, Viewed in an Equality Perspective. The Danish Example* (Copenhagen: Danish Equal Status Council), pp. 167–80.

Bradshaw, J., Ditch, J., Holmes, H. and Whiteford, P. (1993) *Support for Children: a Comparison of Arrangements in Fifteen Countries*, Department of Social Security Research Report, no. 21 (London: HMSO).

Bradshaw, J., Ditch, J., Holmes, H., Whiteford, P. and Ray, J-C. (1994) 'Une comparaison internationale des aides aux familles', *Recherches et prévisions*, no. 37, pp. 11–26.

Brannen, J. and O'Brien, M. (eds) (1995) *Childhood and Parenthood, Proceedings of ISA Committee for Family Research Conference on Children and Families, 1994* (London: Institute of Education).

Brannen, J. and Wilson, G. (eds) (1987) *Give and Take in Families: Studies in Resource Distribution* (London: Allen & Unwin).

Brannen, J., Mészáros, G., Moss, P. and Poland, G. (1994) *Employment and Family Life: a Review of Research in the UK (1980–1994)*, Employment Department Research Series, no. 41 (London: University of London, Institute of Education).

Bridgwood, A. and Savage, D. (1993) *General Household Survey 1991*, vol. 22 (London: HMSO).

Brin, H. (1991) '2e rapport présenté au nom du Conseil Économique et Social', in Conseil Économique et Social, 'La politique familiale française', *Journal officiel de la République française*, séances des 24 et 25 septembre, pp. 33–161.

Burgoyne, J. and Clark, D. (1982) 'Reconstituted Families', in R.N. Rapoport, M.P. Fogarty and R. Rapoport (eds), *Families in Britain* (Henley-on-Thames: Routledge & Kegan Paul), pp. 286–302.

Burke, H. (1991) 'Changing Demography, Changing Needs and Unprotected Families', in G. Kiely and V. Richardson (eds), *Family Policy: European Perspectives* (Dublin: Family Studies Centre), pp. 31–8.

Calot, G. (1980) 'Niveau de vie et nombre d'enfants. Un bilan de la législation familiale et fiscale française de 1978', *Population*, vol. 35, no. 1, pp. 9–56.

Carlsen, S. and Larsen, J.E. (eds) (1993) *The Equality Dilemma: Reconciling Working Life and Family Life, Viewed in an Equality Perspective. The Danish Example* (Copenhagen: Danish Equal Status Council).

Central Statistical Office (1995) *Social Trends 25* (London: HMSO).

Chamberlayne, P. (1993) 'Women and the State: Changes in Roles and Rights in France, West Germany, Italy and Britain, 1970–1990', in J. Lewis (ed.), *Women and Social Policies: Work, Family and the State* (Aldershot/Vermont: Edward Elgar), pp. 170–93.

Chauvière, M. (1991) 'Les mouvements familiaux', in F. de Singly (ed.), *La famille: l'état des savoirs* (Paris: Éditions La Découverte), pp. 288–93.

Chester, R. (1994) 'Flying without Instruments or Flight Plans: Family Policy in the United Kingdom', in W. Dumon (ed.), *Changing Family Policies in the Member States of the European Union* (Brussels: Commission of the European Communities, DG V/European Observatory on National Family Policies), pp. 271–301.

Christensen, H.T. (ed.) (1964) *Handbook of Marriage and the Family* (Chicago: Rand McNally & Company).

Collectif (1984) *Le sexe du travail: structures familiales et système productif* (Grenoble: Presses Universitaires de Grenoble).

Collins, H. (1992) *The Equal Opportunities Handbook. A Guide to Law and Best Practice in Europe* (Oxford: Blackwell).

Commaille, J. (1993) *Les stratégies des femmes: travail, famille et politique* (Paris: Éditions La Découverte).

Commaille, J. (1994a) 'France: from a Family Policy to Policies towards the Family', in W. Dumon (ed.), *Changing Family Policies in the Member States of the European Union* (Brussels: Commission of the European Communities, DG V/European Observatory on National Family Policies), pp. 123–49.

Commaille, J. (1994b) *L'esprit sociologique des lois* (Paris: PUF).

Commission of the European Communities (1987) 'Community Law and Women', *Women of Europe*, supplement no. 25, X/152/87-EN.

Commission of the European Communities/Directorate-General Employment, Industrial Relations and Social Affairs (1994) *Social Protection in Europe 1993* (Luxembourg: Office for Official Publications of the European Communities).

Commission of the European Communities/Eurydice and Cedefop (1991) *Structures of the Educational and Initial Training Systems in the Member States of the European Community* (Luxembourg: Office for Official Publications of the European Communities).

Cooper, D. (1972) *The Death of the Family* (Harmondsworth: Penguin).

Council of Europe (1990) 'Household Structures in Europe', *Population Studies*, no. 22 (Strasbourg: Council of Europe).

Cuelenaere, B. and Van Doorne-Huiskes, A. (1995) 'National Report: the Netherlands', in J. Millar and A. Warman (eds), *Defining Family Obligations in Europe* (University of Bath: Centre for the Analysis of Social Policy), pp. 249-68.

Dahlström, E. (1989) 'Theories and Ideologies of Family Functions, Gender Relations and Human Reproduction', in K. Boh, M. Bak, C. Clason, M. Pankratova, J. Qvortrup, G.B. Sgritta and K. Waerness (eds), *Changing Patterns of European Family Life: a Comparative Analysis of 14 European Countries* (London and New York: Routledge), pp. 31–51.

Dale, A. and Glover, J. (1987) 'Women's Work Patterns in the UK, France and the USA', *Social Studies Review*, vol. 3, no. 1, pp. 36–9.

Danish Ministry of Social Affairs (1993) *Report from the Conference: Fathers in Families of Tomorrow, June 17–18, 1993* (Copenhagen: Danish Ministry of Social Affairs).

Daune-Richard, A-M. (1988) 'Gender Relations and Female Labor. A Consideration of Sociological Categories', in J. Jenson, E. Hagen and C. Reddy (eds), *Feminization of the Labor Force: Paradoxes and Promises* (Cambridge and Oxford: Polity Press), pp. 260–75.

Daune-Richard, A-M. (1993) 'Activité et emploi des femmes: des constructions sociétales différentes en France, au Royaume-Uni et en Suède', *Sociétés contemporaines*, no. 4, pp. 125–44.

Daune-Richard, A-M. and Devreux, A-M. (1992) 'Rapports sociaux de sexe et conceptualisation sociologique', *Recherches féministes*, vol. 5, no. 2, pp. 7–30.

Davisse, A. (1983) *Les femmes dans la fonction publique: rapport au Ministre de la Fonction publique et des réformes administratives* (Paris: La Documentation Française).

de Hoog, K., Presvelou, C. and Cuyvers, P. (1993) *Family Arrangements and Policy in the Netherlands* (The Hague: Netherlands Family Council).

Del Re, A. (1993) 'Vers l'Europe: politiques sociales, femmes et État en Italie entre production et reproduction', in A. Gautier and J. Heinen (eds), *Le sexe des politiques sociales* (Paris: Côté-Femmes Éditions), pp. 37–57.

Del Re (1995) 'Social and Family Policies in Italy: Comparisons with France', *Cross-National Research Papers*, vol. 4, no. 3, pp. 68–79.

Delphy, C. (1970) 'L'ennemi principal', *Partisans*, nos. 54–5, July–October, pp. 112–39.

Delphy, C. (1984) *Close to Home: a Materialist Analysis of Women's Oppression* (London: Hutchinson).

Department of Health (1989) *An Introduction to the Children Act 1989* (London: HMSO).

Desplanques, G. (1987) 'Calendrier des familles', *Données sociales 1987* (Paris: INSÉÉ), pp. 477–95.

Desplanques, G. (1993) 'Les familles recomposées en 1990', in M-T. Meulders-Klein and I. Théry (eds), *Les recompositions familiales aujourd'hui* (Paris: Nathan), pp. 81–96.

Desrosières, A. (1984) 'La nouvelle nomenclature des professions et catégories socioprofessionnelles', *Données sociales: édition 1984* (Paris: INSÉÉ), pp. 538–46.

Desrosières, A. (1993) *La politique des grands nombres: histoire de la raison statistique* (Paris: Éditions La Découverte).

Desrosières, A. (1996) 'Statistical Traditions: an Obstacle to International Comparisons', in L. Hantrais and S. Mangen (eds), *Cross-National Research Methods in the Social Sciences* (London: Pinter), pp. 17–27.

Dex, S. (1984) *Women's Work Histories: an Analysis of the Women and Employment Survey*, Research Paper no. 46 (London: Department of Employment).

Dex, S. and Shaw, L.B. (1986) *British and American Women at Work: Do Equal Opportunities Policies Matter?* (London: Macmillan).

Dex, S., Walters, P. and Alden, D.M. (1993) *French and British Mothers at Work* (Houndmills and London: Macmillan).

Dienel, C. (1992) Weniger Geburten: die Diskussion über Empfängnisverhütung und Bevölkerungspolitik in Deutschland und Frankreich bis zum Ersten Weltkrieg, Inaugural-Dissertation zur Erlangung des Doktorgrades der Philosophie an der Ludwig-Maximilians-Universität zu Münich.

Dienel, C. (1995) 'The Institutionalisation and Effectiveness of Family Policy in Europe', *Cross-National Research Papers*, vol. 4, no. 3, pp. 33–42.

Donzelot, J. (1979) *The Policing of Families* (London: Hutchinson).

Dumon, W. (ed.) (1991) *National Family Policies in EC-Countries in 1990* (Brussels: Commission of the European Communities/ European Observatory on National Family Policies), V/2293/91-EN.

Dumon, W. (ed.) (1993) *National Family Policies in EC-Countries in 1991*, vol. 2 (Brussels: Commission of the European Communities/ European Observatory on National Family Policies).

Dumon, W. (1994) 'National Family Policies in the Member States: Current Trends and Developments', in W. Dumon (ed.), *Changing Family Policies in the Member States of the European Union* (Brussels: Commission of the European Communities, DG V/European Observatory on National Family Policies), pp. 303–26.

Durán, M.A. (1986) *La jornada interminable* (Barcelona: Icaria).

Durán, M.A. (ed.) (1988) *De puertas adentro* (Madrid: Instituto de la Mujer).

Edgell, S. (1980) *Middle Class Couples: a Study of Segregation, Domination and Inequality in Marriage* (London: Allen & Unwin).

Eggerickx, T. and Bégeot, F. (1993) 'Les recensements en Europe dans les années 1990. De la diversité des pratiques nationales à la comparabilité internationale des résultats', *Population*, vol. 48, no. 6, pp. 1705–32.

Ekert-Jaffé, O. (1986) 'Effets et limites des aides financières aux familles: une expérience et un modèle', *Population*, vol. 41, no. 2, pp. 327–48.

Esping-Andersen, G. (1990) *The Three Worlds of Welfare Capitalism* (Cambridge: Polity Press).

European Commission (1994) *Employment in Europe 1994* (Luxembourg: Office for Official Publications of the European Communities), COM(94) 381.

European Commission (1995) *The Demographic Situation in the European Union. 1994 Report* (Luxembourg: Office for Official Publications of the European Communities), COM (94) 595.

European Commission Network on Childcare and other Measures to Reconcile Employment and Family Responsibilities (1994) *Leave Arrangements for Workers with Children. A Review of Leave Arrangements in the Member States of the European Union and Austria, Finland, Norway and Sweden* (Brussels: European Commission Directorate-General V), V/773/94-EN.

Eurostat (1985) *Labour Force Survey. Results 1983* (Luxembourg: Office for Official Publications of the European Communities).

Eurostat (1988) *Labour Force Survey. Methods and Definitions* (Luxembourg: Office for Official Publications of the European Communities).

Eurostat (1992) *Labour Force Survey 1983–89* (Luxembourg: Office for Official Publications of the European Communities).

Eurostat (1994a) *Definitions and Methods of Collecting Demographic Statistics in the European Community Countries* (Luxembourg: Office for Official Publications of the European Communities).

Eurostat (1994b) 'Social Protection in the European Union', *Rapid Reports. Population and Social Conditions*, no. 5.

Eurostat (1995a) *Demographic Statistics 1995* (Luxembourg: Office for Official Publications of the European Communities).

Eurostat (1995b) 'Households and Families in the European Economic Area', *Statistics in Focus. Population and Social Conditions*, no. 5.

Eurostat (1995c) 'Labour Force Survey. Principal Results 1994', *Statistics in Focus. Population and Social Conditions*, no. 6.

Eurostat (1995d) *Labour Force Survey. Results 1993* (Luxembourg: Office for Official Publications of the European Communities).

Eurostat (1995e) 'The Population of the European Union on 1 January 1995', *Statistics in Focus. Population and Social Conditions*, no. 8.

Eurostat (1995f) *Women and Men in the European Union: a Statistical Portrait* (Luxembourg: Office for Official Publications of the European Communities).

Fagnani, J. (1992) 'Les Françaises font-elles des prouesses? Fécondité, travail professionnel et politiques familiales en France et en Allemagne de l'Ouest', *Recherches et prévisions*, no. 28, pp. 23–38.

Fagnani, J. (1994) 'A Comparison of Family Policies for Working Mothers in France and West Germany', *Cross-National Research Papers*, vol. 3, no. 3, pp. 26–34.

Family Policy Studies Centre (1991) *Supporting our Children: the Family Impact of Child Maintenance*, Briefing Paper (London: Family Policy Studies Centre).

Fernández Cordón, J.A. (1994) 'Spain: Adjusting to the New Family Structures', in W. Dumon (ed.), *Changing Family Policies in the Member States of the European Union* (Brussels: Commission of the European Communities, DG V/European Observatory on National Family Policies), pp. 105–22.

Finch, J. (1983) *Married to the Job: Wives' Incorporation in Men's Work* (London: Allen & Unwin).

Flandrin, J-L. (1976) *Familles: parenté, maison, sexualité dans l'ancienne société*, 1st edn (Paris: Éditions du Seuil).

Flaquer, L. and Soler, J. (1990) *Permanencia y cambio en la familia española* (Madrid: Centro de Investigaciones Sociológicas).

Freund, V. (1991) *Vie professionnelle, vie familiale, activité féminine. Inventaire des recherches françaises (1980–1990)* (Paris: ERISFER/CNAF).

Frotiée, B. (1994) 'A French Perspective on Family and Employment in Spain', *Cross-National Research Papers*, vol. 4, no. 2, pp. 30–40.

Gastines, B. de and Sylvestre, J-M. (1992) *Le guide SVP de l'Europe 1993* (Paris: Éditions SVP).

Gershuny, J. and Jones, S. (1987) 'The Changing Work/Leisure Balance in Britain: 1961–1984', in J. Horne, D. Jary and A. Tomlinson (eds), 'Sport, Leisure and Social Relations', *Sociological Review Monograph*, no. 33 (London: Routledge & Kegan Paul), pp. 9–50.

Giroud, F. (1976) *Cent mesures pour les femmes* (Paris: La Documentation Française).

Gittins, D. (1993) *The Family in Question: Changing Households and Familiar Ideologies*, 2nd edn (Houndmills and London: Macmillan).

Glendinning, C. and McLaughlin, E. (1993) *Paying for Care: Lessons from Europe* (London: HMSO).

Glover, J. (1994) 'Concepts of Employment and Unemployment in Labour Force Data', *Cross-National Research Papers*, vol. 4, no. 2, pp. 10–18.

Goldthorpe, J.H., Lockwood, D., Bechhofer, F. and Platt, J. (1968) *The Affluent Worker: Industrial Attitudes and Behaviour* (Cambridge: Cambridge University Press).

GRACE (1991) *Women's Studies in the European Community*, GRACE Project Report Phase 1 (Brussels: GRIF/Commission of the European Communities, DG V, Equal Opportunities Unit)).

GRACE (1992) *Women's Studies in the European Community*, GRACE Project Report Phase 2 (Brussels: GRIF/Commission of the European Communities, DG V, Equal Opportunities Unit).

Grieco, M.S. (1982) 'Family Structure and Industrial Employment: the Role of Information and Migration', *Journal of Marriage and the Family*, vol. 44, no. 3, pp. 701–7.

Grignon, M. (1994) 'Conceptualising French Family Policy: the Social Actors', *Cross-National Research Papers*, vol. 3, no. 1, pp. 49–58.

Grignon, M. and Villac, M. (1993) 'Le problème du coût de l'enfant', *Recherches et prévisions*, no. 32, pp. 1–7.

Gross, I., Wiedenhofer, B. and Vötsch, W. (1994) *The Economic and Social Role of Women in Austria: Statistical Analysis* (Vienna: Austrian Federal Ministry of Labour and Social Affairs).

Grossin, W. (1992) *La création de l'inspection du travail: la condition ouvrière d'après les débats parlementaires de 1881 à 1892* (Paris: L'Harmattan).

Guillemot, D. (1993) 'Marché du travail: embellie jusqu'en 1990, rechute au-delà, *La société française. Données sociales 1993* (Paris: INSÉÉ), pp. 130–7.

Haicault, M. (1984) 'La gestion ordinaire de la vie en deux', *Sociologie du travail*, special issue, no. 3, 'Travail des femmes et famille', pp. 267–77.

Hantrais, L. (1990) *Managing Professional and Family Life: a Comparative Study of British and French Women* (Aldershot/Vermont: Dartmouth).

Hantrais, L. (1992) 'La fécondité en France et au Royaume-Uni: les effets possibles de la politique familiale', *Population*, vol. 47, no. 4, pp. 987–1016.

Hantrais, L. (1993) 'The Gender of Time in Professional Occupations', *Time and Society*, vol. 2, no. 2, pp. 139–57.

Hantrais, L. (1995) *Social Policy in the European Union* (Houndmills and London: Macmillan).

Hantrais, L. and Walters, P. (1994) 'Making it in and Making out: Women in Professional Occupations in Britain and France', *Gender, Work and Organization*, vol. 1, no. 1, pp. 23–32.

Harris, C.C. (1969) *The Family: an Introduction* (London: Allen & Unwin).

Haskey, J. (1993) 'Trends in the Numbers of One-Parent Families in Great Britain', *Population Trends*, no. 71, pp. 26–33.

Haskey, J. and Kiernan, K. (1989) 'Cohabitation in Great Britain – Characteristics and Estimated Numbers of Cohabiting Partners', *Population Trends*, no. 58, pp. 23–32.

Haut Conseil de la Population et de la Famille (1987) *Vie professionnelle et vie familiale, de nouveaux équilibres à construire* (Paris: La Documentation Française).

Herpin, N. (1990) 'La famille à l'épreuve du chômage', *Économie et statistique*, no. 235, pp. 31–42.

Hoem, B. (1993) 'The Compatibility of Employment and Childbearing in Contemporary Sweden, *Acta Sociologica*, vol. 36, no. 2, pp. 101–20.

Iglesias de Ussel, J. (1988) 'La situación de la familia en España y los nuevos modelos familiaris', in J. Iglesias de Ussel (ed.), *Las familias monoparentales*, Seminario hispano frances celebrado en Madrid diciembre 1987 (Madrid: Ministerio de Asuntos Sociales, Instituto de la Mujer), pp. 23–40.

Iglesias de Ussel, J. and Flaquer, L. (1993) 'Familia y análisis sociológico: el caso de España', *Revista de investigaciones sociológicas*, no. 61, pp. 57–75.

ILO (1968) *International Standard Classification of Occupations* (ISCO), 2nd edn (Geneva: ILO).

Izquierdo, J., Del Río, O. and Rodríguez, A. (1988) *Las desigualdades de las mujeres en el uso del tiempo* (Madrid: Instituto de la Mujer).

Jani-Le Bris, H. (1993) *Family Care of Dependent Older People in the European Community* (Shankill: European Foundation for the Improvement of Living and Working Conditions), EF/93/27/EN.

Johansson, L. and Thorslund, M. (1993) 'Suède: importance et limites des ressources formelles', in F. Lesemann and C. Martin (eds), *Les personnes âgées: dépendance, soins et solidarités familiales. Comparaisons internationales* (Paris: La Documentation Française), pp. 115–34.

Joshi, H. (1990) 'The Cash Opportunity Cost of Childbearing: an Approach to Estimation Using British Data', *Population Studies*, vol. 44, pp. 41–60.

Joshi, H. and Davies, H. (1992) 'Daycare in Europe and Mothers' Forgone Earnings', *International Labour Review*, vol. 132, no. 6, pp. 561–79.

Kamerman, S. (1980) 'Managing Work and Family: a Comparative Policy Overview', in P. Moss and N. Fonda (eds), *Work and the Family* (London: Temple Smith), pp. 87–109.

Kamerman, S.B. and Kahn, A.K. (eds) (1978) *Family Policy: Government and Families in Fourteen Countries* (New York: Columbia University Press).

Kaufmann, J-C. (1994) 'Les ménages d'une personne en Europe', *Population*, vol. 49 nos. 4–5, pp. 935–58.

Kaul, H. (1991) 'Who Cares? Gender Inequality and Care Leave in the Nordic Countries', *Acta Sociologica*, vol. 34, pp. 115–25.

Kempeneers, M. and Lelièvre, E. (1991) 'Employment and Family within the Twelve', *Eurobarometer*, no. 34, V/383/92-EN.

Kiely, G. and Richardson, V. (1994) 'Ireland: Family Policy in a Rapidly Changing Society', in W. Dumon (ed.), *Changing Family Policies in the Member States of the European Union* (Brussels: Commission of the European Communities, DG V/European Observatory on National Family Policies), pp. 151–72.

Kiernan, K.E. and Estaugh, V. (1993) *Cohabitation, Extramarital Childbearing and Social Policy*, Occasional Paper 17 (London: Family Policy Studies Centre).

Kirkham, L. and Loft, A. (1993) 'Gender and the Construction of the Professional Accountant', *Accounting, Organizations and Society*, vol. 18, no. 6, pp. 507–58.

Köcher, R. (1993) 'Lebenszentrum Familie', in Bundesministerium für Familie und Senioren (ed.), *40 Jahre Familienpolitik in der Bundesrepublik Deutschland: Rückblick/Ausblick* (Bonn: Luchterhand), pp. 37–51.

Koch-Nielsen, I. (1987) *New Family Patterns: Divorces in Denmark*, Danish National Institute of Social Research Booklet no. 23 (Copenhagen: Danish National Institute of Social Research).

Labourie-Racapé, A., Letablier, M-T. and Vasseur, A-M. (1977) 'L'activité féminine: enquête sur la discontinuité de la vie professionnelle', *Cahiers du Centre d'Études de l'Emploi*, no. 11 (Paris: PUF).

Land, H. and Parker, R. (1978) 'United Kingdom', in S.B. Kamerman and A.K. Kahn (eds), *Family Policy: Government and Families in Fourteen Countries* (New York: Columbia University Press), pp. 331–66.

Laslett, P. (1977) *Family Life and Illicit Love in Earlier Generations: Essays in Historical Sociology* (Cambridge: Cambridge University Press).

Laslett, P. and Wall, R. (eds) (1972) *Household and Family in Past Time: Comparative Studies in the Size and Structure of the Domestic Group over the Last Three Centuries in England, France, Serbia, Japan and Colonial North America, with further Materials from Western Europe* (Cambridge: Cambridge University Press).

Le Bras, H. (1991) *Marianne et les lapins: l'obsession démographique*, 1st edn (Paris: Olivier Orban).

Lefaucheur, N. (1986) 'How the One-Parent Families Appeared in France', in F. Deven and R.L. Cliquet (eds), *One-Parent Families in Europe: Trends, Experiences, Implications*, Proceedings of the CBGS International Workshop on One-Parent Families, Brussels, October 8–10, 1985, vol. 15 (The Hague/Brussels: NIDI/CBGS Publications), pp. 73–81.

Lefaucheur, N. (1991) 'Les familles dites monoparentales', in F. de Singly (ed.), *La famille: l'état des savoirs* (Paris: Éditions La Découverte), pp. 67–74.

Lefaucheur, N. and Martin, C. (1993) 'Lone Parent Families in France: Situation and Research', in J. Hudson and B. Galaway (eds), *Single Parent Families: Perspectives on Research and Policy* (Toronto: Thompson Educational Publishing), pp. 31–50.

Le Gall, D. and Martin, C. (1990) *Recomposition familiale, usages du droit et production normative* (Paris/Caen: Caisse Nationale des Allocations Familiales/Centre de Recherche sur le Travail Social, Université de Caen).

Leira, A. (1993) 'The "Woman-Friendly" Welfare State?: the Case of Norway and Sweden', in J. Lewis (ed.), *Women and Social Policies: Work, Family and the State* (Aldershot/Vermont: Edward Elgar), pp. 49–71.

Lenoir, R. (1995) 'L'invention de la démographie et la formation de l'État', *Actes de la recherche en sciences sociales*, no. 108, pp. 37–61.

Lesemann, F. and Martin, C. (eds) (1993) *Les personnes âgées: dépendance, soins et solidarités familiales. Comparaisons internationales* (Paris: La Documentation Française).

Letablier, M-T. and Daune-Richard, A-M. (1994) 'Conceptualising Women's Unemployment from a Cross-National Perspective', *Cross-National Research Papers*, vol. 3, no. 4, pp. 48–57.

Lévy, M.L. (1985) 'Regards sur la politique familiale', *Population et sociétés*, no. 194.

Lewis, J. (1992) 'Gender and the Development of Welfare Regimes', *Journal of European Social Policy*, vol. 2, no. 3, 159–73.

Lewis, J. and Åström, G. (1991) 'Equality, Difference and State Welfare: the Case of Labour Market and Family Policies in Sweden', *The Study of Power and Democracy in Sweden*, English Series. Report no. 44, Uppsala.

Lister, R. (1995) 'Dilemmas in Engendering Citizenship', *Economy and Society*, vol. 24, no. 1, pp. 1–40.

Lohkamp-Himmighofen, M. (1993a) 'Ansätze für Förderung der Vereinbarkeit von Familie und Beruf', in E. Neubauer, C. Dienel and M. Lohkamp-Himminghofen (eds), *Zwölf Wege der Familienpolitik in der Europäischen Gemeinschaft. Eigenständige Systeme und vergleichbare Qualitäten? Studie im Auftrag des Bundesministeriums für Familie und Senioren*, vol. 22.1 (Stuttgart/Berlin/Köln: Verlag W. Kohlhammer), pp. 313–67.

Lohkamp-Himmighofen, M. (1993b) 'Deutschland', in E. Neubauer, C. Dienel and M. Lohkamp-Himmighofen (eds), *Zwölf Wege der Familienpolitik in der Europäischen Gemeinschaft. Eigenständige Systeme und vergleichbare Qualitäten? Studie im Auftrag des Bundesministeriums für Familie und Senioren*, vol. 22.2, *Länderberichte* (Stuttgart/Berlin/Köln: Verlag W. Kohlhammer), pp. 81–148.

Luckhaus, L. (1994) 'Individualisation of Social Security Benefits', in C. McCrudden (ed.), *Equality Treatment between Women and Men in Social Security* (London: Butterworths), pp. 147–61.

Mallet, S. (1969) *La nouvelle classe ouvrière* (Paris: Éditions du Seuil).

Malpas, N. and Lambert, P-Y. (1993) 'Europeans and the Family', *Eurobarometer*, no. 39.0, V/72/94-EN.

Marry, C. (1989) 'Femmes ingénieurs: une (ir)résistible ascension?', *Social Science Information sur les sciences sociales*, vol. 28, no. 2, pp. 291–344.

Marsh, A. and McKay, S. (1993) *Families, Work and Benefits* (London: Policy Studies Institute).

Martin, C. (1995) 'Father, Mother and the Welfare State: Family and Social Transfers after Marital Breakdown', *Journal of European Social Policy*, vol. 5, no. 1, pp. 43–63.

Martin, J. and Roberts, C. (1984) *Women and Employment: a Lifetime Perspective*, The Report of the 1980 DE/OPCS Women and Employment Survey (London: HMSO).

Martínez, M. (1992) *Mujer, trabajo y maternidad: problemas y alternativas de las madres que trabajan* (Madrid: Instituto de la Mujer).

McLaughlin, E. and Glendinning, C. (1994) 'Paying for Care in Europe: Is there a Feminist Approach?', *Cross-National Research Papers*, vol. 3, no. 3, pp. 52–69.

Melsted, L. (1988) 'Election Year '88. Swedish Family Policy and the Election this Autumn', *Current Sweden*, no. 361.

Messu, M. (1994) 'Les finalités des prestations familiales', *Revue d'action sanitaire et sociale*, vol. 30, no. 4, pp. 575–94.

Metcalf, H. (1992) 'Hidden Unemployment and the Labour Market', in E. McLaughlin (ed.), *Understanding Unemployment:*

*New Perspectives on Active Labour Market Policies* (London and New York: Routledge), pp. 160–80.

Meulders-Klein, M-T. (1992) 'Vie privée, vie familiale et droits de l'homme', *Revue internationale de droit comparé*, vol. 44, no. 4, pp. 767–94.

Meulders-Klein, M-T. (1993) 'The Status of the Father in European Legislation', in Danish Ministry of Social Affairs (ed.), *Report from the Conference: Fathers in Families of Tomorrow, June 17–18, 1993* (Copenhagen: Danish Ministry of Social Affairs), pp. 107–50.

Meulders-Klein, M-T. and Théry, I. (eds) (1993) *Les recompositions familiales aujourd'hui* (Paris: Nathan).

Meulders-Klein, M-T. and Versailles, P. (1994) 'Family Policies in Belgium: Diversity, Pluralism and Uncertainty', in W. Dumon (ed.), *Changing Family Policies in the Member States of the European Union* (Brussels: Commission of the European Communities, DG V/European Observatory on National Family Policies), pp. 11–34.

Michel, A. (1974) *Activité professionnelle de la femme et vie conjugale* (Paris: CNRS).

Michel, A. (ed.) (1978) *Les femmes dans la société marchande* (Paris: PUF).

Millar, J. (1991) *The Socio-Economic Situation of Solo Women in Europe. Revised Final Report to the European Commission* (Brussels: Commission of the European Communities), V/1368/91-EN.

Millar, J. and Warman, A. (1996) *Family Obligations in Europe: the Family, the State and Social Policy* (York: Joseph Rowntree Foundation).

Millward, N. (1968) 'Family Status and Behaviour at Work', *Sociological Review*, vol. 16, pp. 149–64.

Ministry of Health and Social Affairs (1995) 'Shared Power Responsibility'. Unpublished National Report by the Government of Sweden for the Fourth World Conference on Women in Beijing 1995.

MISSOC (1995) *Social Protection in the Member States of the Community: Situation on July 1st 1994 and Evolution* (Brussels: Commission of the European Communities).

Morgan, D.H.J. (1975) *Social Theory and the Family* (London and Boston: Routledge & Kegan Paul).

Morris, L. (1990) *The Workings of the Household: a US–UK Comparison* (Cambridge: Polity Press).

Moss, P. (ed.) (1990) 'Childcare in the European Communities 1985–1990', *Women of Europe*, supplement no. 31.

Moss, P. (1993) 'Strategies to Promote Fathers' Involvement in the Care and Upbringing of their Children: Placing Leave Arrangements in a Wider Context', in Danish Ministry of Social Affairs (ed.), *Report from the Conference: Fathers in Families of Tomorrow, June 17–18, 1993* (Copenhagen: Danish Ministry of Social Affairs), pp. 210–29.

Moussourou, L.M. (1994) 'Family Policy in Greece: Traditional and Modern Patterns', in W. Dumon (ed.), *Changing Family Policies in the Member States of the European Union* (Brussels: Commission of the European Communities, DG V/European Observatory on National Family Policies), pp. 87–104.

Murdock, G.P. (1949) *Social Structure* (New York: Free Press).

Myrdal, A. and Klein, V. (1956) *Women's Two Roles: Home and Work*, 1st edn (London: Routledge & Kegan Paul).

Nave-Herz, R. and Markefka, M. (eds) (1989) *Handbuch der Familien- und Jugendforschung*, vol. 1, *Familienforschung* (Neuwied and Frankfurt/M: Luchterhand).

Neubauer, E. (1993) 'Familienpolitische Ansätze zum Ausgleich der Aufwendungen für Kinder', in E. Neubauer, C. Dienel and M. Lohkamp-Himmighofen (eds), *Zwölf Wege der Familienpolitik in der Europäischen Gemeinschaft. Eigenständige Systeme und vergleichbare Qualitäten?* Studie im Auftrag des Bundesministeriums für Familie und Senioren, vol. 22.1 (Stuttgart/Berlin/Köln: Verlag W. Kohlhammer), pp. 267–312.

Neubauer, E., Dienel, C. and Lohkamp-Himminghofen, H. (1993) *Zwölf Wege der Familienpolitik in der Europäischen Gemeinschaft. Eigenständige Systeme und vergleichbare Qualitäten?* Studie im Auftrag des Bundesministeriums für Familie und Senioren, vol. 22.1 (Stuttgart/Berlin/Köln: Verlag W. Kohlhammer).

Neyens, M. (1994) 'A Leading Sector in Luxembourg Social Policy: Family Policy, from its Genesis to its Diversity. Its Future Challenges', in W. Dumon (ed.), *Changing Family Policies in the Member States of the European Union* (Brussels: Commission of the European Communities, DG V/European Observatory on National Family Policies), pp. 199–224.

Nicole, C. (1984) 'Les femmes et le travail à temps partiel: tentations et perversions', *Revue française des affaires sociales*, vol. 38, no. 4, pp. 95–109.

Nousiainen, K. (1995) 'Family Law and Parental Patterns of Time Allocation', in B. Arve-Parès (ed.), *Building Family Welfare. Report from a Nordic Seminar on Families, Gender and Welfare Policy* (Stockholm: The Network of Nordic Focal Points for the International Year of the Family 1994), pp. 49–52.

Nunes de Almeida, A., das Dores Guerreiro, M., Torres, A. and Wall, K. (eds) (1992) *Familles et contextes sociaux: les espaces et les temps de la diversité*, Actes du Colloque de Lisbonne, 10–12 avril 1991 (Lisbon, GREF/CIES).

O'Brien, M. (1995) 'Fatherhood and Family Policies in Europe', *Cross-National Research Papers*, vol. 4, no. 3, pp. 48–56.

Oakley, A. (1974) *The Sociology of Housework* (Oxford: Robertson).

OECD (1993) *Education at a Glance: OECD Indicators* (Paris: OECD).

Ostner, I. (1993) 'Slow Motion: Women, Work and the Family in Germany', in J. Lewis (ed.), *Women and Social Policies: Work,*

*Family and the State* (Aldershot/Vermont: Edward Elgar), pp. 92–115.

Pahl, R. (1984) *Divisions of Labour* (Oxford: Basil Blackwell).

Parsons, T. and Bales, R.F. (1956) *Family: Socialization and Interaction Process* (London: Routledge and Kegan Paul).

Pauti, A. (1992) 'La politique familiale en Suède', *Population*, vol. 47, no. 4, pp. 961–85.

Peemans-Poullet, H. (1984) *Partage des responsabilités professionnelles, familiales et sociales* (Luxembourg: Office for Official Publications of the European Communities).

Pitrou, A. (1978) *Vivre sans famille? Les solidarités familiales dans le monde d'aujourd'hui* (Toulouse, Privat).

Pitrou, A. (1992) *Les solidarités familiales* (Toulouse: Privat).

Pitrou, A. (1994) *Les politiques familiales: approches sociologiques* (Paris: Syros).

Pitrou, A. and Gaillard, A-M. (1989) 'Familles de France et de Suède: à la recherche de nouveaux modèles', *Cahiers des sciences humaines*, vol. 25, no. 3, pp. 415–28.

Popay, J., Rimmer, L. and Rossiter, C. (1983) *One-Parent Families: Parents, Children and Public Policy* (London: Study Commission on the Family).

Prioux, F. (1989) 'Fécondité et dimension des familles en Europe occidentale', *Espace, populations, sociétés*, no. 2, pp. 161–76.

Prost, A. (1984) 'L'évolution de la politique familiale en France de 1938 à 1981', *Le mouvement social*, no. 129, pp. 7–28.

Pruzan, V. (1994) 'Family Policy in Denmark: towards Individuation and a Symmetrical Family Structure', in W. Dumon (ed.), *Changing Family Policies in the Member States of the European Union* (Brussels: Commission of the European Communities, DG V/European Observatory on National Family Policies), pp. 35–55.

Ramos, R. (1990) *Cronos dividido: uso del tiempo y desigualdad entre mujeres y hombres en España* (Madrid: Instituto de la Mujer).

Rapoport, R. and Rapoport, R.N. (1971) *Dual Career Families* (Harmonsworth: Penguin).

Rapoport, R.N., Fogarty, M.P. and Rapoport, R. (1982) *Families in Britain* (London: Routledge & Kegan Paul).

Rebérioux, M. (1982) *Les femmes en France dans une société d'inégalités*, Rapport au Ministre des Droits de la femme (Paris: La Documentation Française).

Renaudat, E. (1989/90) 'L'appel de propositions de 1985: une multitude de questions ... des réponses', *Recherches et prévisions*, nos. 18–19, pp. 1–5.

Roll, J. (1991) *What is a Family? Benefit Models and Social Realities* (London: Family Policy Studies Centre).

Roll, J. (1992) *Lone Parent Families in the European Community. The 1992 Report to the European Commission* (London: European Family and Social Policy Unit).

Room, G. (ed.) (1991) *Second Annual Report of the European Community Observatory on National Policies to Combat Social Exclusion* (Brussels: Commission of the European Communities/ European Community Observatory on National Policies to Combat Social Exclusion).

Roussel, L. (1989) *La famille incertaine* (Paris: Éditions Odile Jacob).

Roussel, L. (1992) 'La famille en Europe occidentale: divergences et convergences', *Population*, vol. 47, no. 1, pp. 133–52.

Roy, C. (1990) 'Les emplois du temps dans quelques pays occidentaux', *Données sociales 1990* (Paris: INSÉÉ), pp. 223–5.

Rubery, J. and Fagan, C. (eds) (1992) *Bulletin on Women and Employment in the EC*, no. 1, October.

Rubery, J. and Fagan, C. (1993) 'Occupational Segregation of Women and Men in the European Community', Network of Experts on the Situation of Women in the Labour Market, Synthesis Report, *Social Europe Supplement*, 3/93.

Rubery, J. and Fagan, C. (1994) 'Wage Determination and Sex Segregation in Employment in the European Community', *Social Europe Supplement*, 4/94.

Ruggie, M. (1984) *The State and Working Women: a Comparative Study of Britain and Sweden* (Princeton, New Jersey: Princeton University Press).

Saurel-Cubizolles, M-J., Romito, P. and Garcia, J. (1993) 'Description of Maternity Rights for Working Women in France, Italy and in the United Kingdom', *European Journal of Public Health*, vol. 3, no. 1, pp. 48–53.

Schultheis, F. (1990) 'Familles d'Europe sans frontières: un enjeu social par dessus le marché', *Actes du Colloque: Familles d'Europe sans frontières, 4–5 December 1989* (Paris: Institut de l'Enfance et de la Famille), pp. 73–80.

Schultheis, F. (1991) 'Affaires de famille – affaires d'État: des visions et des divisions inter-culturelles d'une réflexion sociologique', in F. de Singly and F. Schultheis (eds), *Affaires de familles, affaires d'État* (Jarville-La-Malgrange: Éditions de l'Est), pp. 7–22.

Segalen, M. (1981) *Sociologie de la famille*, 1st edn (Paris: A. Colin).

Sgritta, G.B. and Zanatta, A.L. (1994) 'Families and Family Policy in Italy: Constraints and Promises', in W. Dumon (ed.), *Changing Family Policies in the Member States of the European Union* (Brussels: Commission of the European Communities, DG V/European Observatory on National Family Policies), pp. 173–98.

Siim, B. (1993) 'The Gendered Scandinavian Welfare States: the Interplay between Women's Roles as Mothers, Workers and Citizens in Denmark', in J. Lewis (ed.), *Women and Social Policies: Work, Family and the State* (Aldershot/Vermont: Edward Elgar), pp. 25–48.

Simões Casimiro, F. and Calado Lopes, M.G. (1995) 'Concepts and Typologies of Household and Family in the 1981 and 1991 Population Cenuses in the Twelve Community Countries'. Unpublished report for Eurostat (Lisbon: Instituto Superior de Estatistica e Gescào de Informaçào).

Singly, F. de (1987) *Fortune et infortune de la femme mariée: sociologie de la vie conjugale* (Paris: PUF).

Singly, F. de (1991) 'La sociologie', in F. de Singly (ed.), *La famille: l'état des savoirs* (Paris: Éditions La Découverte), pp. 424–34.

Singly, F. de and Thélot, C. (1988) *Gens du privé, gens du public: la grande différence* (Paris: Bordas).

Skrede, K. (1995) 'The Nordic Model for Family Welfare – Major Trends and Present Challenges', in B. Arve-Parès (ed.), *Building Family Welfare. Report from a Nordic Seminar on Families, Gender and Welfare Policy* (Stockholm: The Network of Nordic Focal Points for the International Year of the Family 1994), pp. 127–45.

Sosson, J. (1993) 'Le statut juridique des familles recomposées en Europe: quelques aspects de droit comparé', in M-T. Meulders-Klein and I. Théry (eds), *Les recompositions familiales aujourd'hui* (Paris: Nathan), pp. 299–312.

Spicker, P. (1991) 'The Principle of Subsidiarity and the Social Policy of the European Community', *Journal of European Social Policy*, vol. 1, no. 1, pp. 3–14.

Standley, K. (1993) *Family Law* (Houndmills and London: Macmillan).

Statistics Sweden (1995) *Women and Men in Sweden: Facts and Figures 1995* (Stockholm: Statistics Sweden).

Sullerot, E. (1968) *Histoire et sociologie du travail féminin* (Paris: Gonthier).

Tabah, L. and Maugué, C. (1989) *Démographie et politique familiale en Europe* (Paris: La Documentation Française).

Tálos, E. and Wörister, K. (1994) *Soziale Sicherung im Sozialstaat Österreich: Entwicklung – Herausforderungen – Struckturen* (Baden-Baden: Nomos Verlagsgesellschaft).

Tauberman, A-C. (1995) 'Swedish Family Policy – Main Steps and Present Concerns', in B. Arve-Parès (ed.), *Building Family Welfare. Report from a Nordic Seminar on Families, Gender and Welfare Policy* (Stockholm: The Network of Nordic Focal Points for the International Year of the Family 1994), pp. 23–6.

Taylor-Gooby, P. (1991a) *Social Change, Social Welfare and Social Science* (London, New York: Harvester Wheatsheaf).

Taylor-Gooby, P. (1991b) 'Welfare State Regimes and Welfare Citizenship', *Journal of European Social Policy*, vol. 1, no. 2, pp. 93–105.

Teirlinck, M. (co-ordinator) (1994) 'The European Union and the Family', *Social Europe*, 1/94.

Théry, I. (1993) 'Introduction générale: le temps des recompositions familiales', in M-T. Meulders-Klein and I. Théry (eds), *Les recompositions familiales aujourd'hui* (Paris: Nathan), pp. 5–21.

Tilly, L.A. and Scott, J.W. (1987) *Women, Work, and Family*, new edn (London and New York: Methuen).

Titmuss, R. (1974) *Social Policy: an Introduction* (edited by B. Abel-Smith and K. Titmuss) (London: Allen & Unwin).

Tobío, C. (1994) 'The Family–Employment Relationship in Spain', *Cross-National Research Papers*, vol. 4, no. 3, pp. 41–7.

Trost, J. (1988) 'Conceptualising the Family', *International Sociology*, vol. 3, no. 3, pp. 301–8.

Ungerson, C. (ed.) (1990) *Gender and Caring: Work and Welfare in Britain and Scandinavia* (London: Harvester and Wheatsheaf).

United Nations Statistical Commission/Economic Commission for Europe Conference of European Statisticians (1987) 'Recommendations for the 1990 Censuses of Population and Housing in the ECE Region: Regional Variant of the World Recommendations for the 1990 Round of Population and Housing Censuses', *Statistical Standards and Studies*, no. 40 (New York: United Nations).

Utting, D. (1995) *Family and Parenthood: Supporting Families, Preventing Breakdown* (York: Joseph Rowntree Foundation).

Valetas, M-F. (1992) 'Le nom de famille ou l'éviction du nom de la femme: analyse socio-démographique des représentations', in A. Nunes de Almeida, M. das Dores Guerreiro, A. Torres and K. Wall (eds), *Familles et contextes sociaux: les espaces et les temps de la diversité. Actes du Colloque de Lisbonne, 10–12 avril 1991* (Lisbon: GREF/CIES), pp. 29–42.

Valiente, C. (1994) *Políticas públicas para la mujer trabajadora en Italia y España (1900–1991)* (Madrid: Instituto Juan March).

Valiente, C. (1995) 'Rejecting the Past: Central Government and Family Policy in Post-Authoritarian Spain (1975–94)', *Cross-National Research Papers*, vol. 4, no. 3, pp. 80–96.

Van den Brekel, J.C. and Van de Kaa, D.J. (1994) 'The Netherlands: Aspects of Family Policy in the Setting of the Second Demographic Transition', in W. Dumon (ed.), *Changing Family Policies in the Member States of the European Union* (Brussels: Commission of the European Communities, DG V/European Observatory on National Family Policies), pp. 225–54.

Villeneuve-Gokalp, C. (1993) 'La recomposition du paysage familial après la séparation des parents', *La société française. Données sociales 1993* (Paris: INSÉÉ), pp. 322–9.

Voegeli, W. (1991) 'Familles mono-parentales et "État-père": tendances à la socialisation des "risques familiaux"', in F. de Singly and F. Schultheis (eds), *Affaires de familles, affaires d'État* (Jarville-La-Malgrange: Éditions de l'Est), pp. 109–16.

Walby, S. (1986) *Patriarchy at Work: Patriarchal and Capitalist Relations in Employment* (Cambridge: Polity Press).

Wall, K. (1992) 'Pour une sociologie des formes familiales dans la société rurale', in A. Nunes de Almeida, M. das Dores Guerreiro,

A. Torres and K. Wall (eds), *Familles et contextes sociaux: les espaces et les temps de la diversité. Actes du Colloque de Lisbonne, 10–12 avril 1991* (Lisbon: GREF/CIES), pp.163–82.

Wall, K. (1995) 'National Report: Portugal', in J. Millar and A. Warman (eds), *Defining Family Obligations in Europe* (University of Bath: Centre for the Analysis of Social Policy), pp. 307-24.

Willmott, P. and Willmott, P. (1982) 'Children and Family Diversity', in R.N. Rapoport, M.P. Fogarty and R. Rapoport (eds), *Families in Britain* (London: Routledge & Kegan Paul), pp. 338–54.

Wilson, D. (1979) *The Welfare State in Sweden: a Study in Comparative Social Administration* (London: Heinemann).

Wingen, M. and Stutzer, E. (1994) 'Germany: Family Policy as a Cross Party Social Policy', in W. Dumon (ed.), *Changing Family Policies in the Member States of the European Union* (Brussels: Commission of the European Communities, DG V/European Observatory on National Family Policies), pp. 57–86.

Witherspoon, S. (1989) 'Interim Report: a Woman's Work', in R. Jowell, S. Witherspoon and L. Brook (eds), *British Social Attitudes. The 5th Report* (London: SCPR, Gower), pp. 175–200.

Young, M. and Willmott, P. (1957) *Family and Kinship in East London* (London: Routledge and Kegan Paul).

Young, M. and Willmott, P. (1973) *The Symmetrical Family: a Study of Work and Leisure in the London Region* (London: Routledge & Kegan Paul).

# INDEX